CW01625129

AR[illegible]

and

Vincent van Gogh

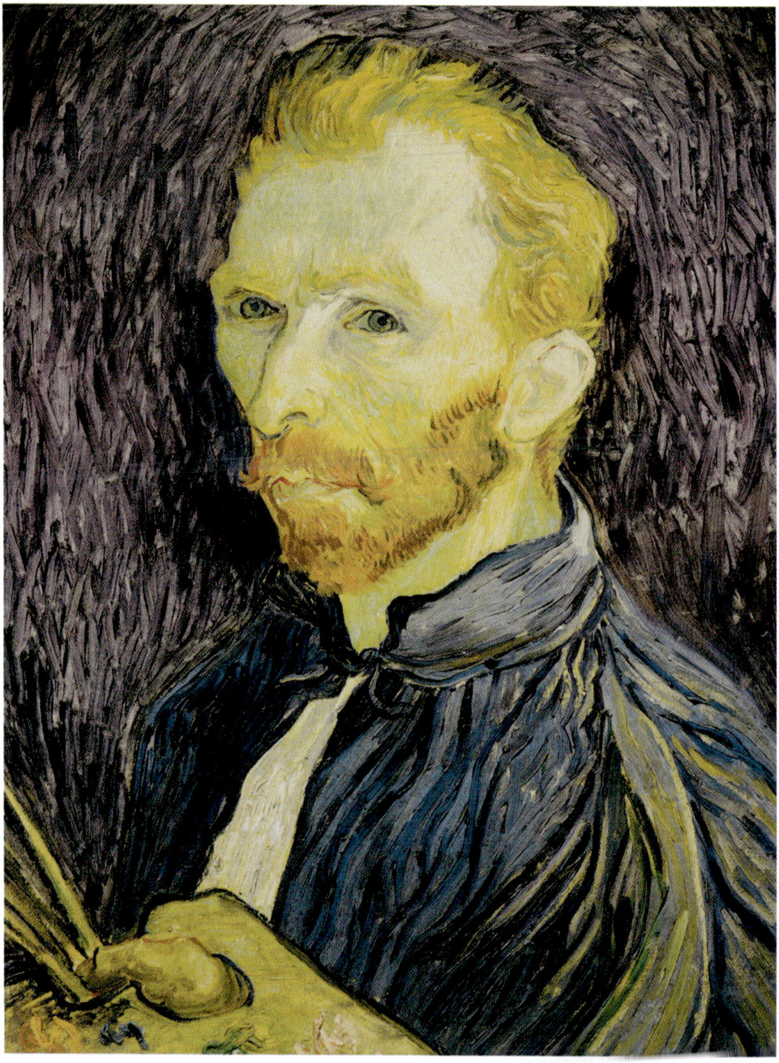

Vincent van Gogh, *Self-Portrait*
JH1770, F626, 57 × 43.5 cm
August 1889, Saint-Rémy

ARTQUAKES

and

Vincent van Gogh

Bouwe Jans

Pillar
Publications

Weybridge, England
2001

British Library Cataloguing in Publication Data:

Jans, Bouwe
Artquakes and Van Gogh

ISBN 0 9513127 5 8

Copyright © Bouwe Jans 2001

The moral right of Bouwe Jans to be identified as the author of this work has been asserted in accordance with the Copyright Designs and Patents Act of 1988.

Published 2001
by
Pillar Publications Limited
Weybridge, Surrey KT13 9EQ
pillarpub@bjhc.demon.co.uk
All rights reserved. No part of this publication may be reproduced, stored in a retrieval system, or transmitted, or reproduced, in any form or by any means, without the permission of the copyright owner.

www.artquakes.com

Typeset in 11/12 Garamond by Jonathan Rolls, Eton
Printed in Great Britain by
Ian Allan Printing Ltd, Hersham, Surrey KT12 4RG

To my wife, Barbara

Contents

Foreword

To many readers this book will come as a surprise. It certainly is astonishing that the author, Bouwe Jans, could have discovered a so far unknown painting of *Two Spitters* [*Two Diggers*] by Vincent Van Gogh at an auction somewhere in the Netherlands.

However it must be considered a still greater surprise that the author should have had the greatest difficulty in convincing the so-called "establishment"—the staff of the Van Gogh Museum and closely associated experts—of the validity of his find.

Bouwe Jans's tale epitomises the frustration of scholars and other researchers, (who are sometimes even derided as 'amateurs'), but who open-mindedly come forward with new findings

Jan Hulsker

Victoria BC
July 2001

Preface

This story came to life in May 1993. Some fifteen years earlier, after working for thirty years on textile industrial projects in Africa and the Far East, I decided on a retirement hobby. Always interested in art, I had, at times, been an amateur painter, and I collected art. Therefore, establishing an contemporary art gallery in 1978 in Spain seemed the perfect answer to my ambitions.

In 1981 I moved home and hobby to England. At the time I did not bargain for my new occupation getting out of hand, but it soon became an absorbing and enjoyable full-time occupation.

During my years in art dealing I have been fortunate in establishing relationships with artists and art collectors alike, many of which have turned into lasting friendships. I was successful and content with my 'stable' of contemporary artists and had no intention of handling any paintings by any of the great masters. In May 1993, however, I became involved with the painting, probably by Vincent van Gogh, my unexpected experiences with which were the spur to write this book.

Artquakes

Artquakes can not only do to works of art what earthquakes can do to the earth, they sometimes also erupt and behave like volcanoes. They can be very destructive indeed.

Acknowledgements

From the early beginning after acquiring the painting with the fortunes and misfortunes of which this book deals, I have been very fortunate in receiving substantial and invaluable support, information, and the benefit of the knowledge of a large number of people, some named, some not named in these pages.

Two art collectors, Goran Strok and Derek Markland, spontaneously gave not only moral but also substantial financial support at an early stage. As soon as they saw *The Diggers*, they believed it to be possibly genuine and offered to become its sponsors. Without their support I would not have had the time or the resources to undertake the amount of research required.

Other early believers in the painting were Frits Bolkestein, who made time to edit an early draft of this story as, later, did the late Dr James Bentley. Final editing was in the hands of Dr Hugh de Glanville, an expert in Dutch English, whose enthusiasm was spurred both by the painting and by the story, as was that of Jonathan Rolls who greatly assisted with the final production.

David Brooks kindly permitted me to download images from his website (*www.vangoghgallery.com*) to illustrate this book.

To my house artists and to all the regular visitors to my gallery I offer my apologies for having restricted access to it from seven days a week to 'by appointment only'. *The Diggers* demanded more and more of my time, unfortunately at the expense of The Eton Art Gallery.

And last but not least, I must express my gratitude to my son Julian for his computer skills and his additional input and to my wife, who has graciously put up with the late hours of work and study and the not inconsiderable but unavoidable travel that my quest has involved. With deep understanding she has lovingly sustained me and eased the strain throughout.

No words of thanks I can write here can be adequate.

Bouwe Jans

Chapter One

Introduction

In May 1993, quite by chance, I was tipped off by a relative involved with auctions in Holland about a painting which he thought could be by van Gogh that was about to be sold at a provincial auction of household goods. Although my first, almost automatic, reaction was that it was highly unlikely this would turn out to be a genuine van Gogh, I had an 'ear' for the possibility. I knew that a number of paintings by this artist, especially from his very early period in Holland, have never as yet surfaced, and—one never knows.

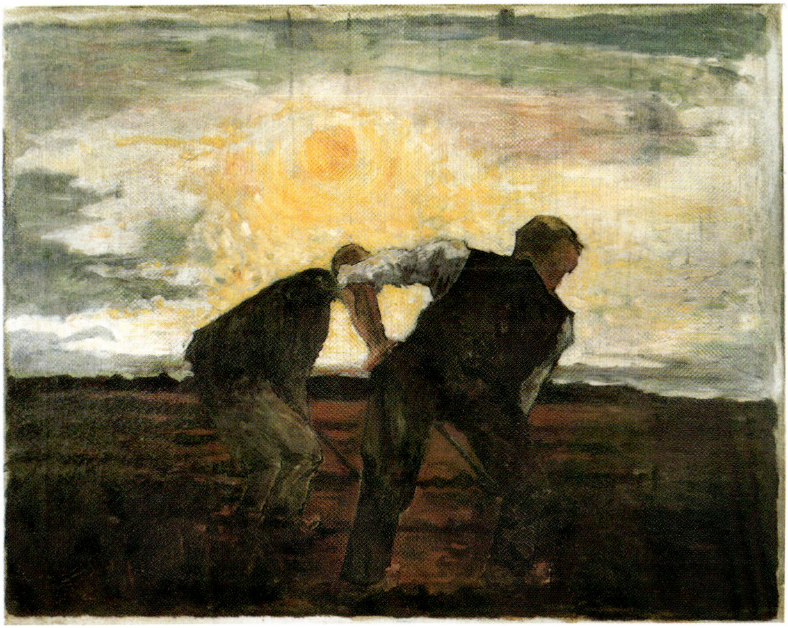

Two Diggers in the Afternoon Sun (The Diggers)
Oil on canvas, 47 × 61 cm
After restoration by Dr Paolo Cadorin

Amateur photographs of the painting showed two men digging in an afternoon sun, a typical subject of the artist whom Vincent van Gogh most admired, Jean-François Millet. Throughout his career, van Gogh used Millet subjects as models and as sources of inspiration for some of his own paintings and drawings. Careful observation made me feel that the painting might indeed be by van Gogh, it certainly had some features characteristic of him. In addition to having had an ear for it, I was also developing an eye for it. Sometimes one gets a hunch. But of course it would be too good to be true.

The date of the auction was getting close and I needed to check that I was not dreaming. I took the photographs to Sotheby's in Bond Street, London. They agreed that there was a chance that the painting might indeed be genuine and suggested I seek the opinion of Mr Sjraar van Heugten, a curator of what was then the Rijksmuseum Vincent van Gogh in Amsterdam. (This had opened in 1973 under this name but in 1994 had become an independent foundation, officially the Stichting Van Gogh Museum, though it is commonly known as the 'Van Gogh Museum, Amsterdam'.)

Having no inkling of the possible consequences, on 11 May 1993 I innocently enclosed photographs of *The Diggers* with a letter to the Rijksmuseum Vincent van Gogh asking for an opinion. Receiving no response, I telephoned and managed to get an appointment for the afternoon of 17 May, the same day the painting was to be auctioned in Groningen (in the north of Holland) in the evening.

At the museum I handed over a new set of photographs to Ms Martine Kilburn, the secretary to the chief curator, Mr Louis van Tilborgh. Asking me to sit down and wait, she went away for the expert's opinion. After some forty minutes she returned with the photographs and asked me whether I was the owner of the painting. I did not think I could very well say "not yet", so I said "No". She then explained, regretfully, that the Museum could only give an opinion to the actual owner of a painting. If that was indeed their policy, I wondered why it had taken so long to tell me so and whether the forty-minute delay was an indication that the expert who had looked at the photographs had also considered a possible connection with Vincent?

I asked whether the Museum had been approached about this painting in the past by anyone else. The answer was a definite no, they had not seen this image before. It seemed rather amazing that a possible van Gogh was being offered for sale in Holland and nobody had bothered to ask for an opinion from the Van Gogh Museum or even tell them that it was coming up for auction.

I then went straight to the auction house, where I was still in time to view the painting before the auction began. It was a reasonably strong work, not a finished oil painting, but a study in oil on canvas. (Who had been talking about studies all his life? Vincent, of course.) The painting was rather dirty, and covered in a greyish varnish. Judging by the age of the canvas and the stretcher it was nailed to, it looked at least a hundred years old. The stretcher was of good quality, a size 12 as it was called at the time, measuring approximately 47 × 61 cm.

Traces could be seen of an earlier painting underneath that had not been totally overlaid by the final image. Only a painter not painting with a view to selling would have left such traces still visible. Equally, only a serious painter experimenting with a composition purely for himself would not bother to completely obliterate earlier efforts on the same canvas.

The figures of the diggers had been drawn in bold outline. The bodies had subsequently been painted in skilfully, partially overlapping the outlines. The depth of field in the painting was excellent, and whoever the painter might have been he was obviously potentially a true and strong artist. Apart from some areas of damage, especially one near the left foot of the foremost digger which had been clumsily repaired (see illustration page 57), the study was in excellent condition.

In the right-hand bottom corner, barely visible, was the indistinct signature 'Vincent' (page 36). It was this that had made the auctioneer believe that the painting might be by van Gogh, a suspicion he had shared with my relative and later also with the local newspaper.

The auctioneer, Mr J. van den Enden, told me that the vendor had bought the painting a few years before at a nearby flea market. The family then selling had originally acquired it many years earlier when they lived in Breda. The auctioneer had not attempted to have the painting authenticated or attributed by the Van Gogh Museum—he said that the Museum's answer was always 'no' anyway. Nor had he told the Museum about the sale or announced it nationally, let alone internationally. Only local buyers were expected, although, as a result of the mention in the paper, local television had been alerted. There were very few paintings in the auction, which comprised mainly furniture and household goods. The auction was due to start at 7p.m. but I had to stop viewing by 6p.m. when the TV crew started setting up lights and cameras in the sale room.

I arranged to enter the bidding by telephone and at approximately

7.40p.m. the painting was hammered down to my final bid of Hfl 9,000, too much if the painting was not by van Gogh, perhaps, but a pittance if it should turn out to be genuine. In any case, I liked the painting and considered it to be worth the price, whoever the painter. The following day the local newspaper reported that an 'English art dealer' had bought the 'van Gogh'. This made me smile, since as far as I was concerned I am Dutch and all I had bought was an attractive painting. The formal title I gave the painting is *Two Diggers in the Afternoon Sun*, but in the rest of this book it willl be referred to simply as *The Diggers* or just *Diggers*.

At this stage only one artist's name had so far presented itself as the possible creator of my new acquisition—Vincent van Gogh. There were certainly some positive indications that it might indeed be by him. But was it really? Could it be one of the most desirable finds imaginable, a painting by the most sought-after artist in the world?

I soon realised that I had landed myself a new task: I would have to endeavour to eliminate all doubt about the author of the painting. A cuckoo's egg had been laid in my art dealer's world. The main question—to whom should the study be attributed—led to a multitude of subsidiary questions, to some of which there were already answers, not infrequently contradictory. And because my painting turned out not to be the only 'van Gogh?' currently involved in debate over authentication it became unwittingly caught up in other controversies.

At the time, I naively thought that a definitive conclusion on the attribution could probably be reached within, say, six months. How wrong can one be! Now, some eight years later, although a number of internationally acknowledged experts have firmly attributed *The Diggers* to van Gogh, the Van Gogh Museum has, as predicted by the auctioneer, so far not been willing to agree.

Indeed, the Museum appears to have adopted the general rule candidly described in Daniel Wildenstein's *Marchands d'Art*. This famous art dealer tells us that, in the fifties, he asked the Brooklyn Museum's Curator of Egyptian antiquities, a Dr Cooney, about his uncanny knack of detecting fakes: "I just cannot understand your knack . . . I myself am incapable of distinguishing genuine from fake." Cooney replied: "It is not difficult—every time someone shows you an item, just say 'That's a fake'." He added, "you won't be wrong more than one time in a hundred."

Museums well know that this is the best way to avoid making more than a very occasional mistake in judging unknown and incompletely provenanced works of art—they are also mindful of past cases in which their predecessors or colleagues would have done better to have followed Cooney's advice. For it is highly likely that when an expert does make a mistake of not recognising a genuine work, the owners will neither themselves be sufficiently knowledgeable nor sufficiently confident to argue. They will normally accept the expert's verdict on the strength of his status, and a search for authenticity may then die a natural death. The authority of a verdict from a major museum is thus formidable: it blinds many a later eye, and is a serious challenge for external experts to rebut.

Yet there have been numerous instances in the past where even paintings acquired by museums as 'van Goghs' have turned out to have been painted by another hand. This happened, for example, to the Berlin National Gallery, to the Metropolitan Museum in New York, to the Kröller-Müller Museum in Otterlo, to the Museum of Oslo, and to others among whom last but not least is the Van Gogh Museum in Amsterdam. For instance, in 1982 the Rijksmuseum Vincent van Gogh bought a study, a canvas on panel that they believed to be the missing second *View of Amsterdam* referred to by Vincent in a letter of October 1885:

> The two wood panels I painted in Amsterdam were done in a hurry, one, believe it or not, in the waiting room of the train station, when I was too early for the train and the other in the morning at 10 o'clock before going to the museum. I am sending them to you as two tiles on which one has thrown something with a few strokes. (LT 426)

When another panel, previously believed to be a *View of The Hague,* turned out to be the second *View of Amsterdam,* the Van Gogh Museum had no choice but to acknowledge its mistake. A gifted eye would have given a warning signal, but sometimes the painting's qualities are overlooked when there seems to be enough evidence from the archives.

Similarly, once a painting has been accepted as authentic it becomes difficult to change that status if doubts, however justified, arise. Incorrect authentication can be very embarrassing, and some museums have been less ready to admit mistakes than others.

There are exceptions, but when the Van Gogh Museum disputes the authenticity of a presumptive van Gogh, its value is negligible, but if a dubious painting has their imprimatur it has real marketing potential. The Museum thus largely 'dictates the market'. Sotheby's themselves advised me to get an opinion from the Amsterdam Museum.

The international auction houses still trim their sails to Amsterdam's wind and are understandably reluctant to go against it, almost certainly because of potential legal consequences if they do. In this position of excessive influence, it is not surprising that museums are unwilling, as will appear, to accept the opinions of outside experts on authenticity: what *is* surprising is that they are often reluctant or unable to substantiate their opposing verdicts at all convincingly.

One good reason, one bit of sound evidence, would have been sufficient for me to accept that my painting is not a genuine van Gogh, and this story would never have been written.

The Diggers has aroused bizarre and unbelievably contradictory opinions amongst the most influential experts in the van Gogh world. Some say it is authentic, and give good reasons: others say it is not, but refuse to give any sound basis for dismissing it. Because of this I have inadvertently become entangled as a bit-player in perhaps the most important war that has ever taken place in the art world, between the 'establishment' and the independent experts outside it, over the authenticity of a number of paintings that are currently attributed to van Gogh by some but which other experts believe to be by another hand. Some of these battles have reached enormous proportions in the last few years, with vast sums of money at stake, and their commotion has caused serious 'artquakes'.

If *The Diggers* is genuine, my innocent sharing of pre-auction information may not have helped my chances of getting a willing and objective opinion from the people who seem at this moment still to matter most. The Van Gogh Museum, having seen photographs of *The Diggers* at a time when they could still have bought it for next to nothing, would not be too keen to authenticate it now and so admit that they had missed a major opportunity. I had to take the opinions of independent experts and do my own research, and persevere until either a sound reason emerged why *The Diggers* could not be by van Gogh or until it could be fully accepted as a genuine early work by him.

I would need to focus my research on two main areas: first, a detailed study of his paintings, mainly the early works but not ignoring the later part of the oeuvre, so that I could recognise his working methods from careful study of his 'handwriting' in oils. Secondly, I would need to make a detailed study of *The Letters* and other relevant literature.

A number of internationally acclaimed experts on van Gogh—including the author of the latest *catalogue raisonné* [descriptive catalogue] of the oeuvre, Dr Jan Hulsker—have come to believe that *The Diggers* is a genuine painting by van Gogh, and have stated clear reasons for their belief, yet the Museum authorities will not agree, nor will they give any sensible and acceptable reasons for their verdict.

In having a controversial attribution *The Diggers* is in noteworthy company. A similar debate is raging about much better-known paintings by—or not by—van Gogh, such as:

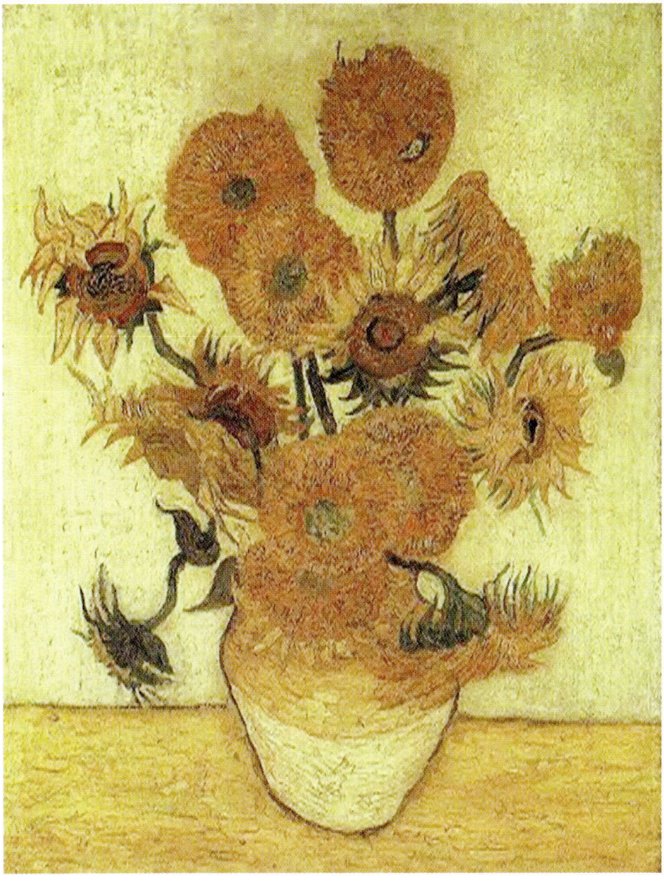

The copy of *Fourteen Sunflowers in a Vase* (JH1666, F457), now owned by the Yasuda Fire and Marine Insurance Company of Japan . . .

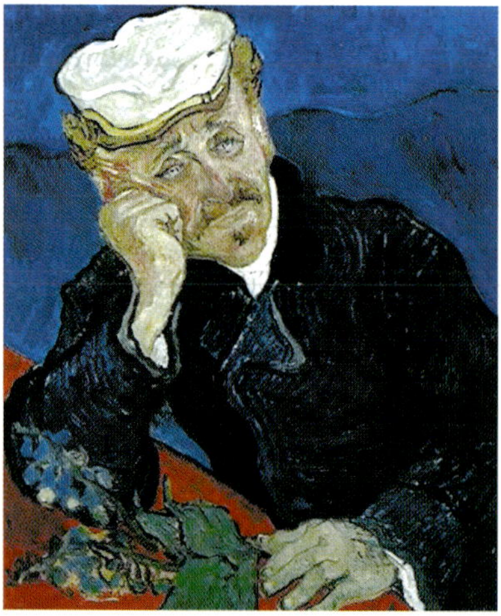

. . . the copy of the *Portrait of Dr Gachet* (JH2014, F754, above) belonging to the Musée d'Orsay in Paris . . .

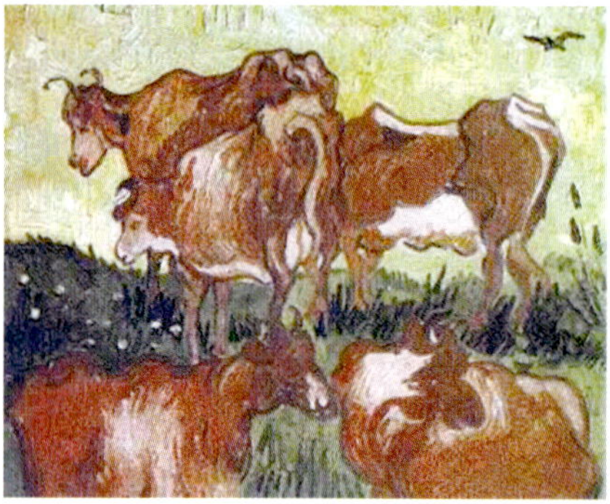

. . . *Cows* (JH2095, F822, left) owned by the Musée des Beaux-Arts in Lille . . .

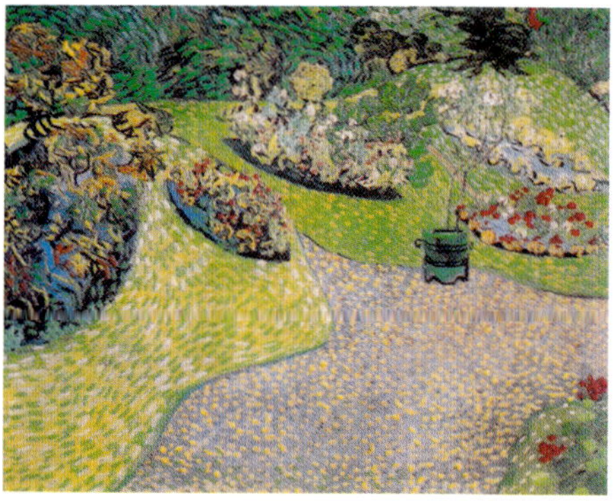

. . .*The Garden at Auvers* (JH2107, F814, right), which has been and perhaps still is the subject of legal action in France . . .

. . . *The Garden of the Asylum* (JH1850, F659, below) owned by the Vincent van Gogh Foundation in Amsterdam

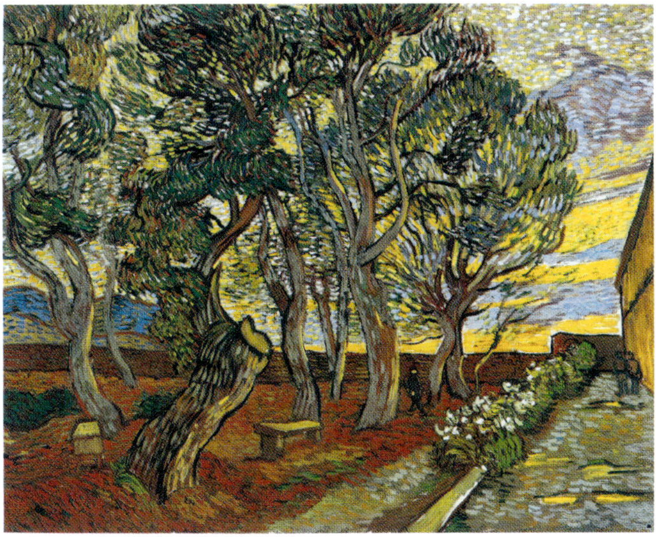

and a number of other works.

All these paintings are involved in the fascinating battle between, on the one hand the Van Gogh and other museums and owners who want and believe them to be authentic, and on the other hand critics, individual scholars, and researchers who—with no financial axe to grind but an academic desire to purify the oeuvre—have *prima facie* valid arguments for disagreeing about their authenticity.

For *The Diggers* and some other paintings in the same boat the reverse is the case—a number of independent scholars and experts believe they are genuine but the Museum and its associated 'experts' refuse to agree.

The final word on the authenticity of a number of paintings has not yet been spoken. The Van Gogh Museum may be right or wrong about *The Diggers*, and also about many other more famous paintings. A clearer, cleaner, more universally acceptable result will eventually emerge on these matters. Until that time the debate will continue, and from time to time major potential authentication upsets will continue to cause 'artquakes'.

Chapter Two

Vincent van Gogh and Diggers

Vincent van Gogh was born on 30 March 1853. He died on 29 July 1890, aged 37. After attempts at art dealing and at becoming a preacher, in 1880 he finally chose to become an artist. Following a period of learning to draw while living with his parents in Etten, near the border between Holland and Belgium, his actual painting career lasted from August 1882 until his death, a mere eight years, in which, according to the *catalogues raisonnés,* he produced some 879 paintings, 1,245 drawings, one etching, and a few lithographs. This entire oeuvre had to be researched to confirm, or otherwise, characteristics in common with *The Diggers*.

The first complete *catalogue raisonné* was published, in four volumes, after eleven years' work, in 1928 by Dr J.B. de la Faille. He followed this in 1929 with *Les Faux Van Gogh*, in which he listed misattributions in his 1928 catalogue, comprising 135 works in all. In 1939 he produced his revised catalogue, of the paintings only, called *The Hyperion*, translated into English by Prudence Montague-Pollack, published by William Heineman in one volume. When he died in 1959, de la Faille left a manuscript for a further revised edition. It took a group of experts more than eight years to edit this manuscript for the revised edition that was eventually published in 1970. The editorial board—also called the Van Gogh Committee—for this revised, augmented, and annotated edition included A.H. Hammacher as President, Dr J. Hulsker, and five other experts. Preliminary work was undertaken by Ms Annet Tellegen-Hoogendoorn and Dr Martha Op de Coul, both from the Netherlands Institute for Art History in The Hague, and by Evert van Uitert, then at the Research Centre for Art History of the University of Utrecht.

In 1978 Hulsker published *Van Gogh en zijn Weg, Het Complete Werk*, a follow-up to de la Faille's catalogue. His revised edition, *The New Complete Van Gogh*, published in 1996, covers the complete oeuvre—all the known paintings and drawings, and even the sketches in Vincent's letters, giving the dates of their creation in, as far as possible, chronological order.

Van Gogh's creativity was not only expressed in images, but also in words that are preserved in his many letters to his brother Theo and other members of his family and to artists he befriended. His brother's widow, Johanna van Gogh-Bonger, was first to publish most of his letters to his brother, in 1914. In the same year Paul Cassirer of the Paul Cassirer Art Gallery in Berlin published an edition in German.

To avoid dispersion of the family collection of works, the Vincent van Gogh Foundation was established on 10 July 1960. In 1962, with the consent of the Dutch Parliament the State purchased the entire collection on behalf of the Foundation, the city of Amsterdam provided the site, and on 2 June 1973 the Rijksmuseum Vincent Van Gogh was officially opened. An updated and more complete edition of *The Letters* in their original language, including letters to and from artist friends and to his sister, was published on the occasion of the opening, thanks to Vincent Willem van Gogh, Theo's son.

At that time the van Gogh family handed over the management of not only the works of art but also of the letters and documentation to the Stichting [Foundation] Vincent van Gogh. Under the editorship of Han van Krimpen, curator of the Rijksmuseum Vincent van Gogh from its opening in 1973, and Monique Berends-Albert of his staff, the latest improved edition, *De Brieven van Vincent van Gogh* [*The Letters of Vincent van Gogh*] in four volumes in Dutch, totalling over 2,250 large closely printed pages, was published in 1990.

Vincent van Gogh has given of himself extensively and clearly in his letters. He often related what he had been or was doing, drawing, or painting. Not infrequently his letters contained sketches of the paintings he was working on and descriptions of the colour schemes he was using. The development of the painter's choice of subject matter, his choice of brush strokes, of palette, of quality of paints and of materials used, can be followed throughout his career. He speaks about his habits and state of health and, from time to time, of his relationships with his fellow men and women.

A vast amount has been written about Vincent van Gogh, about his work, about his lifestyle and character, his state of health, and more, and this accumulated literature is a substantial source of information. These publications are referred to under the collective name of 'the literature', but it is *The Letters* that are the key to 'Vincent', as he always called himself.

* * *

After some preliminary efforts in 1881—five studies and two watercolours painted during visits to his cousin, the artist Anton Mauve in The Hague—van Gogh's painting career can be divided into six specific periods.

The first period—a period of only six weeks from August 1882, in which he painted studies in oils in The Hague, followed by another spell of approximately six weeks there a year later, and then a period of some eleven weeks at the end of that same year, 1883, in Drenthe. Only 32 known oil paintings are attributed to Vincent van Gogh from this entire period, and the whereabouts of twelve of these are unknown.

The second period—this was in Nuenen and lasted just under two years, from 5 December 1883 until his departure for Antwerp on 24 November 1885. It was in this period that he painted the local environment, the churches, the weavers and their cottages, many portraits of the farming population, male and female, and also his greatest achievement of that period, *The Potato Eaters*. He is credited with some 190 oil paintings from this second period.

The third period—after a short spell of approximately three months in Antwerp from the end of 1885, mainly devoted to art studies, Vincent went to live with his brother Theo in Paris for nearly two years from 1886–1888. Just over 230 oil paintings are attributed to him from this period.

The fourth period—this was the Arles period of approximately one year from 1888–1889, a time of great productivity and achievement, in which over 180 oil paintings by him are listed.

The fifth period—at Saint-Rémy-de-Provence, also lasting approximately one year (1889–1890), which saw spells of great productivity but interspersed with periods when illness prevented him from working. Nevertheless over 140 oil paintings are attributed to him for this period.

The sixth and last period—the last months of his life, at Auvers-sur-Oise, a period of less than 70 days but in which he painted, according to Hulsker's 1996 *The New Complete Van Gogh* some 76 oil paintings.

* * *

Tsukasa Kodera, a well known van Gogh scholar, noted in his book *Vincent van Gogh, Christianity versus Nature*, that diggers occur more frequently in van Gogh's oeuvre—eighty-five times in all—than any other specific type of figure. Diggers (and the sun) were evidently very important to Vincent, but from his entire work in Holland, Antwerp, and Paris, that is from the first six years of his entire oil-painting career of some eight years, not one oil painting of a figure or figures digging under a full face sun has surfaced until now. None of his *Digger Sweating it out in the Afternoon Sun* studies have been found, although his own letters confirmed that he had painted such studies in his very first period of oil-painting in 1882; none appears in his known oeuvre. We only know his paintings of diggers in the sun painted after he had reached Arles in the South of France in February 1888.

This might be an indication that until then he had felt that he had solved his problems about depicting two diggers in a satisfactory manner when he painted that subject in The Hague. Had he not he would have tried and tried again. Such was his character. When something was haunting him he had to solve it and diggers had haunted him from an early stage in his career.

There are numerous known drawings of figures digging, even from before he ever started painting in oils. Long before he became a painter he had written to Theo:

> Also remember that Millet has made an etching *The Diggers*. If you ever come across that you won't easily forget it.

He later made two drawings, see below, from a photograph of this etching.

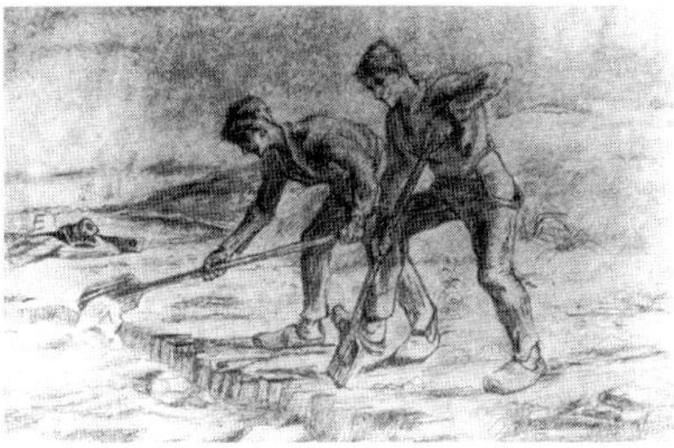

F 828, pencil, 35 × 55 cm

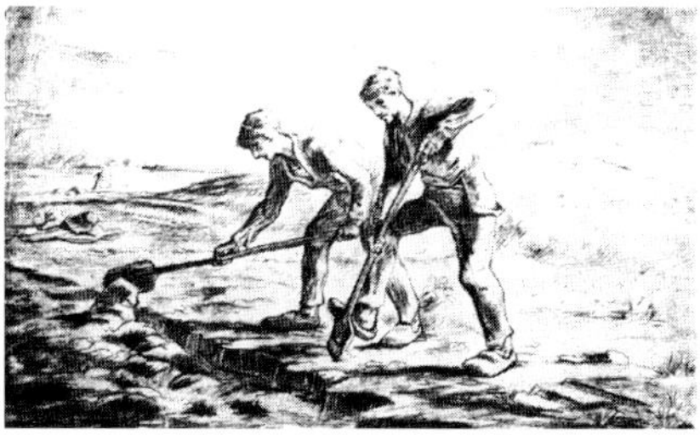

JHD, F 829, pencil, stumped charcoal, 37 × 62 cm

If *The Diggers* is indeed a painting by Vincent van Gogh, then from its style and method of execution, it can only be from his very earliest period in The Hague; otherwise it has to be a forgery. There are very few forgeries, purporting to be from his earliest periods so, clearly, my research needed to concentrate on Vincent.

Soon after his death in 1890 a market developed for his paintings from the French periods, but his works from the early Dutch periods were hardly seen in public before the 20th century. It is a reasonable assumption that no van Gogh painting purporting to be from his period in The Hague [1882–1883] would have been forged before 1903 because most of his work from that period was lying hidden in an attic in Breda and was therefore not available to any aspiring forger. The apparent age of the painting and its stretcher—at least a hundred years old in 1993— also means the painting had to have been painted in the 19th century. Vincent's detailed descriptions of his palette in his early references to a sun in an afternoon sky in *The Letters* would also have assisted a forger, but these were also not widely available until his letters were published in 1914.

Accurate dating of the painting could be decisive. Absolute proof that the painting is from the end of the 19th century would be strong evidence for its authenticity. Unfortunately, precise dating by scientific methods is not yet available.

Other evidence against it being a forgery is needed. For instance, why would a forger copy this kind of study and not a finished painting? *The Diggers* had been painted over an earlier study without completely obliterating it—hardly the sign of an artist painting for sale, or even with the intention of only showing it to others. In any case, there is no known record of any attempt to sell *The Diggers* as a genuine van Gogh during its entire life, although it is signed 'Vincent'. It is more reasonable to believe that it was created by an artist as a study for his own purposes, perhaps, to be used as a reference in his own studio.

All these seemed logical reasons tentatively supporting the painting's authenticity and reducing the possibility of it being a forgery.

Unfortunately, *catalogues raisonnés* are bound to be incomplete and not totally reliable. Some paintings, although, because of previous attributions by others, still in Dr Jan Hulsker's latest catalogue, *The New Complete Van Gogh* of 1996, do not necessarily carry his personal support for their attribution. He clearly states on page 6 of his catalogue, "*This does not mean that all the works reproduced here should be considered authentic.*" It is believed that at least some forty, possibly even up to a hundred works not created by Vincent van Gogh still appear in this latest *catalogue raisonné* as attributed to him. Hulsker himself indicates his reservations about the actual date of creation or other details of some of these doubtful works by placing question marks against their dates of creation in his *The New Complete Van Gogh*. The listing of a painting in this reference book does not therefore always guarantee its authenticity.

The same applies, even more so, to de la Faille's *catalogue raisonné* of 1928. This and subsequent editions contained an even greater number of doubtful attributions.

This confusion was unavoidable. The first *catalogue raisonné* did not appear until some thirty-eight years after Vincent's death. Details of provenances, especially for those paintings that were not transferred to the family at his death, had to be elicited years later, often from whoever were then the owners, and such information was not always reliable. In any case, to get a painting attributed to van Gogh in the first 1928 catalogue of his oeuvre was not too difficult, a fact which was undoubtedly exploited (see Chapter 15).

Not all these incorrect attributions have as yet been identified and eliminated from later *catalogues raisonnés*, and many of his paintings are still missing and therefore not listed; this has made the task of researching *The Diggers* all the more difficult.

Everybody familiar with the oeuvre of van Gogh who has seen *The Diggers* agrees that, if it is indeed by van Gogh, it can only be from his very first period of painting in oil in The Hague or Drenthe.

From this first period, lasting only six weeks in August–September 1882 in The Hague, eleven works are known to have survived out of the total of some thirty.* Five are in private hands; the whereabouts of three are not known; one is in the Van Gogh Museum in Amsterdam; and two are in the Rijksmuseum Kröller-Müller in Otterlo.

None of these are of comparable subject matter requiring a comparable palette, but even so, these early paintings and *The Diggers* do not clash. They show areas of a similar brush stroke, areas where similar or identical pigments have been used, and areas where the impasto is comparable, but none of the eleven shows large figures or has a sun, let alone a sun in the afternoon sky. The particular light in *The Diggers* obviously called for some different colours and pigments, additional to those used in his other known paintings of that period.

One might try comparison with the paintings from The Hague in 1883 and from later that year from Drenthe. In the early paintings, especially in those from Drenthe there are colours and some poses and subject matter, rendering of figures, positions of working people against the horizon, treatment of the horizon, and depths of field which are similar to features in *The Diggers*. These are some positive indications perhaps, but they still do not offer conclusive evidence for or against its authentication.

* A detailed list of these eleven paintings is given in Appendix B.

Of the fourteen paintings (out of some forty) known to have survived from this time in The Hague in August and September 1883 during which Vincent painted in oil, three are in private hands; of seven the whereabouts are not known; one is in Utrecht in the Stichting van Baaren; one was or is in New York in the Hirschl & Adler Galleries; and two are in the Rijksmuseum Kröller-Müller in Otterlo.** From Drenthe seven paintings are known.***

As can be seen, some of them express the same tragic atmosphere characteristic of Vincent at that time, and one can feel a relationship: *The Diggers* seems to fit in very well.

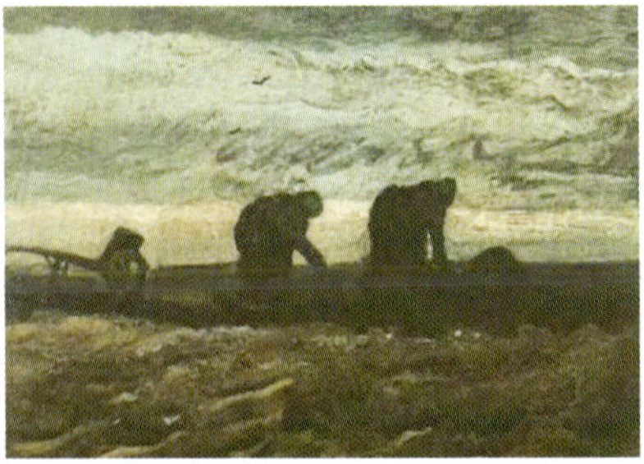

Two Women Working in the Peat
JH 409, October 1883, 27 × 35.5 cm

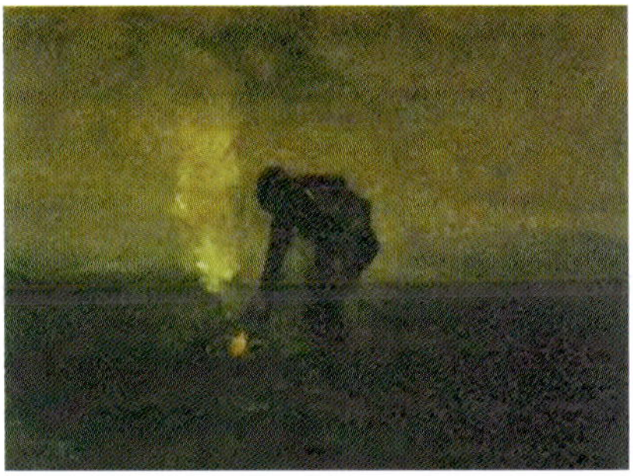

Peasant Burning Weeds
JH 416 , October 1883, 30.5 × 39.5 cm

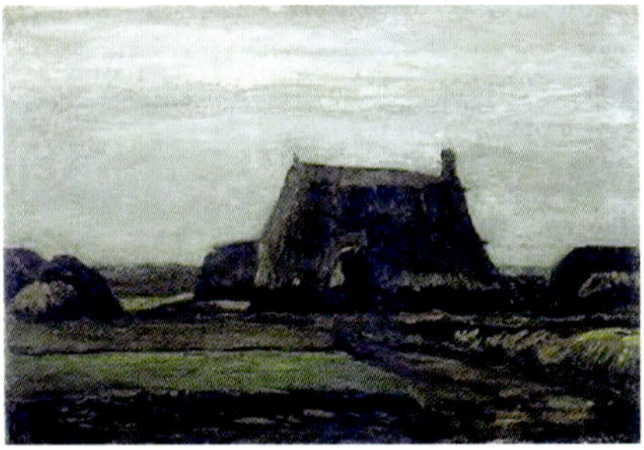

Little Farmhouse
JH 421, November 1883, 37.5 × 55 cm.

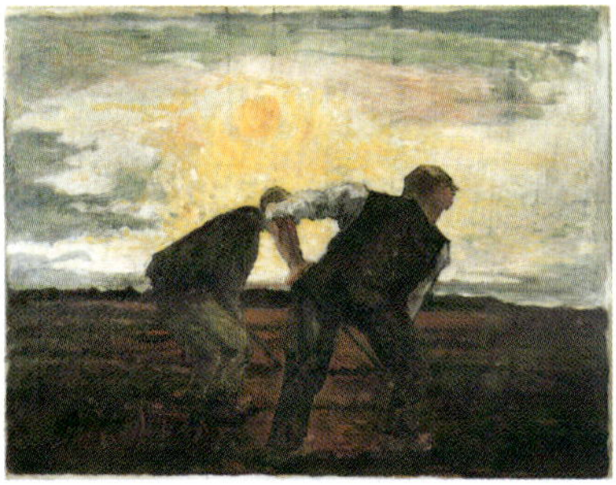

Two Diggers in the Afternoon Sun
September 1882? 47 × 61 cm

Vincent's own words later, if they did refer to this painting, suggest it was one of his most important early studies.

* * *

** These fourteen paintings are listed in Appendix C.
*** These seven are listed in Appendix D.

Now let us turn to the extraordinary story of what befell Vincent's early works. When he left for Drenthe he soon regretted having left his early studies behind in The Hague. In a letter to Theo (LT329 of c. 27 September 1883) he wrote:

> In The Hague are still more than 70 of my painted studies—if only they were here, they would have been more useful to me.

After leaving Drenthe for Nuenen on 5 December 1883, he made a quick visit to The Hague to reclaim his belongings, including the paintings. He told Theo in letter 349 of c. 22–25 December 1883:

> . . . [I] went to The Hague in order to pack up and dispatch my studies, prints, etc, etc.

and in letter 350 of c. 25–28 December, he further related,

> Yesterday evening I returned to Nuenen . . . [after I had] packed up my tools, studies etc. and dispatched them to here.

The Hague studies thus belatedly accompanied him to Nuenen, but some two years later he left them behind a second time when he left for Antwerp. In a much later letter to his sister Wilhelmina, c. 22 June 1888, he wrote from Saint-Rémy in France:

> Tell me, talking about rubbish, maybe it would be worthwhile rescuing whatever is useful out of my rubbish, which, according to Theo, is still in a loft somewhere in Breda.

No immediate action is thought to have been taken as a result of this letter, but it does tell us that at least some of his belongings eventually ended up in a loft in Breda, and this was confirmed by Johanna van Gogh-Bonger, Theo's widow, in 1913, in her introduction to the first publication of *The Collective Letters of Vincent van Gogh* in 1914. She wrote:

> When his mother also left Nuenen, in May 1886, all of Vincent's work was packed up in wooden crates and placed in storage with a carpenter in Breda. The carpenter, in due course, sold everything to a rag and bone merchant.

Benno J. Stokvis noted in his *Investigations about Vincent van Gogh in Brabant,* published in 1926, that the carpenter who stored Vincent's crates and the family furniture was a Mr Schrauwen. The story goes that when the van Gogh family went to reclaim the furniture, one of Vincent's sisters, presumably Wilhelmina, found traces of woodworm in Vincent's crates, and his mother, for fear of her furniture becoming infested, decided to leave the crates where they were. Many years later Schrauwen, who by now considered himself to be the rightful owner, is supposed to have emptied some cases and to have left the contents piled up in a corner of his attic. At some time he is supposed to have given one case with contents to a jobbing gardener in Breda, a Mr Barend den Houter. In 1903 Schrauwen arranged with a second-hand dealer in Breda, J.C. Couvreur, who was buying some brasswork from him, to take away the remainder of the van Gogh cases and loose 'rubbish' as part of the deal. Couvreur obliged and, with his brother, took the lot away to their store. A hundred or so crayon drawings thought to be worthless were torn up on the spot and thrown away, and Couvreur's wife immediately weeded out all of Vincent's drawings from the nude. Some items were apparently sent to a processing plant in Tilburg where they were destroyed. When questioned later by the biographer Benno Stokvis, the Couvreur brothers estimated roughly that after this purge the remainder had consisted of some 60 paintings on stretchers, 150 or so loose canvases, two portfolios with approximately 90 pen drawings, and 100–200 crayon drawings. They filled their pushcart with these, nailed some items to the sides, and sold them off for a penny or two according to size and desirability, at the nearby market. Finally, a Breda art dealer, C. Mouwen jr, reportedly bought what was left on the cart for one guilder. He asked for still more, and Couvreur then realised that he had missed a trick and tried, partly successfully, to locate some of his earlier customers; he bought some back and sold these at a higher price to Mouwen. Mouwen thus managed to acquire quite a few more of these early paintings.

The entire lot at Schrauwen's must have included the more than seventy painted studies from The Hague that Vincent had mentioned in his letters. About thirty of these he is believed to have painted in 1882 and about forty in 1883. Only twenty-five of the seventy have surfaced so far, eleven of which are currently generally attributed to the 1882 period and fourteen to the 1883 period. Some forty-five studies painted in The Hague are still missing.

In his letter to Theo of 14 August 1882, only some ten days after he had started painting in oils for the first time independently, Vincent had described what he saw as the correct colour scheme for a sky in a landscape with a setting sun:

> But it was entirely a matter of colour and tone, the nuances of colours of the sky, first a lilac haze, wherein the red sun, half covered by a purple cloud with a sparkling red fine edge; near the sun reflections of vermilion, with above a stroke of yellow turning green and higher bluish, the so-called cerulean blue and then here and there lilac and sombre clouds catching reflections from the sun.

Vincent's character was such that he would normally have painted what he had written about not long afterwards. In *The Diggers* there is a lilac haze to the right of the sun; near the sun are reflections of vermilion and, above, an area of yellow turning green, with green above the lilac on the right as well, and higher up, above the green the sky is bluish. On the left of the painting are lilac and sombre clouds catching reflections of the sun.

The spectrum of colours in the painting reflects remarkably closely Vincent's description in this letter to Theo of how he had visualised the sky in a landscape with a sun. It is difficult to imagine that the sky in *The Diggers* could have been painted by anyone other than the writer of, or someone who had read, this description. No other known painting of the Hague and Drenthe periods has colours in the sky such as he described in his letter.

A week later he wrote to Theo, on 20 August 1882:

> I have painted several studies in a short time . . . In a number of studies are small figures; I have also worked on a larger [figure] but already twice scraped it all off, which you would perhaps have called over-hasty if you had seen the effect.

In *The Diggers* it is apparent that large areas have been scraped off and later repainted. In the same letter he continued:

> But it is absolutely essential for a painting that one knows how to draw, with reasonable certainty, the correct proportions and place of the subjects before one starts.

In the study there are two subjects, whose correct proportions and place in the painting it would have been important to establish at the outset. Their outlines were certainly drawn in paint, in bold strokes, at the beginning and filled in later.

These two sentences from this letter match precisely, as far as one can tell, the method of execution of the figures in *The Diggers.*

In a number of letters, between 5 August 1882, when he bought his first oil paints, and 20 August, Vincent described in some detail the pigments and colours, etc. he had purchased. These details have helped to confirm that the actual pigments in the painting do indeed correspond with those we know he bought.

On 2 August, 1883 he wrote to Theo, at the beginning of his second spell of six weeks of painting in oils:

> Recently a great worry has fallen off my shoulders. Last year I repeatedly tried to paint figure studies but I became desperate over the way they turned out. I have started again now and I don't have any problems with the execution now because I draw with much greater ease than last year. At that time I often got confused if I lost the drawn sketch whilst painting . . . the first two figures I painted this year I did just like I tried last year—first drawing and then filling in the outline. This is what I would like to call the dry method.
>
> The other method is that one actually does the drawing last and starts by first searching out the tones without worrying too much about the drawing, except trying to get the tones as near as possible in their correct place and slowly making the form and the subdivision of the colours more precise. The result is then a figure as if surrounded by air and somewhat softer. You will see the difference if you see the first two I have now made, if they remain in their present state.

The statement that "Last year [in 1882] I repeatedly tried to paint figure studies . . ." evidently does not refer to any of the eleven surviving paintings from that period, as none of them are figure studies. There are relatively small figures in three studies from 1882 but they are too small for the technique he described to have been applicable to them. The other figure studies of 1882 he wrote about are not known to us and must therefore be among the nineteen missing studies never found from the 1882 period.

The Diggers is a figure study and the only known candidate to be one of the paintings he was referring to when he wrote in 1883 about his figure studies in 1882 and about his 'dry' method—first drawing the outlines, and afterwards filling them in. He again mentions having painted studies of a digger in the afternoon sun in his letter to Theo of 9 September 1882:

> In the autumn there are two things which particularly appeal to me. There is sometimes a soft melancholy in the falling leaves, in the tempered light, in the haziness of things, in the elegance of small tree-trunks. And then I equally like the more sturdy, rugged side, the strong

> light effects for instance on a digger sweating it out in the afternoon sun. I enclose a few sketches of the studies I made this week.

But none of the painted studies or the sketches of a digger in the afternoon sun, all of which, he tells us, he made in the week before 9 September 1882, have been found till now. A sun in the sky, but hidden behind a tree, does appear in a pen-and-pencil drawing of 1884, done in Nuenen (JH461, left), of the garden of the vicarage where he lived with his parents in 1884. The halo in pen strokes around the sun in this drawing, is seen in brush strokes in *The Diggers*. This halo later became a typical van Gogh trademark.

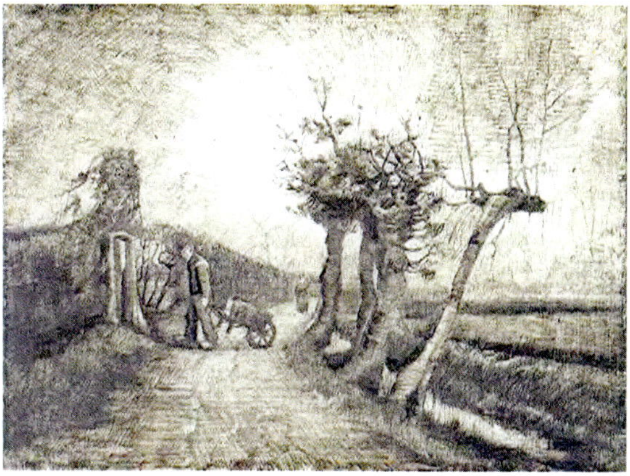

In the same letter of 9 September he also wrote:

> In the meantime my paint is finished, I sincerely hope you are not too hard up. In any case I hope you can send me the usual by 10 September.

Unfortunately, lack of funds made it impossible for him to purchase more oil paints and he stopped painting in oils for some eleven months until August the following year. During this break he concentrated again on his draughtsmanship.

The Diggers may thus have been painted under the stress of a shortage of paint. Although in certain areas the brush strokes incline towards impasto, generally speaking the painting is not executed in heavy impasto. That is no obstacle to authenticity: some paintings needed heavy impasto, others did not, as he said in his letters on a number of occasions. Shortage of paint may also have been why he did not trouble to obscure the underlying painting on the canvas of *The Diggers* completely. This could be supporting evidence that this painting was executed between late August and early September 1882, when his paint ran out.

The close link between what Vincent wrote to Theo and the painting is such that it seems only reasonable to conclude that the writer, or a reader, of *The Letters*, must have painted *The Diggers*.

All this was rather convincing supportive evidence for the authenticity of the study, but Vincent wrote the most important references to it in the last year of his life, while he was in the asylum at Saint-Rémy in 1889–1890. Periods of ill health there forced him either to abandon painting or to paint indoors, and at the end of 1889 he undertook the painting of numerous copies, many after Millet.

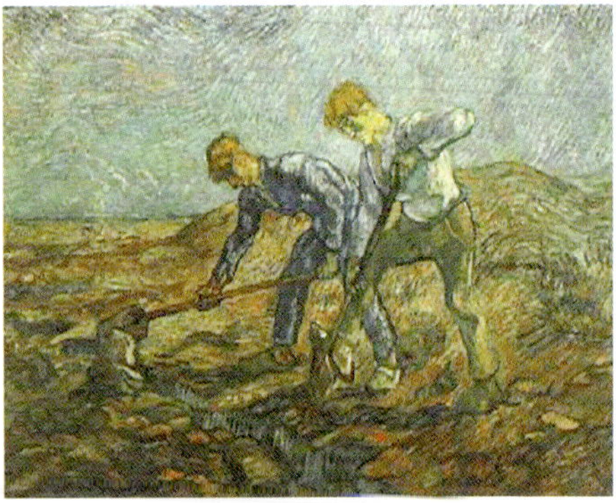

In letter 611, c. 25 October 1889 he wrote to Theo,

I have started on *The Diggers* (JH1833, right) on a canvas size 30

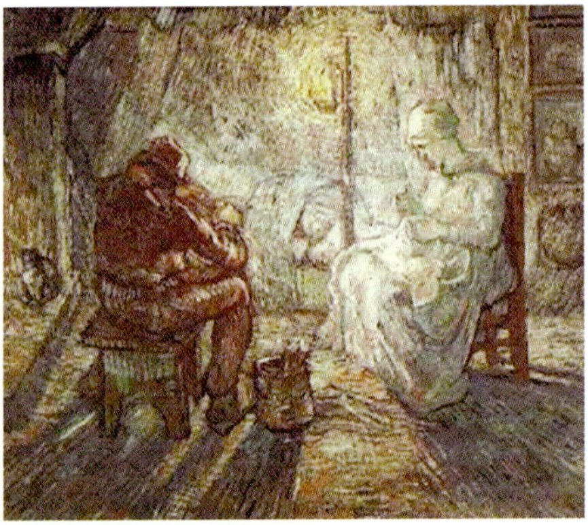

and in letter 613, c. 2 November 1889 he wrote:

Have finished *The Family at Night* (JH1834, left), and am working on *The Diggers* [above] . . .

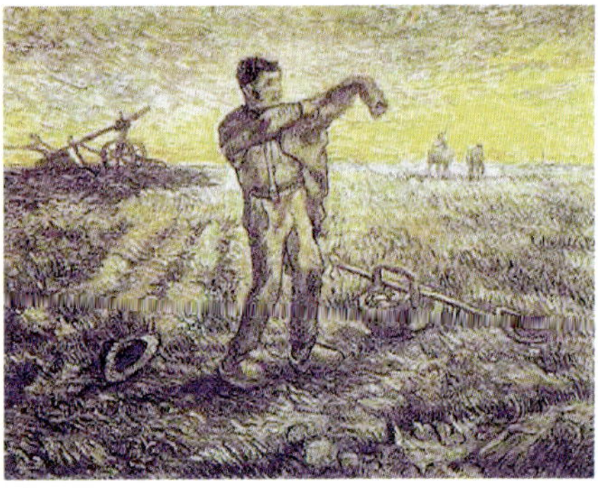

. . . and *The End of the Day* (JH1835, right), canvas size 30,

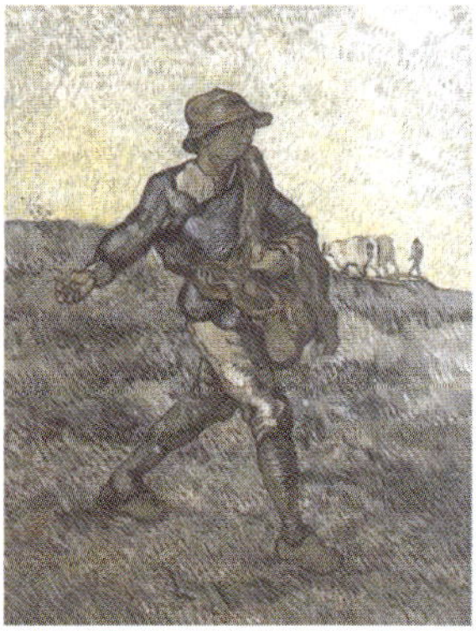

. . . and on *The Sower* (JH1837, left) which is smaller.

In letter 621 of 3 January 1890 he recorded a dispatch of paintings to Theo that day, which included the copy of *The Diggers* he made after Millet.

Vincent became ill again after visiting Arles in February 1890, restricting his ability to work and write until the end of April 1890. When he became a little better, he expressed the desire also to repaint subjects from his early Dutch period. In letter 629 of 29 or 30 April 1890 to his brother, he ordered a quantity of paint and brushes and added:

> Please send me any figure drawings you can find among my old drawings. I am thinking of doing the picture of the *Peasants at Dinner* [better known as *The Potato Eaters*] with the lamplight effect again. That canvas must be quite black now, perhaps I could do it again altogether from memory.
>
> You must especially send me the *Women Gleaning* and the *Diggers* if they are still there. Then, if you like, I will do the *Old Tower of Nuenen* again and the *Cottage*. I think that if you still have them, I can make something better of them now from memory.

The same day, in letter 629a, he wrote to his mother and his sister, Wilhelmina:

> Do you perhaps still have some of my old painted studies and drawings? Even though they may not be very good they could still provide me with memories and information for new work, but I will not need those you may have hanging on your walls. I would rather have the attempts at figures of farmers.

The reference to the *Diggers* in the letter to Theo in Paris is to drawings but the reference to 'figures of farmers' in the letter to his mother and sister can only refer to a study or studies of diggers or farmers that he had made himself in the Netherlands but which have never been found. Vincent had an excellent memory and knew where his works could be.

No early painting of diggers had been sent to Paris, and once again this fits in with the appearance in Breda of the painting of diggers.

Vincent's mentioning of diggers among the early subjects he wants to paint again shows the importance the subject had for him. Could any subject be in better company than that of:

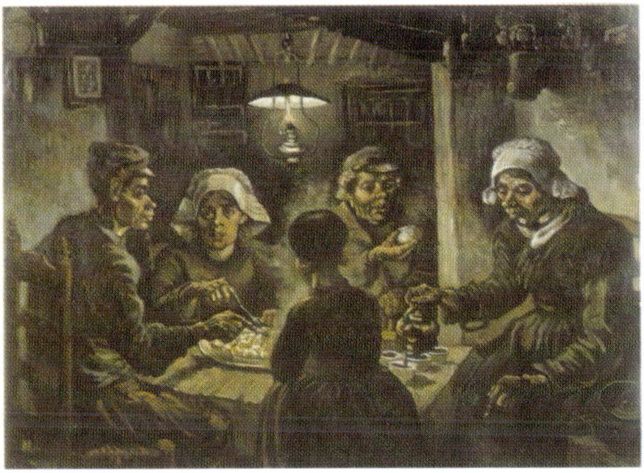

The Potato Eaters (JH764)

The Old Tower of Nuenen (JH772)

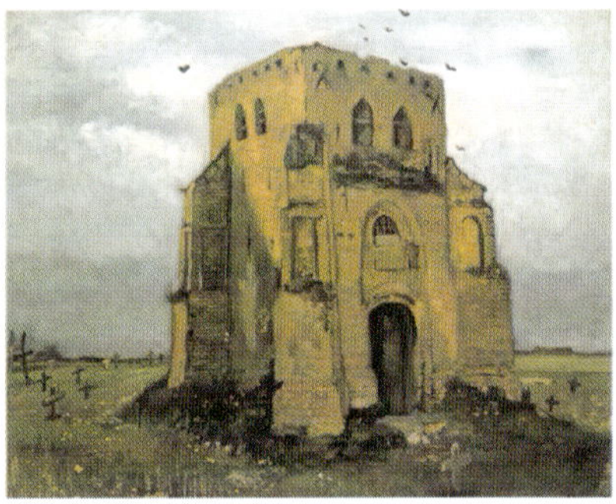

and

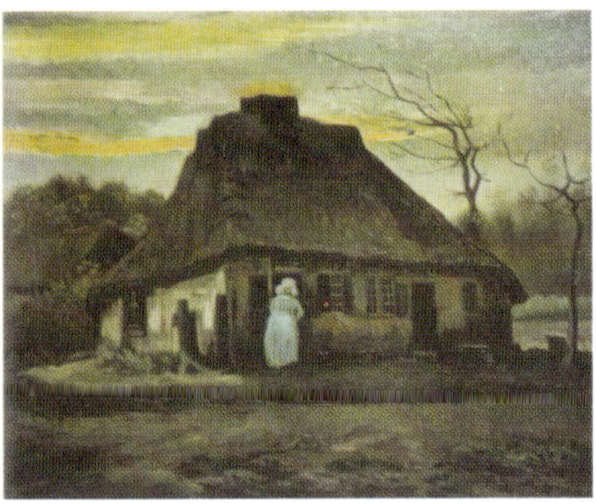

The Cottage (JH777)

* * *

The research so far had taken me deep into Vincent country. A year had passed and it was now May 1994. I had cautiously become a little more confident about my original intuitions, and the time had come to seek outside opinions and try to obtain undeniable proof that the painting was not by him or, alternatively, confirmation that it was.

But there was a snag—many a wishful thinker believes that they have found a masterpiece in grandmother's attic, in a flea market, or elsewhere. Fear of being cast into this category was a restraining factor. I realised if I were just to announce that I had found a previously unknown painting by van Gogh I would meet with a fair amount of perhaps justifiable cynicism. There might well be considerable reluctance to accept the painting as genuine and I had been warned and anticipated that I would get a few 'no' verdicts. But surely the features characteristic of Vincent, the choice of subject matter, the colours, the handling of the paint, the supporting references in the letters could not all be ignored—or so I still naively thought.

The purpose of my endeavours was to find undeniable evidence that the painting was either genuine or not. Finding an undeniable reason that it could not possibly be by van Gogh would end my task and I would accept that as an unfortunate end perhaps, but in a way also as a relief from the considerable and time consuming burden of the research I felt to be committed to. But thinking this way was now a waste of time, I had to take the show on the road and find out. With an open mind.

Chapter Three

On the Road

As a major first port of call, the Kröller-Müller National Museum in Otterlo seemed a good choice. It has two paintings by van Gogh from each of the 1882 and 1883 periods in its collection, more than any other museum, institution, or private collector. Apart from these four early paintings, the museum has over 260 of his paintings, drawings, and other works, which is by far the richest and largest collection outside the Van Gogh Museum in Amsterdam.

I contacted the curator of the museum, Mr Johannes van der Wolk, who readily gave me an appointment. He is the author of *The Seven Sketchbooks of Vincent van Gogh* and a former curator of the Museum Boymans-van Beuningen in Rotterdam, as well as a former director of the then Rijksmuseum Vincent van Gogh in Amsterdam. I felt it to be still a little early to force the painting on him, so I decided to leave it at home.

The Kröller-Müller National Museum is a truly magnificent museum, lying peacefully in the middle of a large National Park, called Den Hoge Veluwe, near Arnhem. It also has a fabulous sculpture garden of some fifty acres, with a lake. Opened in 1938, the museum originally housed the collection of Helene Kröller-Müller. This lady, together with her husband, was guided by H.P. Bremmer (1871–1956), who was a van Gogh aficionado and an impressionist painter himself. He set out to advance the fame of Vincent van Gogh, and built up for her a considerable collection of paintings, which was transferred to the State in 1935. The collection includes works by Seurat, Picasso, Léger, Mondrian, and many more great artists but centres on the impressive number of works by van Gogh. In 1928 an additional some 128 drawings and a lithograph were bought from the Hidde Nijland collection by the Foundation to further augment their collection from Helene Kröller-Müller.

After one reaches a principal gate of the National Park it is still quite a drive to the museum itself through the most beautiful and peaceful scenery imaginable—with one or two farm buildings here and there but for most part without a building in sight, only sandy soil, heather, pine trees, and deer. A more romantic and appealing setting for a museum would be hard to find.

During this visit, in May 1994, van der Wolk made me feel very welcome indeed. He studied the photograph of the painting I showed him with great interest, at length and in detail. He found the painting rather clumsily executed but added that Vincent's early work was known to be rather clumsy. He was certainly not positive that it was by van Gogh but he did not exclude that possibility either, and he could not suggest anyone else who might have painted it.

He said it would be important to check if the painting had previously been subjected to official scrutiny and rejected as a van Gogh, and whether it could possibly be attributed with any certainty to another painter. For this he suggested that I should show it to Dr Martha op de Coul, who had worked on the preparation of the revised *catalogue raisonné* published in 1970 and who is head of the department of 19th century Dutch art at the Netherlands Institute for Art History in The Hague.

He also felt that it would be very important to get an earlier provenance. All I have is the word of the auctioneer that the vendor had bought it around 1990 from people who had acquired it many years earlier when living in Breda, and the evidence of Vincent's own letters.

As he had not said anything adverse after seeing a photograph, I offered to show him the painting itself, and in March 1995 I took *The Diggers* to Otterlo. After careful examination he still felt unable to decide on the author. He said that too little was known about van Gogh's early work and that there was not enough known material with which the work could fruitfully be compared.

At this second visit to Otterlo I had hoped to see the early van Gogh paintings in the collection at close hand, to find whether there were any similarities between materials and canvases used and those used for *The Diggers*. I was taken to the vaults of the museum but unfortunately the backs of all their four paintings from this period were boarded up, so the reverse of the canvases could not be seen. While we were looking at one of the two 1882 paintings, the *Edge of a Wood*, however, I commented to the curator that frankly, if I knew nothing at all about either picture, I would have more difficulty in ascribing his to van Gogh than mine. To my pleasant surprise he said that he himself might have had the same problem, but the all-important difference lay in their provenances.

The earliest recorded owner of the *Edge of a Wood* is the art dealer Mouwen of Breda. He tried to sell it at auction (F. Muller) in Amsterdam on 3 May 1904 but failed. He then sold it to the Oldenzeel Art Gallery in Rotterdam, whence it found its way to the Kröller-Müller Museum. Its provenance is thus acceptable and its attribution reliable.

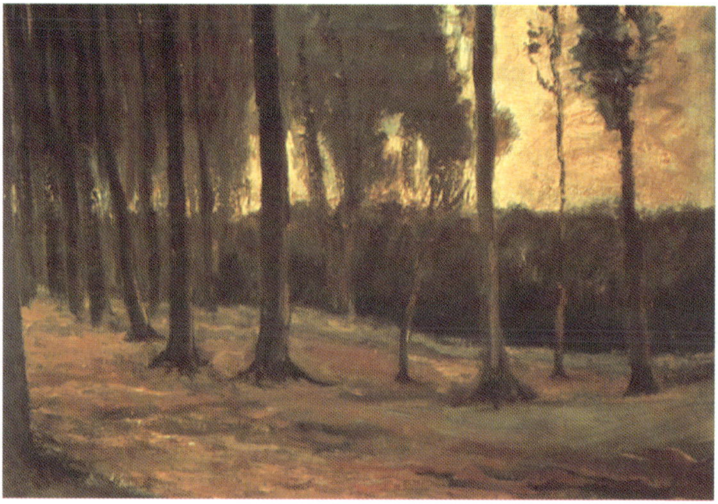

Edge of a Wood (JH184, F192)
Canvas on panel, 34.5 × 45 cm

The absence of such records has left *The Diggers* without an early provenance. Van der Wolk suggested that in some ten or fifteen years' time, when more research has been carried out on the early van Goghs, including their canvas structures, new knowledge may make it easier to make a firm attribution, but until such time he felt unable to attribute it positively to van Gogh. He had no particular suggestion as to what I should do next, but he had not given any reason, either, for me to call a halt to my endeavours.

* * *

In between my two visits to Otterlo, Mr I. Humphreys, a lecturer in painting at the Berkshire College of Art and Design and also a well known painter in his own right, saw *The Diggers* hanging in my Eton gallery. His eye was immediately drawn to it and he studied it closely.

Unsolicited, he drew attention to a number of aspects he described as positive early signs of van Gogh characteristics which, he said, developed further in Vincent's later career.

He thought that the following pigments had been used in the painting: ochres—red, yellow and terra sienna; blues—cobalt, ultramarine and prussian; reds—carmine and vermilion; Naples yellow, sepia, and lead white. All these pigments are known for certain to have been in van Gogh's possession in August/September 1882 because he mentions buying them in his letters to his brother. Humphreys's verdict was that, in his opinion, the painting was definitely an early Vincent van Gogh.

* * *

On 14 September 1994, I showed the painting to Dr Nicholas Penny of the National Gallery in London. He had a close look at it and was clearly rather intrigued by it. He did not think it was very old, perhaps as little as a hundred years, possibly a little older. He suggested it might be doubtful whether it was by van Gogh because he was known not to have been able to draw very well, but the painter of *The Diggers* had obviously not had any such difficulty, as the figures seemed boldly executed without hesitation.

Since van Gogh had in April 1882 produced the famous drawing *Sorrow* (JH129) as well as a boldly drawn scene of *Diggers in a Broken-up Street* and a number of other strong drawings, he can certainly be considered capable of the bold drawing in oil of the two figures in *The Diggers* (below).

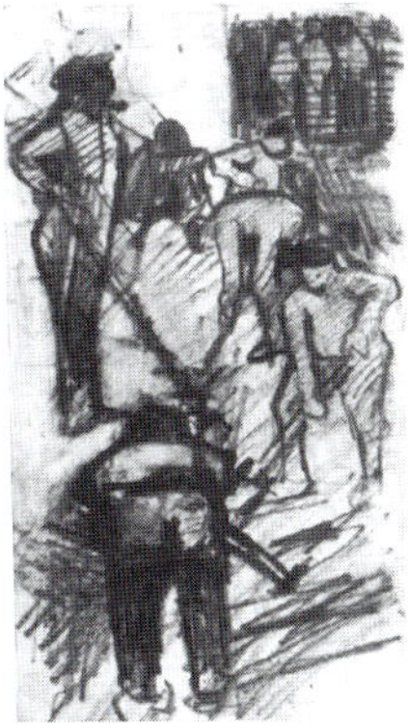

Diggers in Broken-up Street (JH 132) April 1882

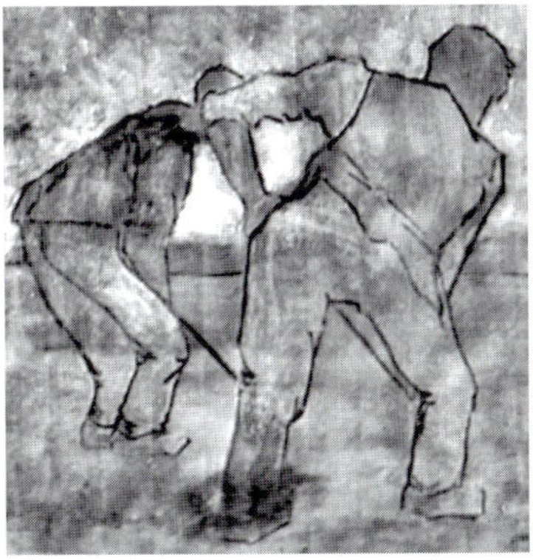

IRR/DP image taken by Dr Eastaugh revealing the base drawing in oil of *Two Diggers in the Afternoon Sun*, September 1882?

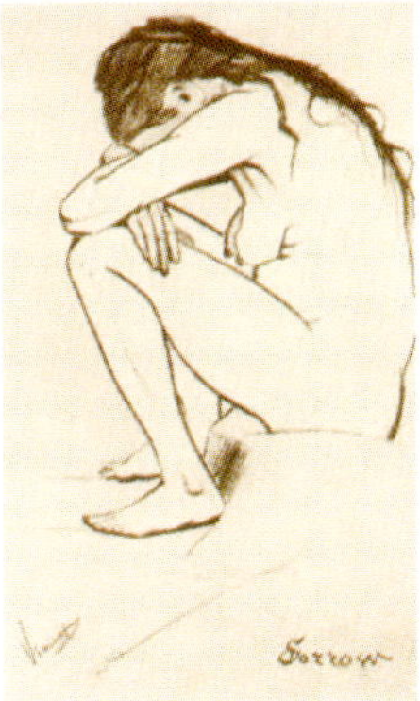

Sorrow (JH 129, F 929a) black chalk 44.5 × 27 cm April 1882

Nevertheless this was the only reason Penny gave for doubting an attribution to Vincent.

He could not think of any other possible artist and his estimate of the painting's age was a helpful statement from an authority. He admitted, however, that John Leighton, not he, was the Gallery's expert on 19th century Continental paintings and said that I should it to him. He would tell Leighton, who was then away, what he had seen and would arrange an appointment for me.

* * *

I now turned to Sotheby's in Bond Street, London, to find out whether they could suggest my next move, and two days after my visit to the National Gallery I showed the painting to Oliver Barker, one of the directors of their Impressionist & Modern Art Department. He had previously seen a photograph, but now felt, on seeing the painting, that it could be dated quite definitely to the end of the 19th century. He became most interested and asked me to come back again for two of his senior colleagues to see the painting. I returned on 24 October 1994, and he showed it to Phillip Hook.

Sotheby's interest was confirmed. It was felt that the painting could be dated to the end of the 19th century and that it might very well be by Vincent van Gogh—neither expert could suggest any other possible author. It was explained to me, however, that for important paintings the larger auction houses depend on reputable specialised expert opinions. They could never risk auctioning a painting as a van Gogh without a formal authentication from, for instance, an authority such as the art dealer Walter Feilchenfeldt of Zürich or, preferably, from the Van Gogh Museum in Amsterdam.

They also wished to confirm their own opinions and asked if I could leave the painting behind to be seen by Michel Strauss, senior director of Sotheby's Impressionist & Modern Art Department, who was away at the time. This was not possible for insurance reasons, but I left a photograph and agreed to bring the painting again when Strauss returned. They wrote to me a few days later that Strauss could not confirm authenticity from the photograph alone and that he would prefer to wait to hear what the Van Gogh Museum would have to say.

I had, as it turned out, an opportunity to show him the actual painting a few weeks later, when his immediate reaction was quite positive and he spontaneously exclaimed, "I like it a lot". As for formal attribution to van Gogh, he suggested I would need to find a sufficiently influential authority who developed a positive 'gut feeling' about it. There are, he said, no easy ways to prove the authenticity of a painting. Scientific research can often provide absolute proof that a painting is *not* by a particular artist but hardly ever that it *is*. At best, it can confirm that there is nothing against a proposed attribution. He estimated that if scientific examination revealed no obstacles, I might have a '50–50' chance of getting the painting attributed to van Gogh. He too could not think of any other possible author for it.

Having seen only a photograph a few weeks earlier but now seeing the painting 'in the flesh', he said that it would be essential to show the painting itself, rather than a photograph, to any authority whose positive opinion would be important. He suggested individual members of the erstwhile 'Van Gogh Committee', or Walter Feilchenfeldt in Zürich, or Louis van Tilborgh, chief curator of the Van Gogh Museum. He also mentioned Dr Roland Dorn, who was said to be in the process of writing a new van Gogh *catalogue raisonné*.

The marketing experts who had seen the painting thus believed that it might indeed be genuine. They considered that a serious attempt at getting an attribution to Vincent van Gogh might well turn out to be successful in the end, but they too recommended that I should not go to the Van Gogh Museum empty-handed. I was given suggestions on how they thought I should proceed, which were essentially to tread carefully—an attribution by the Museum would be ideal, but before going for that I should collect as much positive material about my painting as I could; show it to as many knowledgeable people as would look at it; and if I succeeded in amassing substantial support, then to go for the final shot.

In early November 1994, I telephoned Feilchenfeldt to ask for an appointment to show him the painting. He asked to see a photograph first, which I sent the same day. He is an art dealer based in Zürich. His father was the Walter Feilchenfeldt (1894–1953) who became a partner and director of the Paul Cassirer Art Gallery in Berlin and later Amsterdam, after the suicide of Paul Cassirer. The Gallery had been marketing and promoting Vincent's paintings since around 1905 when, fifteen years after his death, his fame began to spread after exhibitions of his work—one in Paris, two in Holland, and four in Germany. The Gallery operated in Germany from its base in Berlin and Cassirer became the most important dealer in van Goghs in the world at that time.

With the records of the gallery at his disposal, Walter Feilchenfeldt junior had a wealth of information about dealings in and early provenances of van Goghs in Germany. His listing of dealings in van Goghs prior to 1914 was published in 1988 as *Cahier No. 2*, Rijksmuseum Vincent van Gogh, entitled: *Vincent van Gogh and Paul Cassirer, Berlin*. Feilchenfeldt is thus an established scholar and expert on provenances of van Gogh paintings.

And, as other experts before him, he has also had his misadventures. On a trip to the United States in 1990 he declared three self-portraits of Vincent to be forgeries. Glenn Collins reported this in an article in the *New York Times*, and shortly afterwards openly ridiculed Feilchenfeldt's statements in a second article. On the reverse of two of these supposedly forged self-portraits were other genuine paintings by van Gogh, and underneath the third an Xray showed a painting of a peasant from Nuenen peeling potatoes. This experience may have led him to be more cautious in his subsequent judgements.

When I telephoned him again on 14 November 1994, he said he had received the photograph but, before giving an opinion, he would like to show it to his then friend and colleague Roland Dorn. Dorn is a German art historian who had teamed up with Feilchenfeldt on provenances and several other matters to do with van Gogh. Both work in close co-operation with the Van Gogh Museum and are major contributors to its official publications. They and the Museum march to the same drum.

On 26 November 1994 I received a letter from Dorn. He said that, from the photograph, beyond superficial analogies in subject matter *he saw absolutely no reason to attribute this painting of a setting sun with two men digging in the ground to van Gogh*. He felt that neither style nor execution admitted van Gogh's authorship. He did suggest, however, that I ask Messrs van Tilborgh and van Heugten of the Van Gogh Museum for their opinions.

Feilchenfeldt and Dorn, in an article they contributed to the book *The Mythology of Vincent Van Gogh,* by Tsukasa Kodera, declare that 'the time for treasure hunting is over'. I wondered whether they had classified me as a 'treasure hunter', and also why they had closed their minds to the possibility of new discoveries?

* * *

As my next step I arranged a meeting with Dr Martha Op de Coul of the Netherlands Institute for Art History in The Hague, who had been suggested by van der Wolk on my first visit to the Kröller-Müller

Museum. My first meeting with her, at which a colleague Mr W. Rappard from her department was also present, was on 15 November 1994.

Van der Wolk had suggested that this was the best source of advice whether *The Diggers* could possibly be a forgery or, alternatively, whether it might be by any other artist of its time. The department has extensive records on van Gogh forgeries, including those listed by de la Faille in *Les Faux van Gogh*, as well as others which have never been publicised.

After consulting their archives, Dr Op de Coul and Rappard confirmed that the painting was not a known forgery, nor could they suggest any painter of that period, other than van Gogh, who would sign his work 'Vincent'. It was agreed that the painting was from the late 19th century, which confirmed that it had been painted before material that might have inspired any other painter, such as Vincent's descriptions for the colours of a sky with sun, had been publicly available. Nevertheless, though looking at a photograph only, Dr Op de Coul declared that she did not think that the painting could be by van Gogh. I could not get her to say why or give any explanation other than 'for stylistic reasons', and to this day I do not know what stylistic reasons she may have had in mind. Pointing out stylistic features that positively suggested it could be by Vincent did not influence her verdict.

When she later saw the actual painting, she was obviously more impressed than by the photograph. She said spontaneously, *"Dat oogt toch wel heel wat beter"* [That does indeed look a lot better], but was still not inclined to change her mind. It may be that for her, and for some others, there are just too many van Goghs in the catalogues already. She did suggest that I show the painting, rather than the photograph, at the Van Gogh Museum.

She has been interviewed by the makers of the film *The Fake Van Goghs* and has indeed expressed doubts about the authenticity of a number of paintings attributed to van Gogh in the catalogues. She does not like to be specific about precisely which she feels not to be authentic, but she has publicly estimated that there must be forty or more such works.

I had perhaps not yet fully appreciated that what I really needed was an expert with the eye and the talent to be able to understand the burgeoning of the genius of Vincent van Gogh at the very start of his career—not just art historians, who do not necessarily possess the talents a task like this requires. Vincent himself wrote, on 3 September 1882,

> In some ways I am glad that I have not been taught (learned) to paint because then I might have learned to pass by certain effects.

and he went on to suggest that it is better to find out for oneself, by looking and looking again until one achieves the desired result. It may take longer but the result will be better.

At a later stage in the proceedings Dr Evert van Uitert, then professor in Art History at the University of Amsterdam, after seeing only a photograph of *The Diggers* gave as his verdict that it had been painted by someone who could not only not paint but who would never be able to learn to paint. In an interview he also said that he did not think that it would be possible to discover hitherto unknown paintings by Van Gogh any longer.

But where was I to find the kind of gifted expert I needed? There are individuals who have become experts out of love for a certain subject or for the work of a specific artist. This love then fires their inner ambitions, drive, and passion. Such dedicated people make a meticulous study of the area that has caught their imagination and make this the major purpose of their life, becoming greater experts about a specific subject than those who have to cover a wider field and cannot be expected to be experts on every detail. However, if these independent scholars are not in a senior position on the staff of a reputable museum , they are often dismissed as 'amateurs', they are 'not part of the art establishment', and are not given due credit for their skills and knowledge.

I was gradually beginning to understand more and more about where one should and should not go for sound and honest opinions.

* * *

As promised by Dr Penny, I was given an opportunity to show *The Diggers* on 23 November 1994 to John Leighton, the London National Gallery's young expert on 19th century European Art. On this first occasion, clearly intrigued, he spent three-quarters of an hour examining the painting. He said that he liked it, but, unlike Penny, found the drawing of the figures a little weak. He liked particularly the areas to the left and to the right of the two diggers. He thought the painting, canvas, and stretcher were probably from the end of the 19th century and advised me, as had Sotheby's, to show it to more people 'in the business' and to continue to build up a body of relevant knowledge and material on it. He had, he confessed, and as his judgement on the drawing had confirmed, too little detailed knowledge of van Gogh himself to be able to give a definite opinion. He said that he would not like to guess whether the end result would be positive or negative. He did suggest that it might well be worth having the painting examined 'scientifically'—expensive though it would probably be—and for this he recommended a Dr Nicholas Eastaugh, who, he said, did work of this nature for the National Gallery from time to time. After this, however, and after everything else that could be done, the final verdict must come from the experts at the Museum in Amsterdam.

By an ironic twist of history John Leighton a little over two years later became director of the Van Gogh Museum in Amsterdam.

* * *

I therefore went in search of Dr Eastaugh and was able to see him on 1 December 1994. The painting immediately interested him and he suggested various tests in order to estimate the dates of the canvas, the stretcher, and the painting itself better. He also recommended tests on the pigments used, and on the signature and the time of its placing. He suggested infrared, ultraviolet, and Xray examinations. *The Diggers* went to his Teddington laboratory from 12 December 1994 to 9 January 1995.

Dr Eastaugh is a technical expert who provides a professional opinion based on the results of tests and analyses of a painting. Fees are normally agreed in advance and are based on the time taken and complexity of the work; they are not influenced by the outcome. Tests may prove a painting not to be authentic, for instance by finding that it was painted after the supposed artist's death, that it contains material not yet available to him, or if Xray reveals underlying work more recent than its supposed date. If nothing is found to gainsay the attribution, the laboratory can still only certify that nothing has been found that contradicts it. In short, they can only say 'no' or 'possibly', but never 'yes'; but the deeper the investigation goes, the more possible it is that a 'possibly' may one day mature into a 'yes'.

A series of sixteen pigment samples were taken and two methods used for their identification—polarised light microscopy and scanning electron microscopy/energy-dispersive Xray spectrometry. There was considerable matching between the pigments found and those described by Vincent in a letter of 5 August 1882, with a few exceptions that could be explained by further letters telling of additional purchases of paint. The most notable differences were: in the use of ultramarine; the occurrence of a green pigment; the apparent use of a commercially prepared purple/mauve paint; and possibly in the presence of cadmium yellow rather than Naples yellow. All the pigments used would have been available to Vincent in 1882.

Eastaugh also found that the canvas was of an unusual weave. The same type was used for an 1870 painting by Fantin-Latour, and for an 1872 painting by Monet that is in the National Gallery. As already recounted, I had been unable to examine the canvases of the two 1882 van Goghs in the Kröller-Müller Museum, and had encountered the same problem with the 1883 painting in Utrecht. I have also asked several times to be allowed to examine the one and only 1882 painting in the Van Gogh Museum, but something has always intervened to prevent my having a close look. In any case, the Museum's painting was originally painted on paper or cardboard and later put on a panel that was subsequently removed, damaging the original carrier; it was then placed on canvas. It is unlikely that its canvas is at all comparable with that of *The Diggers*.

Eastaugh noted that the signature, in the lower right-hand corner of the painting, has been abraded but is apparently original, since there was

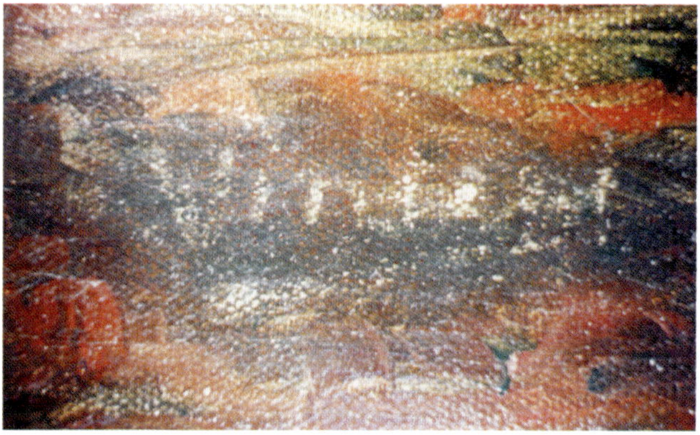

A reproduction from a photograph by the laboratories of
Dr Nicholas Eastaugh Ph.D., Dip.Cons., B.Sc.

no evidence under binocular microscopy that the paint passed over areas of damage or that it had suffered differently from the immediate surroundings. Moreover the paint shows some evidence of incised lines corresponding to the letters.

He also reported that there is a design underneath the present painting, the form and extent of which could not be fully gauged. It appears to consist of various lines of differing width and orientation.

He was uncertain whether these might be part of the preparatory work for the final composition or might belong to an unfinished earlier composition.

Finally, he found evidence that some time had elapsed between the execution of the basic design, laid out in the black lines of the figures and the horizon, and the subsequent painting.

The results from these intensive tests and analyses were that nothing had been found which would prevent 1882 from being the year of creation, or would rule out an attribution to Vincent van Gogh. It meant that I still had to carry on in my quest. I now needed the opinions of other genuine, internationally recognised experts. They too cannot provide absolute proof perhaps, but at least their observations on a painting, their ability to recognise an artist's characteristics, and their ability to spot things others would pass by a hundred times without seeing them, could be helpful. If they can convince fellow experts of their opinions, this can place the matter 'beyond reasonable doubt'. This, combined with favourable results of technical and chemical analysis, and the absence of any dubious episodes in the provenance, might lead to an authentication. The only really positive opinion I had obtained so far, however, was from Humphreys, but however expert he may be on paintings, unfortunately he does not have a known track record or international reputation on paintings by van Gogh.

I wondered if Vincent's description of painters, in a letter to his brother in August 1882, as:

> a family, an unfortunate association of people with conflicting interests in which basically everyone disagrees with all the rest and in which two or more will only agree with each other and combine forces if it is for the purpose of hindering another member of the group.

could apply to art experts as well as to painters.

None the less, with Eastaugh's report I felt a lot of possible doubt had been removed. In particular, I thought that those who had so far only seen photographs of the painting might now, when confronted by *The Diggers* 'in the flesh' as well as by the results of the extensive research, be more positive about it.

* * *

Remembering what I had learned at Sotheby's, I felt that I should now renew my contact with Messrs Feilchenfeldt and Dorn. The auction houses might accept a positive verdict from them. There seemed to be nothing to lose by paying them a visit, if I could..

In February 1995 therefore, I tried to arrange to show Dorn the painting and acquaint him with Eastaugh's findings. I tracked him down by phone in Mannheim, and he said he would be at the Museum in Amsterdam a few days later, and would be happy to look at the painting there, provided I first got permission from the then chief curator, van Tilborgh. I telephoned immediately and was promised that I would be rung back with an answer, but answer came there none. After several more calls, van Tilborgh himself finally came on the line and said I should have applied for his permission much earlier and in writing—my request simply to be allowed to meet Dorn on the Museum's premises was apparently in the same class as asking for their opinion on a painting, which requires a preliminary application well in advance, with a photograph and written details. (I wondered rather unkindly why a photograph is so often requested instead of a painting itself—could it be that it is relatively safe to say 'no' to a photograph because poor quality of the reproduction can later be blamed—should it become necessary—for a mistaken rejection.)

My attempts to show Dorn my painting at the Museum had thus brought it to the attention of van Tilborgh again, a little prematurely under my grand plan. However, I needed the verdict of the Museum or of Messrs Feilchenfeldt and Dorn to calm the auction houses' fear of litigation. I now regretted having shown the Museum the photographs before the auction, as I felt certain they would now be very reluctant to authenticate my painting unless I could provide indisputable provenance or attribution by an expert such as Dr Dorn. Yet I felt I could not really delay any longer but must beard the lion, the mighty Van Gogh Museum, in its den. I might only get a 'no' verdict, but surely they would have to back it up with valid supporting reasons, which could be interesting.

Chapter Four

The Brick Wall—the Van Gogh Museum

The 'Van Gogh Committee' of the sixties, created to edit de la Faille's manuscript after his death with a view to publication of the revised *catalogue raisonné* in 1970, was no longer in existence. At the Van Gogh Museum, it now appeared, the fountain-head of wisdom was the head curator of van Gogh paintings Louis van Tilborgh.

I wrote to him on 9 March 1995, primarily to ask if I could show him the painting at any time convenient to him. I provided details such as size, medium, and subject matter. I also told him how it had come into my possession, and I summed up the story so far: that van der Wolk of the Kröller-Müller museum and Dr Op de Coul of the Netherlands Institute for Art History had seen a photograph of the painting. The latter had also seen the painting itself and had confirmed that the image had never been seen in the Institute before; that it did not resemble any of the known van Gogh copies or forgeries; and that she knew of no other artist to whom it could be attributed. I also mentioned that it had been seen by Leighton of the National Gallery in London and, at his suggestion, it had been thoroughly tested scientifically, without finding any let or hindrance to its being attributed to van Gogh, and I offered to send the full laboratory report.

As requested, I sent photographs of the painting but clearly pointed out that all the experts who had seen both painting and photograph had advised that a photograph was inadequate and that anyone seeking to judge it must see the painting itself. I therefore offered to bring it to Amsterdam at any time convenient to him.

A reply dated 23 March informed me that, under certain conditions, the Van Gogh Museum offers research into the authenticity of works of art, free of charge. These conditions were contained in a separate agreement, two copies of which were sent with the letter, to be signed by the owner or by someone in possession of a power of attorney to sign on his behalf. I was offered confidentiality unless and until I gave written permission for disclosure of my identity.

I was asked to send, when returning the signed agreements, additional documentation relevant to *The Diggers* and was told that all material I sent about the painting, including photographs, would be retained by the Museum for the benefit of their research archives. If no definite verdict could be given on the basis of the material sent, I might be asked to bring the painting to Amsterdam for viewing. In principle, I could expect their report within three months from the date of receipt of the signed agreement. The Museum committed to reasonable care in respect of its research but could not guarantee that its 'expertise' (expert assessment) would be correct. The agreement would be subject to the laws of The Netherlands and any dispute would have to be submitted to the Amsterdam courts.

I returned both agreements and all available relevant material on the painting on 2 May 1995 and duly received back my copy of the agreement, countersigned by van Tilborgh. I now looked forward to receiving the promised expertise not later than the beginning of August. Before going on holiday in July, I telephoned the Museum and was told that the result would probably be available by the end of July, and that I would be advised at both my home and my holiday addresses. In the autumn I rang again, and on 22 September I was told that there had 'been a delay' but that I could definitely expect the results by the end of the month. Early in October I wrote asking when I could expect the expertise but I got no reply. On 12 October I rang van Tilborg's secretary. She told me that he was not available but that all the papers were now on his desk and I would receive the expertise in a week or certainly within two weeks.

Three weeks later I rang van Tilborgh again, and his secretary now told me that he had passed all the papers to the head of restoration and conservation at the museum, Ms Cornelia Peres, and was awaiting her comments. As soon as he received these he would write his report. I said that I would be in Amsterdam from 15 to 18 November and could bring the painting on that occasion, if that would be helpful. The secretary promised to ring me back at the latest by 14 November to let me know. When I telephoned her on 16 November from Amsterdam she seemed very surprised that van Tilborgh had not called me. She told me that the restorer/conservator had finished her examination of the painting, and the papers were back on van Tilborgh's desk. He would write his report, which I would receive within two weeks, that is before the end of November. Nothing came.

By now I was increasingly pessimistic about the verdict—how could they possibly not want to see the painting?—but I was even more curious as to what arguments the final report might contain.

Why were they so reluctant? Did they hope I would simply stop pestering them and go away? I finally received the expertise, promised for early August the previous year, in early January, some five months overdue.

It may be translated as follows:

> 8 January 1996
>
> Dear Mr Jans,
>
> I regret that the result of our research has taken so long. With due regard to the conditions as mentioned in the Agreement dated 2 May 1995 and also to the conditions as stated in my letter of 23 March 1995, I advise you as follows:
> In view of the style we cannot attribute your work, entitled "Two Diggers", to Van Gogh. The painting does not show any of his characteristics. The gay colours (especially in the sky) are different. The clumsy, not very lively method of drawing is clearly different, and it is also noticed that a non-commercial, factory prepared canvas [sic] was chosen—something which is not known from his Dutch period, while the weave of the cloth is also not familiar to us.
> The paint has been placed very thinly, and that also we do not know from his Dutch oeuvre; his works usually show a substantial impasto.
> Hoping to have informed you sufficiently,
>
> I am,
>
> Yours sincerely,
>
> Louis van Tilborgh,
> Head Curator.
>
> P.S. This result is meant exclusively for you personally. Third parties cannot derive any rights against the Van Gogh Museum from this result.

For eight months the top echelon of the Van Gogh Museum had laboured over a snapshot, inventing delay after delay for producing their promised 'expertise' and in the end had come up with this missive of meaningless statements containing under a hundred unconvincing words.

As for the expertise:

The style did not show any of Van Gogh's characteristics?
On the contrary, the painting has distinct van Gogh characteristics—though these may not have been easy to see in a photograph—such as the depth of field and the treatment of the horizon; the accentuating of the warmth and light from the sun by concentric brush strokes; and the general brushwork, the use of colour, and the bold outlines of the figures. And what about the mood, so typical of Vincent's paintings of that time?

The gay colours, especially in the sky, are different?
Trying to judge the colours of an oil painting from a photograph is surely less than professional: one must see the painting itself, nothing else will do. And 'different'—different from what? Different from the colours in the photograph? or from those in other known van Goghs from that period? Of course some of the colours in *The Diggers* are 'different'—none of the very few other known paintings from the period depicts a sun or a comparable light. The actual colours in the painting closely follow what Vincent himself described, in his letter to Theo of 14 August 1882, as being the colours he saw in a sunlit sky.

The clumsy method of drawing being different? Again—different from what? There are no other oil paintings by Vincent of that period with large, drawn figures with which to compare.

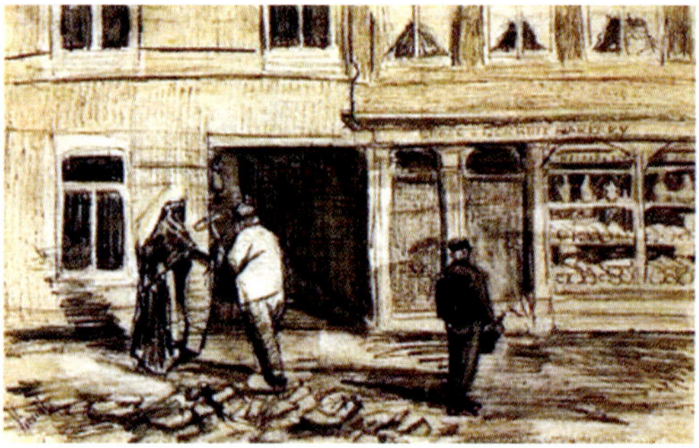

JH112, (left), a pencil, pen drawing from March 1882

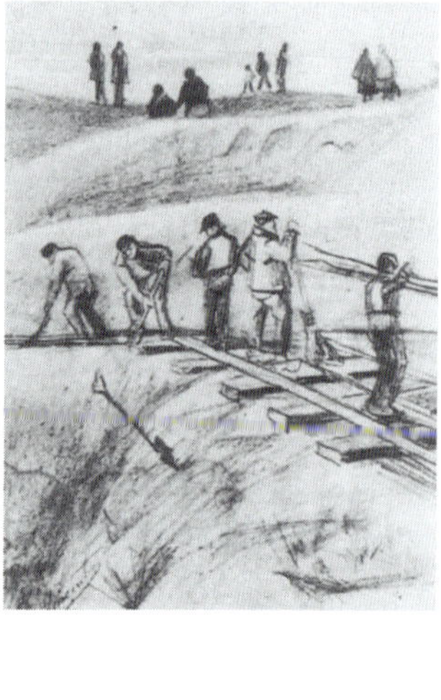

But there are pencil and charcoal drawings (some of which show considerable resemblance to the basic drawing of the figures in *The Diggers*) with similar boldly drawn outlines, as well as comparable poses.

JH114, (right), a pencil drawing from March 1882

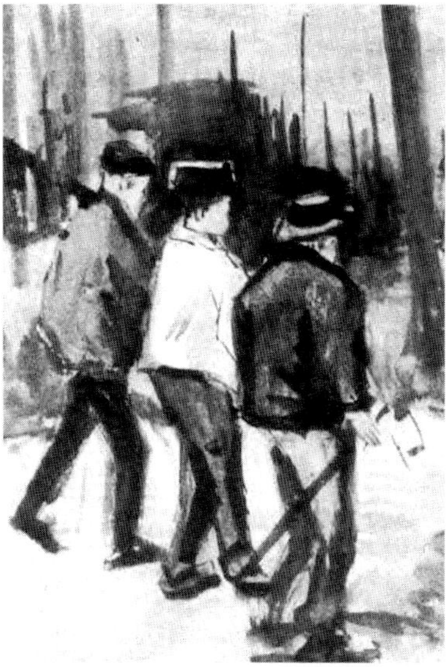

JH171, (left), a watercolour from July 1882

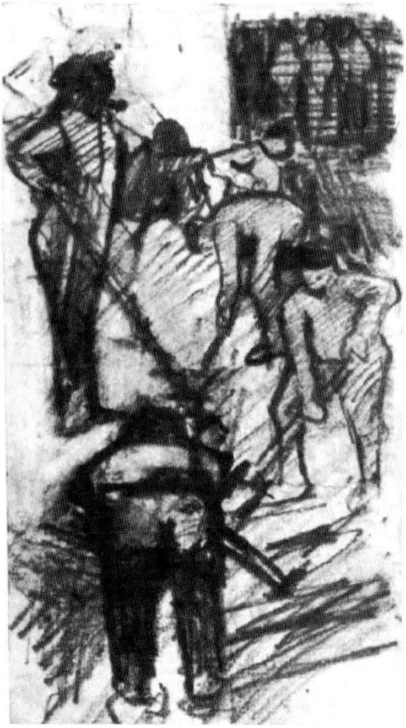

JH132, (above), a sketch reproduced with a letter of April 1882

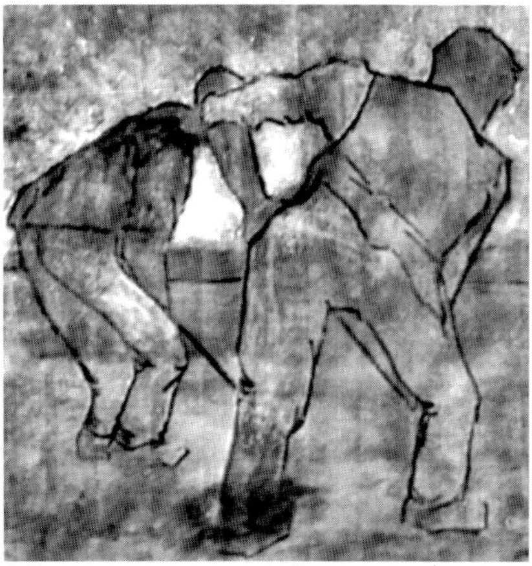

Base drawing for *The Diggers* In oil, September 1882? (left)

The non-commercial, factory-prepared canvas?

What canvas? Van Tilborgh had never seen the canvas: it cannot be seen in the photograph. This statement must have come from reading Eastaugh's report, apparently not too carefully. The scientific examination had shown that the canvas, which appears to be on its original stretcher, seems to have had a commercial priming. It was cut from a larger piece, with one selvedge remaining at the top. Vincent, especially early in his career, was hard up and used any base—paper, board, or canvas—that he could lay hands on or which a friend or his brother gave him. How could this unseen commercially prepared canvas be called a 'non-commercial, factory prepared canvas' [*niet commercieel, fabrieksmatig geprepareerd doek*] and be made an argument against the authenticity of the painting?

The weave of the canvas is also unfamiliar to us?

No detailed study of the canvases of Vincent's early work has yet been made, and there are many examples of his use of unusual and unfamiliar carriers. Eastaugh had already noted that the weave of the canvas was indeed unusual, with two warp threads crossing two weft threads, and he had reported that the same weave could be found in the canvas of an 1870 Fantin-Latour oil painting and also in a 1872 Monet now in the National Gallery in London. How could anyone maintain that van Gogh could not have used this type of canvas?

The paint had been placed very thinly... his work usually show a substantial impasto?

Van Tilborgh seems to have had second thoughts after writing this, because on 23 January 1998 he wrote in the leading Dutch paper, the *NRC-Handelsblad*, that critics disputing the authenticity of certain van Gogh paintings had probably not looked properly or at all at the actual paintings but only at reproductions 'in which van Gogh's typical impasto—the most important element by which the expert can verify authenticity—is lost.' Further comment seems unnecessary.

In fact painting with heavy impasto was exceptional in Vincent's very early days and when he used it he mentioned it, especially, for instance, in the case of painting of a dune (Letter 225, 14 August 1882). In large areas of *The Diggers* the paint has indeed been placed quite thinly but in other areas there is impasto. The brushwork throughout, however, indicates an inclination towards impasto—in some places it can be seen that the paint was hardly mixed on the palette. The impasto in this painting appears to be fully in keeping with Vincent's dilemma between heavy impasto and saving paint. In August 1882 he wrote to his brother Theo:

> It would become too expensive if one is not economical with the paint . . .

and again on 3 September:

> It is not dependent on the use of a lot of paint, to enable one to paint well . . . Sometimes the subject matter indicates that one should paint thinly, sometimes, the material, the nature of things indicate themselves that they require more impasto.

I do not say that van Tilborgh or anyone else could not possibly be right in suggesting that the painting is not by Vincent, but his reasons given for the rejection did not seem to hold water. It would have been more helpful if they had been convincing. Could he not have produced at least one solid reason which would have enabled me to discontinue my quest?

On receipt of this 'expertise' I immediately telephoned the Museum to ask for an interview with him and also for an opportunity to see the only 1882 van Gogh work in their collection, *The Beach at Scheveningen in Stormy Weather*, at close quarters. I hoped this would give me an opportunity, among other things, to look at the weave of its canvas. I was told that that particular painting was going to be sent to Vienna for an exhibition, so I should ring again on 16 February when I would be given an appointment and also an opportunity to study the painting before its departure. When I telephoned on the 16th, I was given the appointment—for 21 February 1996—but told that I would not be able to see the 1882 painting after all, as it had already been crated up for Vienna.

I packed up *The Diggers* and drove to Amsterdam. Not wishing to give the impression that I was forcing the painting on him I left the parcel containing it in my car and met van Tilborgh at the appointed time for a meeting that was to last about an hour. I began by saying that I could not really accept his letter of 8 January as a formal expertise. I had been promised an expert report and after a long delay had only received a short letter, very unlike what is usually expected from an expertise. I said that I felt entitled to a more detailed and substantiated report on their findings. He replied that I must accept that the Museum had to deal with many requests such as mine, and some got short, others more detailed, answers.

I told him that I was not able—nor did I think anyone else would be able—to accept any of the six reasons listed in his letter as a valid argument for not attributing *The Diggers* to van Gogh. His short answer was that he did not have a monopoly on knowledge of the work of van Gogh, and the opinions he had given in his letter were his own and must be accepted as such. (An 'expertise' from the Museum was just the opinion of one curator, based on a photograph, although part of the delay had been because all the papers were with one of his colleagues?)

Seeming unwilling to get involved in detail, he explained that one cannot judge a painting in isolation, but only in the context of an artist's entire oeuvre, from knowledge of which one learns the artist's 'handwriting'. He had been unable to detect in *The Diggers* Vincent's 'handwriting' as we know it from his South of France paintings. (Was his suggestion that the characteristics typical of van Gogh's later years should have been visible in his first efforts in oils in the first few weeks when he began to paint?)

It seemed as though at this stage he would not admit that anything at all in *The Diggers*, not even the most obvious feature, the subject matter itself, was characteristic of van Gogh!

I then suggested that *The Diggers* had been painted in the manner Vincent himself had described in his letter of 2 August 1883 to his brother Theo, drawing the outlines first and filling them in later, and I pointed out that the concentric brush strokes around the sun were a very typical van Gogh characteristic, as was the bold drawing and the pose of the figures. I asked him to agree on the skill displayed in the rendering of the foreground, the depth of field, and other features.

He replied that *The Letters* could not be used to prove such a point, adding that *The Diggers* had none of the forceful brush strokes we know so well from, for instance, his Arles period. I readily agreed that the painting was definitely not of the Arles period: so far everyone who had seen it had agreed that it could only have been one of his very first paintings from his first period in The Hague.

I said that I had been surprised that he had not wanted to see the painting itself but that I had it with me now and could show it to him. He said he had expected such a request and he would take a look at it if I insisted but added that, whether he saw it or not, he would not change his mind. I could hardly believe what I thought I had just heard, and John McEnroe's famous remark to a Wimbledon umpire*, rose to my lips, but I managed to hold my tongue as I nevertheless very much wanted to see how he would react to the actual painting.

I fetched it and was motioned to place it on the floor, where van Tilborgh first had a look at it from a distance. I pointed out that the brush strokes did have van Gogh characteristics and that the paint had not been placed thinly everywhere, but clearly had been applied by a painter inclined towards generous impasto. Coming closer to the painting he did agree that there were areas where the brush strokes showed an inclination towards more impasto. This seemed to knock out another of his reasons for denying an attribution to van Gogh and, *ipso facto*, his earlier claim that the painting did not show anything characteristic of Vincent. I again pointed to the concentric brush strokes around the sun, an early appearance of a later very typical van Gogh characteristic further developed in Arles, but I could not draw him on this important point.

* "You cannot be serious."

I then turned to the 'gay colours' he had mentioned as being 'different'—presumably he had meant different from the colours of the very few other van Gogh paintings of that period—and I pointed out that the colours in the actual painting differed from those in the photograph and that one could not really call the colours of the sky gay. He wavered a little but would not accept my point of view when I tried to build a bridge between the colours in the sky of *The Diggers* and the words of Vincent's letter of 14 August 1882 to his brother:

> . . . first a lilac haze, wherein the red sun, half covered by a lilac cloud, with a sparkling red fine edge, near the sun reflections of vermilion, with above a stroke of yellow, turning green, and higher bluish, the so-called cerulean blue and then here and there lilac and sombre clouds catching reflections of the sun.

Not only do the colours described in this letter correspond closely with those in *The Diggers*, but also the reflections of the sun in the 'lilac and sombre clouds' are clearly seen in this painting. How could anyone ignore these undeniable facts?

He said that he did not know of any use of similar colours in van Gogh's other skies of that period—again no argument, as all the skies by Vincent of that period differ one from another and none from that period with a sun in it has surfaced.

There is no getting round the fact that Vincent wrote that he saw a sky with these colours when he was in The Hague. When, some six years later, in 1888, in Arles, he painted concentric brush strokes around sources of light (and sometimes round people's heads in portraits), this was a resumption of the manner used in the study in oils of a hot sun in his period in The Hague described in his letter of 9 September 1882 to Theo:

> I love . . . strong light effects for instance on a digger sweating it out in the afternoon sun.

When I moved on to his comment about the clumsy and not lively method of drawing in the painting being 'different', and suggested that it was not at all unlike, for instance, drawing JH132, of the end of April 1882, *Diggers in a Broken-up Street* (see page 43), which is in the Van Gogh Museum, he just said "that does not mean anything", and every time I quoted Vincent's words he repeated that one cannot really derive anything from his letters. (Coming from someone who has himself quoted at length from *The Letters* to substantiate an argument, has quoted them in interviews, and has based many articles on them, this was rich.)

Finally, I could get no explanation for his statement that the painting was on a non-commercial, factory-prepared canvas. I pointed out that under scientific examination the canvas used for *The Diggers* in fact appeared to have a commercial priming. Who was right? The man in the laboratory, or the man who, when he wrote his expertise, had only seen a photograph? The man who had only seen a photograph also had a copy of the report of the man in the laboratory in his possession at the time.

I asked what he thought of the painting. His answer was that he felt that it was not all that strong, and asked me what I thought of it. I told him that I liked it a lot, that I considered it to be a study, rather than a finished painting, that I felt that it had been painted by a very dedicated, talented artist who was still trying to find himself, but because he was lacking in experience, it was still a little clumsy in execution. He said that he could agree with that description.

I then asked him whether he thought the painting to be a deliberate forgery or whether he thought that it had been painted by another artist using the name Vincent, but I got no clear answer. When I pointed out the obvious age of the canvas, from the end of the 19th century, and the fact that Eastaugh had found that the signature had been placed at or close to the time when the painting had been painted, van Tilborgh said that van Gogh forgeries had started appearing as early as 1903. At that moment I did not have the courage to remind him that at least two forged van Gogh paintings, shown in an exhibition in 1901, had already been unmasked by then. (Since then I have seen a demonstration showing that two forgers had been at work as early as 1893.) He added that they had extensive material on the forgeries of van Gogh's work in the Museum.

When I asked whether any of the fakes they knew about showed any resemblance to *The Diggers* or were representative of van Gogh's early period, he answered that he had not studied these fakes for a long time but intended to do so shortly, and if and when he did find any similarities or comparable work he promised to let me know (I am still waiting). It did not seem that he had in fact consulted the Museum's material on forged van Goghs before writing his opinion on *The Diggers*.

I suggested that it would be very odd, if the painting were indeed an early forgery, that it had not surfaced earlier in an attempt to become recognised as a genuine work. And why would a forger choose to forge a very early work, far less popular and less valuable than a later work? It is on the later works that all the known forgers have concentrated. No answer.

When I asked whether the Museum had facilities to date paintings of this kind reasonably accurately, and whether the Museum, or anybody else, had done research on the canvas qualities of the early paintings, he said not. This did seem to undercut the expertise statement that "the cloth is not familiar to us".

I mentioned that a well known curator of an important and well known van Gogh collection had once told me, on being asked, that if the painting *Edge of a Wood* (see Chapter 3), attributed to van Gogh in August/September 1882, had only been found recently, without a provenance, it would have presented at least the same problems in authentication as *The Diggers*. At this he waxed almost indignant. The *Edge of a Wood*, he said, was clearly described in van Gogh's letters—which he had just said could not be relied on in these matters—and was without any doubt genuine. In fact it is not mentioned anywhere in *The Letters*. This whole discussion seemed to be becoming deliberately confusing and more and more like Alice in Wonderland's conversation with the Red Queen!

I expressed my sincere disappointment at his relegating *The Diggers* to outer space—not a fake, not by Vincent, not by anyone else known, a pariah painting!

I told him that his expertise had not cleared up the matter, so I would therefore have to continue to look for cast-iron reasons why either *The Diggers* could not be by van Gogh or that it was. I was not going to desist from my efforts without being satisfied one way or the other: I needed sound arguments.

He said that he did not think I would find any acknowledged van Gogh expert to disagree with his opinion on *The Diggers*, but if I ever did find any who shared my views, he would be willing to debate the matter with them. I asked who, in his opinion, would hold the required status, and he suggested Dr Roland Dorn, who was in process of writing a new van Gogh *catalogue raisonné*, or his own colleague van Heugten at the Museum, or Professor Pickvance, or Mr Tsukasa Kodera.

I asked if I could show the painting to van Heugten there and then but, by now beginning to show some irritation, he said there would be no point in doing so.

I told him that my opinions were backed up by long and serious study, and he agreed that obviously I was well up in the subject, "but then," he added, "of course you have no acknowledged status on the subject."

Asking relevant questions and getting no valid answers or no answers at all was like bashing my head against a brick wall. The Museum refused to treat my perfectly reasonable arguments seriously but had not produced any valid counter-arguments.

Several times during the meeting van Tilborgh had recommended that I should stop any further research, and had seemed keen on my abandoning my efforts, but I had to go on: brick walls do not necessarily hold out for ever. As soon as I reached home I carefully wrote down precisely what had been discussed at the meeting. My task was now far more difficult—it might be almost impossible to convince the van Gogh establishment after the 'no' from van Tilborgh. Yet, so far, not a single valid argument against the painting had been put forward.

Chapter Five

The Search for Genuine Experts

I had been told by van der Wolk, by Sotheby's, and by van Tilborgh himself that the Van Gogh Museum is not the only body that can authenticate a painting by van Gogh. Whether an authentication by any other body would in practice be fully internationally acceptable or not seemed a moot point, but none the less I now had to look elsewhere. Messrs Dorn and Feilchenfeldt had not seen the painting yet, so it seemed sensible to make another attempt to show it to them, preferably at their joint office in Zürich.

By now two and a half years had elapsed since I had acquired *The Diggers.* The painting had sometimes been hanging in my office at my gallery, and on several occasions an important industrialist and art-collector client had seen and been impressed by it and had become quietly confident that it could be genuine. He and a partner now made me a generous offer of financial and moral support in my quest. In exchange, I took them into my confidence, told them in detail about all my efforts so far and provided them with copies of all the documentation that had accumulated.

Not long after this, they discussed matters with their legal advisers in Switzerland, to whom they disclosed some of the details. These had then been shared with an associated but independent art adviser, a Mrs Janet F. Briner,* and it was arranged for me to meet her. From this it transpired that she had had contacts with the Van Gogh Museum in the past and that she also knew Feilchenfeldt in Zürich, which fitted in perfectly with my intention to approach him a second time. Mrs Briner studied the record of my researches so far and offered help and assistance, for which my financial benefactors generously offered to pay.

---

* Independent art appraiser and adviser in Geneva, Member of the Appraisers Association of America, of the Association of Swiss Art Dealers and Restorers, and of the Board of Directors of Nordstern Fine Art Insurance, Switzerland.

As a start, Mrs Briner arranged for us both to meet Dorn and Feilchenfeldt *chez* the latter in Zürich on 26 March 1996. On arrival we were shown into an office, where I unwrapped the painting and placed it on a chair on the far side of the room from Feilchenfeldt, who was seated at his desk with Dorn standing behind him. It was immediately apparent that the latter was going to do the talking, and Feilchenfeldt remained more or less silent throughout.

For no apparent reason and totally unexpectedly, Dorn immediately adopted an adversarial stance, declaring straight out that *The Diggers* was a fake. It is logical, of course, that if one intends to reject a painting signed 'Vincent', one must call it a fake, and he had earlier seen a photograph, but he seemed now to be doing it without even a close look at the original.

Having been told that Dorn knew far more about *The Letters* than van Tilborgh, I quoted the three letters in which Vincent talked about the subject matter, about a colour scheme for a painting with a sun, and about the method of painting, all three of which might very well refer to features of *The Diggers*. I mentioned that these letters had been published for the first time in 1914. He did not disagree that knowledge of Vincent's letters would have been important for producing a forged *Diggers* but said that some of the letters had in fact been published as early as 1893 in the Belgian paper *Van Nu en Straks*. He was not entirely sure but he thought these had included the ones I had quoted and offered to let me have the details.

He has never done so, but I have checked for myself and found that only one of these three letters, the one about the colour scheme, was published in *Van Nu en Straks* in 1893, which by itself would not have given enough information to forge the painting. Nobody, except the writer or recipient of the letters, could have known all that it was essential to know to match all the details before 1914. It could only have been forged after that time, which did not fit with the accepted age of the painting.

I then raised the subject of the some thirty studies in oils painted by Vincent in 1882, of which only eleven have surfaced so far, leaving some nineteen missing. Dr Dorn disputed this figure of nineteen, maintaining that a number of them have now been found underneath other paintings. He would not say which, and I have not been able to find any evidence of this anywhere. Perhaps he was confusing them with some canvases from the Nuenen period (1884–1885) which van Gogh reused for other paintings by overpainting them or by using the reverse.

Dorn now offered yet a third opinion on the canvas used for *The Diggers*, suggesting it was a non-commercial canvas, prepared by the artist by hand (the first—that it *was* commercially prepared—had come from the laboratory examination; the second was van Tilborgh's deduction from a photograph).

Looking at the painting from a distance, Dorn announced that, the scientific findings notwithstanding, the signature had been placed some fifteen years after the rest of the painting. (I remember thinking at the time how could anyone say such an extraordinary thing without a closer look than from across a room—he might as well have said the signature was five years older than the painting!)

He went on: "The figures are not of the Hague period, the left leg of the foremost digger is too short and the foot crooked, making it look as if the digger's leg is deformed" (see page 57). At this time, the damage to the left foot had not yet been properly restored and he did not seem to understand that the tear in the canvas in the area of the foot had only been clumsily restored by some unknown hand. I don't think he realised the area he was criticising was a part of the painting *not* painted by the original artist!

His statement that the figures were not of the Hague period was particularly odd, as at least twenty drawings from that period show one or more diggers (see *The Diggers* after Millet page 13) *Diggers in a Broken-up Street* (page 43), and *Torn-up Street with Diggers* (below) as examples. There are also other drawings, from before Vincent started painting in oils, with figures comparable to, if smaller than, those in *The Diggers.*

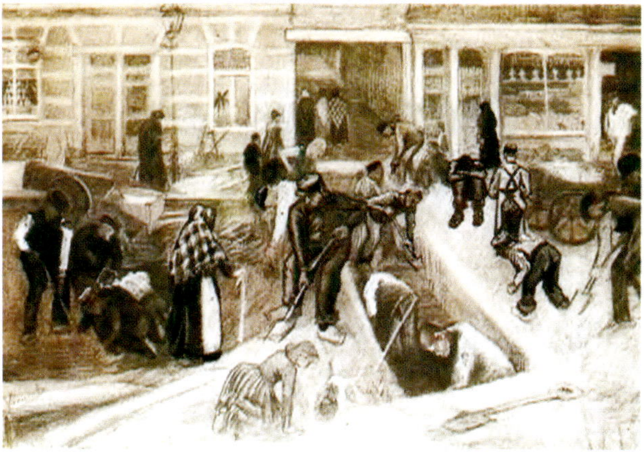

Torn-up Street with Diggers JH 131, F 930a, (left), pencil with white and colours, April 1882, The Hague

When I pointed out the characteristic concentric brush strokes around the sun, he smiled and said they were such a typical van Gogh characteristic that every forger would have employed it. (H'm—van Tilborgh could not find any similarities to van Gogh, nor, in 1994, could Dorn, but now . . .)

Dorn concluded that he felt *The Diggers* to be the work of a Belgian forger, likely to have been painted around 1914–1915, after the 1914 van Gogh exhibition in Belgium, where he could have studied comparable subject matter. (And the forgery was signed 15 years later, say in 1930?—odder and odder!) I asked whether he thought the signature had been placed by the forger or by someone else, and why the painting had never surfaced in any attempt to sell it as a van Gogh, but he did not answer.

I have since obtained the list of the ninety-six paintings and drawings exhibited at the exhibition in Belgium of 1914, and there was not one from The Hague period among them. The only painting of diggers was that by van Gogh, JH1833, after Millet (see page 22), which was painted between 25 October and 7 December 1889 in a style that could never have been the model for a painting pretending to be from his early Dutch period.

There seemed to be rather a gap between Dorn's opinion of 2 November 1994 when he had written:

> To my regret, I see absolutely no way of attributing this painting of a setting sun with two men digging in the ground to the hand of Vincent van Gogh. Beyond superficial analogies in subject matter which point towards its author's admiration for van Gogh's early work, neither style nor execution admit van Gogh's authorship.

and this day in March 1996 when he declared it to be a forgery in the style of van Gogh.

When I asked whether he would be kind enough to confirm his view in writing he was at first reluctant to do so—the painting was definitely not by van Gogh and any further time spent on it would be wasted. As had van Tilborgh, he strongly recommended me to stop my efforts to obtain an authentication for it. I persisted, however, and he agreed to send me a letter but said he would have to charge around SFr 1000 for it. After exchanging glances with Feilchenfeldt, he then talked of SFr 2000 or 3000, increasing it to 4000 or 5000, saying that a lot of extra work would be involved. Then he said that no further work would really be necessary and he would simply write me a letter confirming the points discussed.

This I never received, because three days later, I received his fax asking for SFr 2500 before he would send it. This seemed to me exorbitant for a short letter simply to confirm our discussion and I declined the offer. Dorn was obviously a man having difficulties in making up his mind.

* * *

The Diggers had not been very lucky with sources recommended by Sotheby's. So far the result had been two very negative opinions, from van Tilborgh and from Dorn, two sources who, I had meanwhile learnt, were in close co-operation with each other. It seemed as if they had discussed *The Diggers* and agreed to reject it but had not bothered to agree on the reasons to be given.

How could two people so eminent in the art world be so unable to provide someone new in the field with convincing arguments? Why was it necessary for them to be so derogatory and unco-operative? The atmosphere during the meeting with Dorn and Feilchenfeldt had been downright unfriendly and unpleasant from beginning to end, which made me feel that they were not being very truthful, that they were hiding something. This made me all the more determined to persist.

It was fortunate that Mrs Briner had been present during the entire interview and witnessed this almost incredible tale of woe. She was as taken aback as I by Dorn's attitude and as perplexed by his ill-conceived arguments but was equally unwilling to be defeated in this manner. She suggested that we take the painting to another expert in Switzerland, Dr Paolo Cadorin, who had once been head restorer at the Kunstmuseum in Basle and now had his own research laboratories in Basle. This seemed to me to be an excellent idea. Mrs Briner managed by phone to get an appointment with Dr Cadorin and we set off, with the painting, to his laboratory.

I quote from her report:

> After the disappointing result of a visit to have the *"Two Diggers in the Afternoon Sun"* examined by Mr Roland Dorn at Mr Feilchenfeldt's residence in Zürich, I spontaneously decided to have this painting shown to Dr Paolo Cadorin.
>
> Dr Cadorin has worked on several van Goghs over the years and has also published reports on various technical aspects of the work of van Gogh.
>
> Before his retirement, Dr Cadorin was the head of the restoration

department at the Kunstmuseum in Basle. He at present has his own restoration laboratory and works with Ms Monique Veillon, who also was present at the meeting.

Without wanting to know any of the history of the painting, Dr Cadorin first carefully studied it with a magnifying glass, then under the microscope and under the ultraviolet lamp.

He at first stated that the painting, if executed by van Gogh, was surely not of very high quality.

He noted that the lower part of the painting had suffered considerable restoration and partly been overpainted, that the anatomy of the digger on the right was not quite correct and that the signature was overpainted too.

Dr Cadorin also questioned if there might have been a marine painting underneath the *Two Diggers in the Afternoon Sun*, either by van Gogh or by another artist (visible vertical lines in the painting). He suggested that Xrays should be taken in order to know more about the painting under the top layer. The canvas also has an old varnish, which seems to have oxidized and been revarnished at a later date.

After having said this, Dr Cadorin, without any hesitation took a mixture of alcohol and acetone and carefully wiped the layer of paint away, which was covering the signature "Vincent" to a large degree. He confirmed that the signature, which appears at present in a very bright colour, and underlined, was made at the same time as the painting itself and was surely not added at any later moment.

Dr Cadorin suddenly became very enthusiastic about the painting. Somebody had evidently tried to cover the signature, probably at the time the hole in the area of the left foot, of the digger standing on the right, was restored. Dr. Cadorin also cleaned the overpainting of this restoration with the result, that the left leg appears longer. Now the anatomy of the body is correct too!

Dr Cadorin suggested to have the painting also shown to Ms Cornelia Peres, restorer at the Vincent van Gogh Museum in Amsterdam and a former pupil of Dr Cadorin. (This presented a difficulty as by this time Mr van Tilborgh, head curator of that museum had already issued his expertise.)

Dr Cadorin was of the opinion that the painting could be authentic and was prepared to undertake the restoration of the left foot and the cleaning of it in order to try and give the painting its original 'look'—then the painting should be shown in its new light to Mr van Tilborgh.

Geneva, March 28, 1996

* * *

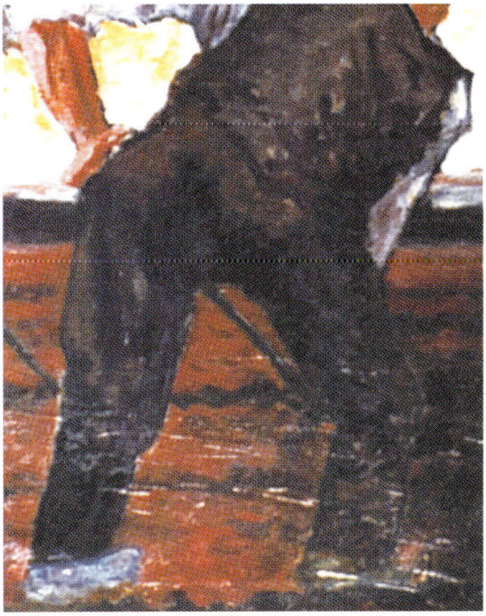

Bottom of left foot before restoration

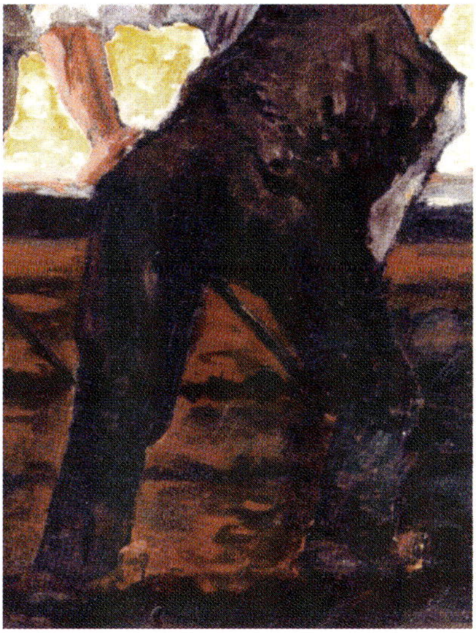

Bottom of left foot after restoration
Note extended trouser leg length and position and colour of the left wooden shoe

Dr Cadorin indeed became very excited about the painting. At one point, after studying it carefully under a microscope and removing some surface matter by the signature and by the left foot of the foremost digger, he suddenly got up and shook me by the hand congratulating me on my find. I told him about the expertise by van Tilborgh but he said that from his experience van Tilborgh was not the right person to judge it and Cornelia Peres should have had a chance to see the picture itself as she was better qualified to give an opinion. However, as I had been told that she had seen all the papers and reports on *The Diggers*, I doubted that she would give an opinion dissenting from that of her superior.

As Mrs Briner had noted in her report, it did seem that now, after the letter from van Tilborgh, it would be difficult for me to show the painting to Ms Peres, but Dr Cadorin there and then rang her up in Amsterdam, and she agreed to see the painting at my private address in Amsterdam. An early appointment was made and on 3 April I took *The Diggers* by road to Amsterdam to meet Ms Peres at 7 o'clock at my small ground-floor apartment in the Jordaan, a well known district in central Amsterdam.

In the meantime I had told my financial backers about my experiences in Zürich and Basle and they had become rather excited about it all. They were flying around various destinations in Europe in their private Learjet at the time, and were due on 4 April in Vienna. They now arranged to be dropped off in Basle so the plane could fetch the painting and me from Amsterdam after I had shown it to Ms Peres, and I could then take it back to Cadorin.

Although I had been more than pleased with the developments at the Cadorin laboratory in Basle, I was still a little bruised by the events with Dorn in Zürich, and I was not too happy about this almost clandestine meeting with Ms Peres—if van Tilborgh should hear about it, her job might be jeopardised. And even if she became as convinced as her previous tutor, Dr Cadorin, had been, how could we ever make use of a favourable opinion by her? To go on record against the opinion of her superior at the Museum might well ruin her career. Indeed, she might well have spoken with van Tilborgh and discussed what she should say.

She arrived at my apartment by bicycle. She seemed nervous, would not let me put her bicycle safely inside, and said immediately that she could not stay long, as she had to meet her fiancé, who was flying in from Rome. Even before having had a good look at the painting, which was on a chair in the corner, she said that she did not quite understand what was expected of her. In her opinion my painting was not by van Gogh, as it had nothing in common with any of his other paintings of the same period. When I pointed out that none of the very few other known paintings from the early first period in The Hague depicted a sun or were in any other way suitably comparable, she insisted that there were many, though she could not, of course, give a single example when challenged. Instead, she said she was living with van Gogh paintings all the time and so had an excellent feeling for his work. She avoided further discussion on the Hague period and appeared slightly irritated by my questions. However, when asked, she confirmed that she had not seen photographs of *The Diggers* before. ("All the papers are now with the restorer," I had been told. I wondered if I was getting the whole story or had the delay while Ms Peres looked at the papers been invented to account for some of the long delay of van Tilborgh's report. It was also curious that she had already decided that my painting was not genuine, without, as she now said, ever having seen its photograph.)

Under these circumstances it was obviously difficult for her to examine the painting properly and discuss it in any detail. She had said that she wanted to leave quickly: now she left. When all was said and done, she was under no real obligation to discuss a painting already rejected by her superior.

I now had to take *The Diggers* back to Basle, where I rejoined Mrs Briner and my sponsors and recounted events in Amsterdam. We decided that all four of us should go together to see Cadorin, who did not seem to react very much to my story—perhaps he had even spoken to Ms Peres since I had seen her. I also had the feeling that he was slightly taken aback by the unexpected number of visitors, but he and his associate Monique Veillon, also a restorer, made us all very welcome.

Despite the negative result of my Amsterdam visit, Cadorin was still willing to research the painting in detail, restore the damaged areas, and clean it thoroughly, and it remained with him for several weeks while this was being done. I was able to collect it on 27 August 1996 and was delighted with the result of the cleaning and of the restoration of the earlier clumsy repair of the tear in the area of the left foot of the foreground figure. The signature he had obscured again to be as he had originally found it.

Dr Cadorin submitted a report on the painting, illustrated by some fourteen photographs of various details. It reads:

> *The composition underneath the 'Two Diggers'*
> The painting 'Two Diggers', executed in oil on canvas, mounted on a stretcher with nails, was executed on top of an earlier composition, most likely of a harbour with boats.
>
> Vertical and oblique dark lines, visible through the transparent top layer of the actually visible composition, suggest the presence of a port, with several boats; in the first layer, in the lower part of the painting, parallel and horizontal impastos evoke the shapes of waves on water.
>
> Xrays and infrared reflectograms show, among others things, in the right-hand lower part, the prow of a boat on the quayside.
>
> In his letters from The Hague to Theo of July and August 1882, Vincent mentions his sketches of boats on several occasions, some letters are even illustrated with drawings.
>
> *The support*
> The painting, before it was mounted on the actual stretcher, was fixed on a flat surface by means of four drawing pins (the holes these made are still visible in the four corners), a common technique for painters working in the open air.
>
> The fact that the two compositions superimposed on one another

cover the left side of the canvas to the edge of the stretcher, but leave a margin of approximately 1cm unpainted surface on the other 3 sides, allows one to conclude that both compositions were painted before the canvas was mounted on a subsequent support.

Also the second composition was painted several years before the painting was professionally mounted on the actual stretcher, because the original preparation of the canvas is cracked at the lower edge and in the upper right-hand corner; it had lost its elasticity, through ageing.

The nails are original and in their original places and the canvas has never been removed from the stretcher. This type of stretcher with nails is of a type already known in France at the end of the nineteenth century.

The paint

The 'Two Diggers', as well as the underlying composition, is executed in oil paint, which has totally hardened through oxidation. With an appropriate instrument it flakes off easily. The brittle character of the paint and the resulting cracks in the paint surface, due to drying time, indicate that we must date the painting as over 80 years old.

State of conservation

The state of conservation of the painting is generally good except for three areas: in the upper central and upper right parts of the sky one could find lacunae in the paint coverage which became more evident after removal of a layer of non-original varnish.

At the left foot of the digger in the foreground is a tear in the canvas of approximately 3 cm, which has been repaired very badly. This has caused an important loss of paint coverage and of the original preparation of the canvas around the tear.

This had, relatively recently, been 'restored' by attaching a piece of cloth to the back of the painting and by using a mixture of plaster and glue on the front, smoothed over with glass paper, and this layer, after drying, had been brutally abraded. This procedure damaged the surface and the layer of paint around the tear.

Intervention

The painting was most probably varnished at the time of the last restoration. An examination revealed that under this varnish was a second layer of greyish varnish which could not be removed with any of the usual solvents.

We presumed that this layer could consist of animal protein, for example egg white; this material was frequently used for provisional varnishing by artists in the second half of the 19th century while the paintings dried. Van Gogh also used this technique.

Egg white, soluble in water, is reputed to be suitable for oil paintings but hardens after a certain time and becomes insoluble, and for a long time became impossible to remove after such hardening. Only recently a new technique has been found to remove this material and we have used this technique with success on this painting.

As a result a very colourful and bright painting appeared, "in the fauve style" which has given it its strange beauty.

Subject matter

The composition of the two persons presents us with a problem. The one on the left, also in trousers, has a very small head, disproportionate in size to the massive one of his companion. The form of this head, small and rounded, without hair, reminds one of a skull. Are we confronted here with an allegorical representation of Death accompanying the worker step by step in his hard labour?

The style

The presence of a sky, which has a lot of movement and colours—as we know them from the period of Van Gogh's stay in the south of France after 1888—is amazing in a dark landscape which, by subject matter and monochrome tones, would remind one of his period in The Hague, 1882–83.

This was an interesting study by Cadorin in addition to his professional work on the painting. His achievements on cleaning it and restoring the damaged areas had beautified the painting substantially and restored the proportions of the left leg of the foremost digger. He himself was also very satisfied with the results of the cleaning and suggested that showing the painting again to those who had earlier given negative opinions—particularly Dorn and van Tilborgh—might result in at least some changes of mind.

I have offered both of these gentlemen the opportunity to take another look at the painting after the restoration work by Cadorin, but neither has taken up the offer or even responded.

Chapter Six

An 'Artquake' Takes Place

While I was waiting for Cadorin's report I heard about a controversy brewing in France over the *Garden at Auvers* , a painting attributed to van Gogh. It was presumed to have been painted by Vincent very shortly before his death in July 1890 and had attained considerable fame in France.

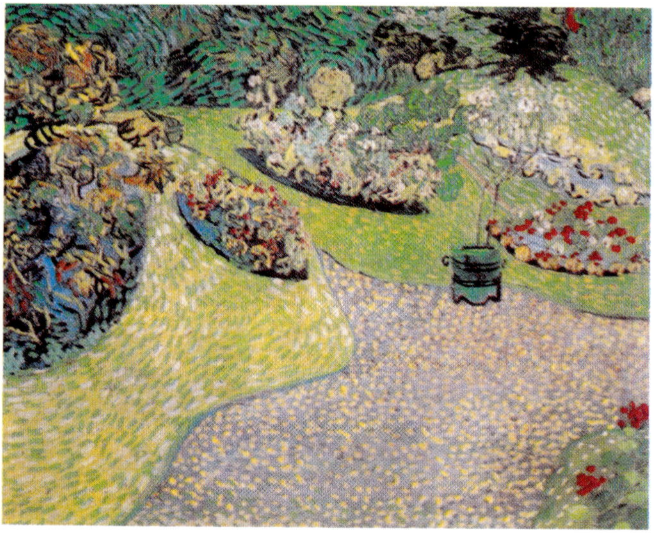

Garden at Auvers (JH2107, F814), 64 × 80 cm, June/July 1890?

This controversy had exploded into a momentous art history dispute, into a real humdinger of an artquake. Although the epicentre was in Paris, it reverberated throughout the international art world and also caused severe cracks in the fortifications of the 'brick wall' at the Van Gogh Museum in Amsterdam.

The official Dutch *catalogue raisonné* of Vincent van Gogh, the revised de la Faille edition published in 1970, lists Amédée Schuffenecker, brother of the painter Emile Schuffenecker, as the first owner in the provenance for the *Garden at Auvers*.

Both brothers, Amédée, a collector/dealer, and Claude-Emile (1851–1934)—commonly referred to simply as 'Emile', a collector-painter, had doubtful reputations. They collected and marketed originals but are also suspected of having created and marketed forgeries, not only of van Goghs. Two paintings with a listed provenance of A. Schuffenecker, previously attributed to van Gogh, are now rejected. For art dealers, a Schuffenecker provenance rings alarm bells.

The *Garden at Auvers*, even on photographs, shows features not characteristic of van Gogh. As a Van Gogh Museum curator might put it, "The gay colours (there is no sky) are different. The clumsy, not very lively method of drawing is clearly different; the canvas has never been examined. In one area the paint has been placed in the pointillist manner, which is not known from van Gogh's Auvers period."

According to the provenance in the 1970 de la Faille catalogue, the *Garden at Auvers* was on loan to the Museum Boymans-Van Beuningen in Rotterdam from 1933 until 1945, from the Paul Cassirer Art Gallery P. Cassirer, of which the father of Walter Feilchenfeldt of Zürich was a director/partner at the time. Afterwards the painting apparently passed, via Mrs Alice Kurtz (U.S.A) and the Wildenstein Art Gallery in New York, to Mr Jacques Walter in Paris in 1955. The price paid by Mr Walter is believed to have been Ffr 15 million. In an exceptional move, the French Government, through the French Minister of Culture, M. Jack Lang, declared the painting an 'historic monument', which meant that it could no longer be exported from France.

The controversy about this work really started when Jacques Walter, who was living in Geneva at that time, put the painting up for sale at auction by the *commissaires-priseurs* Messrs Binoche and Godeau in Paris in 1992. At that time a reasonable estimate for the painting on the international market would have been around 200 million francs but the export ban, of course, seriously affected the selling price. It received a certificate of authenticity from the Musées de France. In the auction catalogue for the 1992 sale, van Heugten, the curator of drawings at the Van Gogh Museum, called the painting an attractive work and because of its pointillist style, an 'echo' of van Gogh's work in the later part of his 'Paris' period. According to him there was no doubt at all that the painting was genuine. Binoche declares that van Heugten saw the painting at the same time as Professor Ronald Pickvance, an English art historian and known authority on van Gogh, who had also remarked on the pointillist brush strokes in the painting, and on the curves, which in his opinion gave the painting a very special quality. He supported the attribution to van Gogh, declaring it to be the fourth in the series of four paintings by Vincent of Daubigny's garden. This was strange, as Cadorin and many other specialists before him had much earlier declared one of the other three of this 'series of four', *Daubigny's Garden with Cat* in the Basle Kunstmuseum, to be a fake, effectively reducing the series to a maximum of three.

Also curiously, in the 1992 auction catalogue Mrs Johanna van Gogh-Bonger was for the first time named as having been the first owner of the *Garden at Auvers,* instead of A. Schuffenecker as in the official de la Faille 1928 provenance. This was not the first time that Johanna van Gogh-Bonger's name has been swapped for that of a Schuffenecker as first owner in a provenance. Some five years earlier, when a version of the *Fourteen Sunflowers in a Vase* came up for sale in their auction in 1987, Dorn had suggested to Christie's that the original de la Faille provenance giving E. Schuffenecker as first owner should be changed to one saying that Theo van Gogh and his wife Johanna had been the first owners.

On 12 December 1992, at the auction in Paris, the *Garden at Auvers* was hammered down by Binoche to the banker Jean-Marc Vernes for a price of Ffr 55 million. The vendor, Jacques Walter, then claimed that his painting would have fetched about four times as much if it could have been sold on the international market and he sued the French Government. He died before the case was settled but it was decided in his favour after his death, and the French Government had to pay the Walter family Ffr 145 million as final compensation, effectively increasing the sale price of the painting to Ffr 200 million.

On 4 April 1996, the new owner of the *Garden at Auvers,* M. Vernes, died after his bank ran into financial difficulties. It was no longer realistic for his heirs to think in terms of presenting the painting to the State, and they put it back on the market. An auction by auctioneer Jacques Tajan was planned for November 1996.

The director of *Le Figaro*'s art department, Jean-Marie Tasset, apparently wrote an article—which the paper did not publish—revealing that, as a result of detailed research, experts had doubts whether the *Garden at Auvers* was a genuine van Gogh. In July, however, the satirical but respected magazine *Le Canard enchaîné* broke the same story. Their article, which also reported the suppression of the story in *Le Figaro*, was even more intriguing than the article in *Le Figaro* would have been. *Le Monde* followed with a full-page article on the *Garden at Auvers* on 27

September 1996, exactly one month after I had collected *The Diggers* again from Cadorin in Basle. This artquake was really shaking terra firma.

The 'historic monument' that had cost the French taxpayer Ffr 145 million was now suspected to be a fake and became an immediate *cause célèbre*. The article in *Le Monde* cited van Tilborgh, the curator of paintings, and van Heugten, the curator of drawings, of the Van Gogh Museum, and Mme Francoise Cachin, director of the French Musées Nationaux, as authorities who had declared the painting to be genuine. Such an array of prestigious opinions and guarantees would surely convince potential buyers.

The article included mention of the fact that originally de la Faille had listed Amédée Schuffenecker as the first owner of the painting. The auctioneer in 1992, M. Binoche, explained that he had quoted the provenance of Johanna van Gogh-Bonger, as first owner, from the Flammarion catalogue (in which there is no mention of a provenance) and has apparently admitted to having 'made an error' in so doing.

Le Monde also drew attention to the atypical pointillist brush strokes in the painting, in which three different coloured oil paints are placed on top of each other. To avoid the colours mixing, a painter has to wait at least three to four days after applying each colour, to let the paint dry, before being able to place the next colour on top. This alone should have been enough to prove that the painting could not possibly be from the hand of van Gogh, as he would not have had the time to paint it, let alone that he did not use that style at the time.

A point in the polemics turned on the fact that van Heugten had said in his certification that there *had* been enough time for the paint to dry in between applications. This was very surprising as, according to the catalogue, Vincent would have had to paint more than one painting a day when in Auvers. That alone should be reason enough to label it as a more than usually time-consuming painting, 'probably not by Van Gogh'. In addition, however, the *Garden at Auvers* is supposed to have been painted after *The Garden of Daubigny,* which, in a letter three days before his suicide, Vincent said he had just painted. If that was the case, he would hardly have had the time to paint it, let alone to indulge, uncharacteristically, in pointillism.

Not surprisingly, despite the opinions of the impressive group of experts, the notion that the painting was not a genuine van Gogh but from the hand of Emile Schuffenecker gained ground, albeit 'underground'.

Mme Cachin appeared on the French TV with M. Tajan. Her message, paraphrased, was more or less, "Please buy the *Garden at Auvers*, we can't have it for the Musées Nationaux as we have already paid too much for it and, even if the painting is not entirely typical of Vincent van Gogh, it is absolutely a genuine van Gogh, the Van Gogh Museum has certified it."

Two weeks before the auction, another article appeared in *Le Monde*, by Michel Guerrin, who stated that he had researched the archives of the Paul Cassirer Art Gallery in Berlin and come to the conclusion that the *Garden at Auvers* had been in the collection of Johanna van Gogh-Bonger, the sister-in-law of the painter. And because it was now supposed to have originated from the collection of Johanna van Gogh-Bonger, Feilchenfeldt and his collaborator Dorn had also concluded that the painting must be genuine.

On 10 December 1996, the day of the sale, Tajan started the bidding at Ffr20 million. The bidding appeared to go up to 32 million, by bids, as the saying goes, 'from the chandeliers'. Finally he indicated someone, who eventually turned out to be a journalist, as the 32 million bidder. He ended the proceedings without the customary *adjugé* [sold] hammer, or by identifying the 'last bidder'.

In fact the painting had not been able to attract a buyer: it had been consigned to a sudden death.

Despite the build-up by the French officials, the curators of the Van Gogh Museum, and by Messrs Feilchenfeldt, Dorn and Prof. Pickvance, potential buyers were 'not having any'. Shockwaves were felt throughout the art world.

On 26 December 1996 *Le Monde* published an article by the French writer Benoit Landais in which he gave ten reasons for rejecting the painting. Among them he argued that the type and style of painting of the *Garden at Auvers* is foreign to the work of van Gogh. A dedicated viewer could "walk into" a van Gogh landscape, he said, whereas the *Garden at Auvers* was a dead end. The colours were not van Gogh colours. The invasion of the pointillist style would have meant Vincent had regressed two years in his painting development. Instead of being by van Gogh it was almost certainly a genuine Emile Schuffenecker, parts of which seem to have been modelled on two other paintings.

These are JH2105, *The Garden of Daubigny with Black Cat*, a fake, and JH1630, *Memory of the Garden in Etten*, a genuine van Gogh. Both were good subjects to use for a painter wishing to create a painting like the *Garden at Auvers*—and both were at one time owned by Schuffenecker.

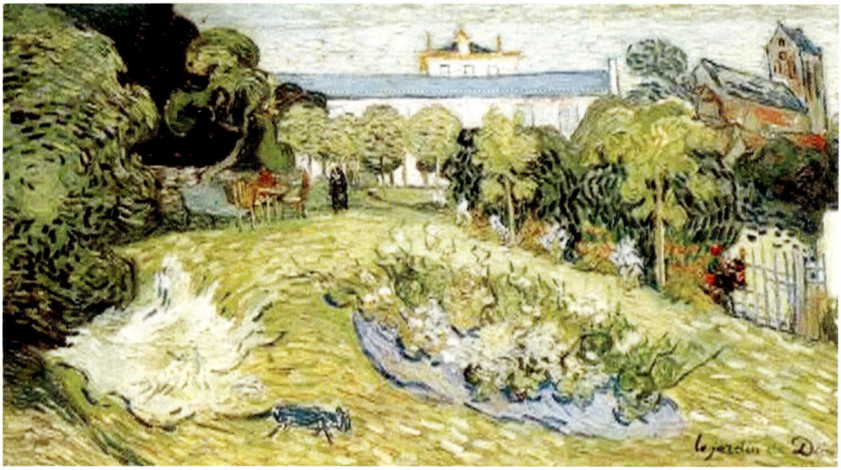

The Garden of Daubigny with Cat, a fake Van Gogh (JH2105, F814 above)
56 × 101.5 cm
10 July 1890?

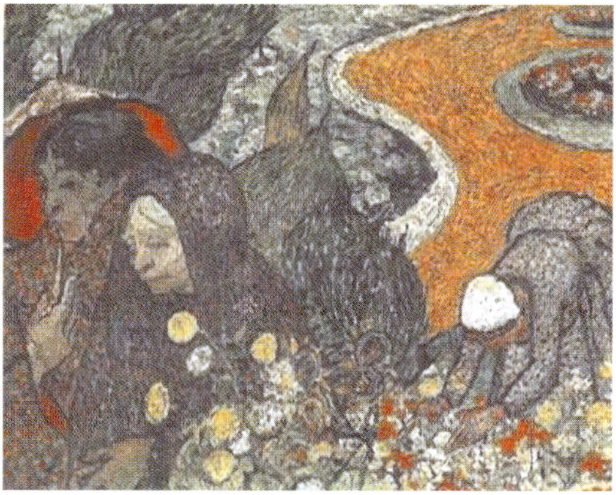

Memory of the Garden at Etten,
(JH1630, F496 right)
73.5 × 92.5 cm

Hulsker, in his latest *catalogue raisonné*, *The New Complete van Gogh*, had also been unable to confirm the authenticity of the *Garden at Auvers*. This was one of the forty-seven works which had received his question mark against its date of production. Uncertainty about dating can throw doubt on a painting's authenticity, and vice versa. Sometimes the actual date of production of a painting attributed to Van Gogh can be after Vincent's death.

In an interview published in *Le Figaro* of 14 January 1997, Hulsker declared that he had often thought about the atypical character of the *Garden at Auvers*. The current public debate about the painting had not surprised him and he felt unable to offer any arguments in favour of the painting. And in another interview—with Bob Witman, in the *Volkskrant* of 14 February 1997—in which he confirmed his misgivings about the authenticity of a number of important paintings, Hulsker said that a *catalogue raisonné* was not the place for revelations. He preferred to leave these to others to present, and he named Landais, whose knowledge on these matters he greatly valued, as a possible such 'other'. (I made a mental note to try and meet Landais for an opinion on *The Diggers*, as I now realised that many valued his expertise and extensive knowledge.)

The claim that *Garden at Auvers* is a fake was being kept very much alive by articles in the international press, such as in an article in *Die Weltwoche* by Hanspeter Born on 7 August 1997; in articles in Holland in the Cultural Supplement of the NRC-*Handelsblad;* in an article by Geraldine Norman in *The New York Review of Books* of 5 February 1998; and in others.

Unable to sell the *Garden at Auvers*, the Vernes heirs later initiated legal proceedings against the auctioneer Binoche, who had sold the painting to their late father in December 1992. *Le Figaro* was the first to break the news, and Binoche took legal action against the paper, explaining that Feilchenfeldt, the Van Gogh Museum, and Pickvance had provided him with the new provenance he had used in his 1992 catalogue. This statement caused some argument and dispute between the parties concerned. In 1998, Feilchenfeldt said that he thought that the van Gogh Museum had given Binoche the provenance he had used, but in 2000 he confirmed in writing to Binoche that, when they had met in 1992, he had read the catalogue and that he had noted particularly that Binoche had taken into account the advice and documents he, Feilchenfeldt, had given him about the provenance.

Van Tilborgh had declared in 1996 that Dorn had recently (after 1992) discovered the 'new' provenance. Pickvance was apparently displeased about Binoche's version of events and refused to confirm it. What confusion!

Both court cases are currently believed to be under appeal.

* * *

Landais, whose articles on fake van Goghs have appeared in the French Magazine *Connaissance des Arts*, in *Journal des Arts*, in *Le Figaro*, *Le*

Monde, and in other publications now became the main target of the 'Van Gogh establishment'.

He was obviously a man to whom I should show *The Diggers* but he equally obviously was very busy. I learned later that he was very much occupied at that time preparing to trigger second and third artquakes of at least the same proportions as the first. He was about to detonate a charge under the Yasuda copy of the *Fourteen Sunflowers in a Vase* (see next chapter) and was also preparing a rope to hang the reputation of the famous Doctor Gachet (Chapter 15).

However difficult the task for *The Diggers* might have become, I still refused to believe that it might not be possible somehow to do better than the flimsy rejection by the Van Gogh Museum. That it had become apparent that *The Diggers* was not the only painting on which some people could have erred in their judgement provided some moral support.

Chapter Seven

The Second Artquake

This 'quake had started being felt a few years earlier, but it really erupted with impact in 1996. Although the first tremors had been felt in Europe, the epicentre had moved to Japan. The painting causing this serious shock wave throughout the international art world was one of the three paintings of *Fourteen Sunflowers in a Vase* attributed to van Gogh.

Vincent van Gogh considered the sunflower to be 'his'. A life-giving flower, a symbol of love and gratitude, and closely related to 'his' sun. He painted a number of sunflower still lifes, and sunflowers appeared in some of his other works as well. His sunflower paintings from the Arles period are the most famous. He created four paintings of sunflowers in a vase there in August 1888: *Three Sunflowers in a Vase* (JH1559), *Five Sunflowers in a Vase* (JH1560), *Twelve Sunflowers in a Vase* (JH1561) and *Fourteen Sunflowers in a Vase* (JH1667).

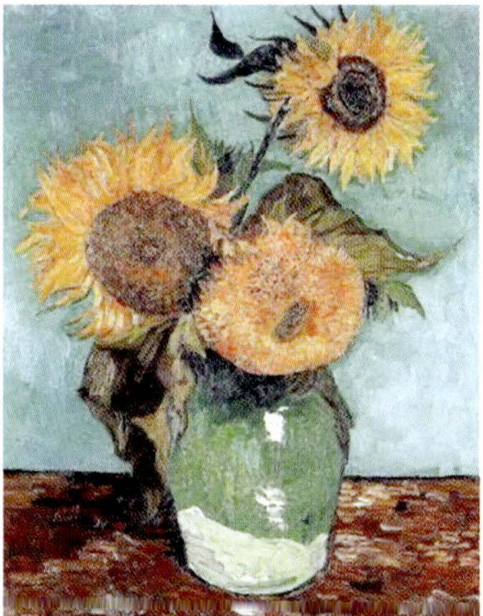

Three Sunflowers in a Vase
(JH1559, F453) 73 × 58 cm
Private Collection, U.S.A.

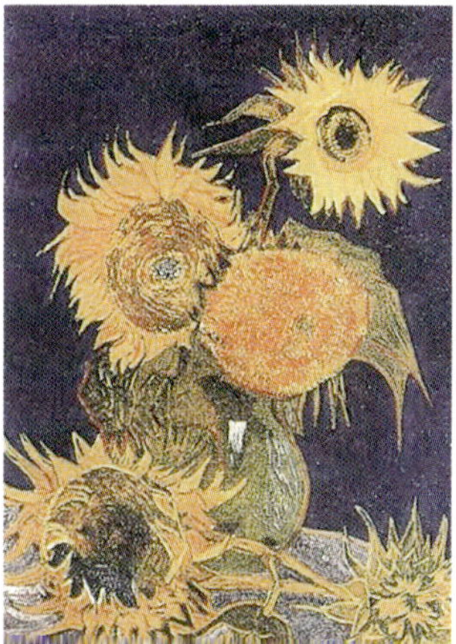

Five Sunflowers in a Vase
(JH1560, F459) 98 × 69 cm
Destroyed by fire, formerly in Yokohama

His *Fourteen Sunflowers in a Vase* (JH1667), painted in August 1888, now hanging in the Van Gogh Museum in Amsterdam, is considered to be one of the greatest masterpieces of his career. A few days earlier he had painted the *Twelve Sunflowers in a Vase* (JH1561) which is now hanging in Munich. Vincent had described them at the time in a few letters to his brother written from the Yellow House, 2 place Lamartine, Arles.

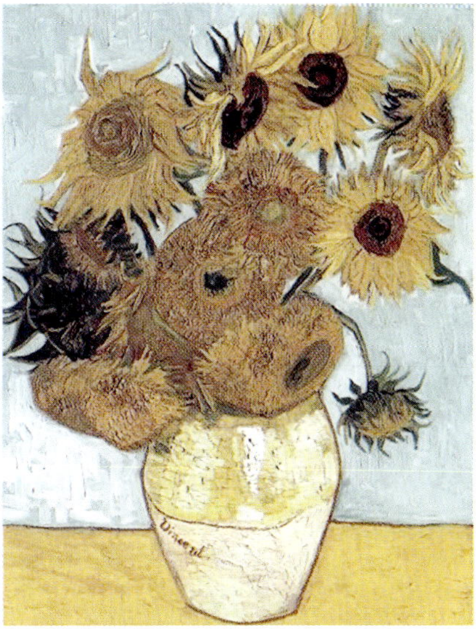

Twelve Sunflowers in a Vase
(JH1561, F456) 91 × 71 cm
Neue Pinakothek, Munich

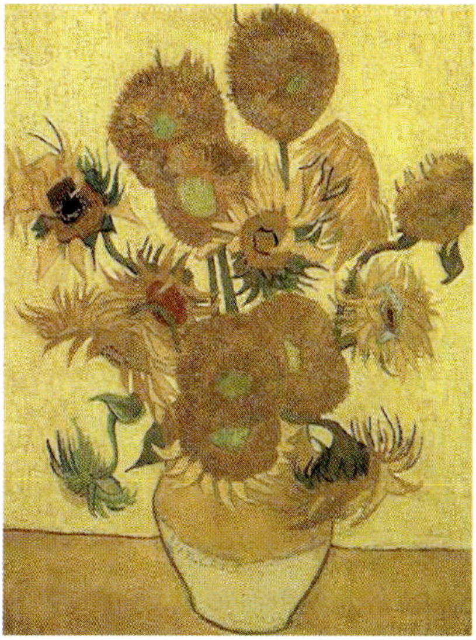

Fourteen Sunflowers in a Vase
(JH1667, F458) 95 × 73 cm
Van Gogh Museum, Amsterdam

These two still lifes were meant to decorate what was hoped would become a 'Studio of the South' and were hung in the room Paul Gauguin would occupy when he came to share the atelier in October 1888. After Gauguin had left in late December 1888, after Vincent's well-known ear accident, he asked, in January 1889 by letter, to be given the *Fourteen Sunflowers in a Vase* but Vincent refused his request.

But at the end of January 1889, Vincent, considering a possible exchange with Gauguin, had completed copies of both the sunflower paintings which were hanging in the Yellow House. These copies are the *Twelve Sunflowers in a Vase* (JH1688), now in Philadelphia and the *Fourteen Sunflowers in a Vase* (JH1562), now in London. The exchange with Gauguin never took place. All six sunflower paintings, the four painted in August 1888 (one of three, one of five, one of twelve, and one of fourteen blooms) and the two copies by Vincent in January 1889 (one of twelve and one of fourteen blooms) are mentioned in Vincent's letters and can be accounted for in the documentation.

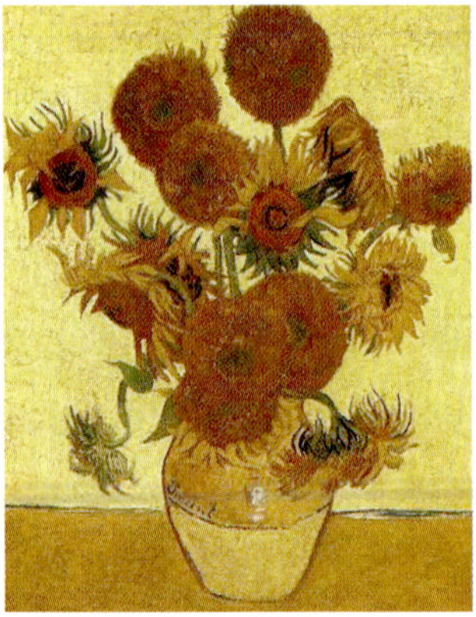

Fourteen Sunflowers in a Vase
(JH1562, F 454) 93 × 73 cm
National Gallery, London

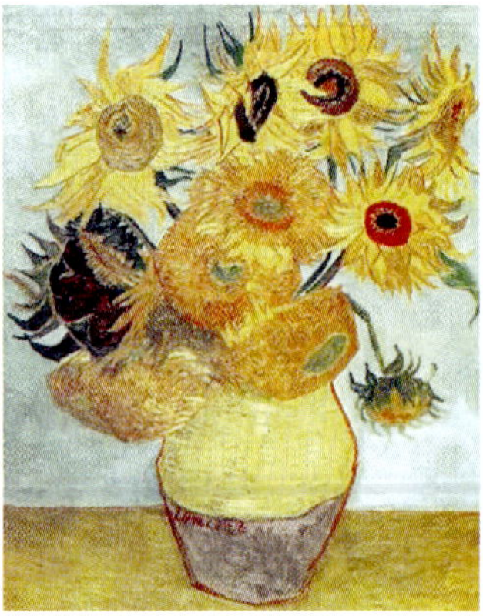

Twelve Sunflowers in a Vase
(JH1668, F 455) 92 × 72.5 cm
Philadelphia Museum of Art

Until recently it had been believed that the version of the *Fourteen Sunflowers* now hanging in Amsterdam was the copy and that the one in London was the original, but Landais has pointed out that the reverse is true and the painting in Amsterdam is the original, that in London the copy. Hulsker agrees with Landais's very strong arguments. No valid dispute on this point is possible. Vincent had written that the background of the original *Fourteen Sunflowers in a Vase* is 'yellow green', and this can only refer to the Amsterdam canvas, as the background of the London painting is lemon yellow.

There is also, however, a third version, in addition to the undisputed original in Amsterdam painted in August 1888 and the copy in London painted by van Gogh himself in January 1889. This third version is not mentioned in Vincent's letters nor does it appear in any of the early stock records. It is the only one of the three versions which is not signed.

This third, mystery version of *Fourteen Sunflowers in a Vase* is a copy of the London painting and therefore a copy of Vincent's own copy, not of the original. It was last sold by Christie's in March 1987.

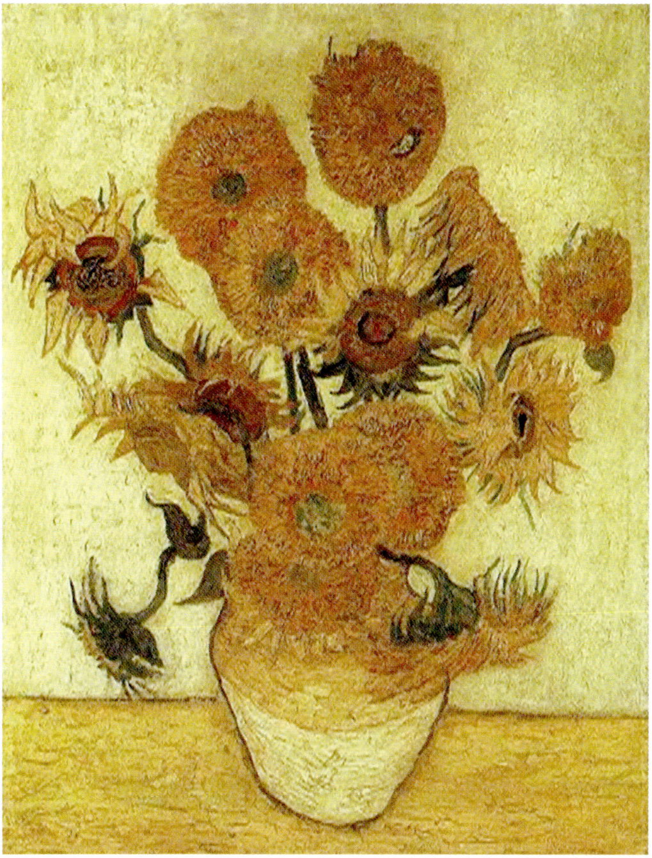

Fourteen Sunflowers in a Vase, (JH 1666 F 457)
100 × 76 cm, Yasuda Kasai Museum of Art, Tokyo

Their auction catalogue for that sale said that this third copy was also painted in January 1889 but, as Landais has pointed out, this was clearly a mistake. Careful reading of Vincent's letters, in which he thrice says that he only made one copy, definitely excludes the possibility of his having painted a third version.

One of the reasons Landais advances to attribute this third version to Schuffenecker appears to be especially valid. In June 1900, six months before this copy appeared in the Schuffenecker collection, Johanna van Gogh had sent the genuine copy (now in London) to Julien Leclerq, an art critic and art dealer in Paris. The painting was damaged on the way and Leclerq had asked his friend Schuffenecker to restore it. In his exchange of letters with Johanna van Gogh, Leclerq avoided mentioning the name of the restorer, which remained unknown to her.

The first acknowledged recording, with certainty, of the third version of *Fourteen Sunflowers in a Vase* was by Julien Leclerq, shortly before the exhibition at the Gallery in Paris in March 1901, some eleven years after Vincent's death. The owner was stated to be Emile Schuffenecker. Julien Leclercq organised this exhibition and also wrote the catalogue, which listed sixty-five paintings. What is believed to have happened is that during the lengthy period of restoration of the genuine copy of *Fourteen Sunflowers* Emile Schuffenecker had ample time and opportunity to make a copy for himself. This also explains why the third version is a copy of the copy in London and not of the original in Amsterdam.

Then, at the time of the exhibition, to which Johanna van Gogh was known not to be coming, as Schuffenecker's copy was not yet sufficiently dry, the friends Leclerq and Schuffenecker cunningly exhibited the genuine copy, Johanna's painting, at this exhibition, but under the name of Schuffenecker as owner. After the exhibition, the Schuffenecker copy, the 'third version', had thus acquired a workable provenance for itself.

This painting was sold some years later by the A. Schuffenecker Art Gallery. It went to Germany, and was later acquired by a London collector. It went on loan to the National Gallery in London and was shown there from 1983 to 1987, near the genuine (van Gogh) copy, which had originally been acquired in 1924 by the Tate Gallery.

I saw the third version at the National Gallery when it was exhibited there and was not the only one who remarked on its inferior appeal. But who, at that time, would have suspected that the National Gallery might be showing a fake van Gogh?

The painting must have acquired some extra credibility with its presence on the walls of the National Gallery before Christie's sold it in 1987. The auction catalogue stated that the van Gogh family (not Schuffenecker) had been the first owner, and the painting was sold on 30 March 1987 at auction in London for the record sum of £24.75 million to the Yasuda Fire and Marine Insurance Company of Japan. Elsewhere in their catalogue Christie's expressed their gratitude to Dorn for having provided them with the information which had enabled them to change the previously accepted [but commercially possibly detrimental] official provenance of E. Schuffenecker.

Geraldine Norman noted in the *Daily Telegraph* that if the Yasuda *Sunflowers* was supposed to have been with Johanna van Gogh in 1891 then there were just not enough sunflower paintings on her known inventory lists, as all her entries of *Sunflowers* can be accounted for elsewhere.

Since alarm bells have rung for more than half a century in the international art market whenever the name Schuffenecker is mentioned, one cannot but realise that the new provenance 'discoveries' by Dorn were very welcome in some quarters. And Christie's could hardly be blamed for using this information from an accepted and acknowledged expert.

Just after the painting had been knocked down to Yasuda, someone in the salesroom public gallery asked whether there was any doubt about its authenticity. This met with chuckles all round and the reaction from the Christie's auctioneer of "What a time to ask!", then a smile and a further "No, I don't think so." This seemed a joke—at the time.

After the auction, in Christie's *Review of the Year*, Professor Pickvance pointed out some of the reasons why Dorn had been mistaken on the provenance, through erroneously attributing a letter about a painting of twelve sunflowers to a painting of fourteen sunflowers.

Four years after the auction, in 1991, the Yasuda Fire and Marine Insurance Company made the generous offer of a gift of some £15 million to the Van Gogh Museum for an extension to their building. In December 1996 it was announced that final building permission to build the controversial new wing to the Van Gogh Museum, the design of a Japanese architect, had been granted. The gift could now be confirmed and utilised.

The first to alert the international art world publicly that all was really not well with 'The Yasuda' was an Italian, Antonio de Robertis, who has made a name for himself as a van Gogh expert. His opinion that it was a fake, published in January 1994 in the Milan *Il Corriere della Sera*, was based on his study of the painting, which he said had revealed various atypical van Gogh aspects, as well as on his analysis of *The Letters*. But despite his conviction that it was a fake, he did not seem to offer an answer at the time as to who might have painted it.

The lead in the debate in France and in Holland was being taken over by Benoit Landais, whose international reputation as a van Gogh fake hunter was steadily growing. He drew attention to the exchange between the Van Gogh Museum and the Stedelijk Museum in Amsterdam in 1997 to acquire their *La Berceuse*. This would make it possible to display a triptych—*Fourteen Sunflowers-Berceuse-Fourteen Sunflowers*—at the opening of their new wing. Vincent had once expressed the idea of a 'grand Arlesian triptych' of his *Fourteen Sunflowers—Berceuse—Twelve Sunflowers* and had suggested this as a decoration for the wall of a ship's saloon to console fishermen at sea. He even made a sketch of such a triptych in letter 592 of 22 May 1889 to his brother but the plan had never been executed.

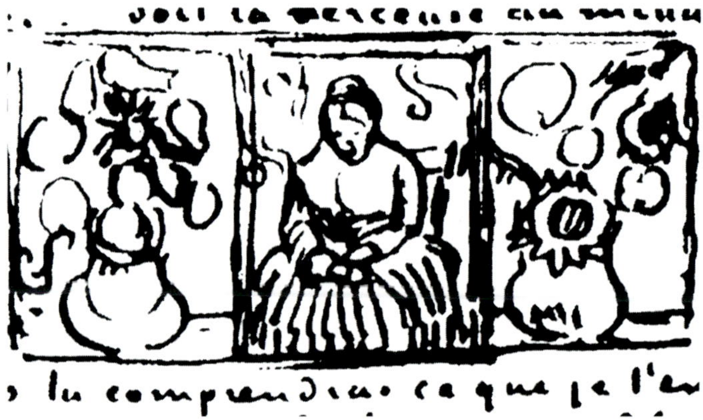

Sketch in letter 592 of 22 May 1889

The Van Gogh Museum, who owned Vincent's original *Fourteen Sunflowers*, now also had *La Berceuse* from the Stedelijk Museum and was ready to welcome the famous Yasuda *Sunflowers* to complete a triptych filling Vincent's spot for *Twelve Sunflowers* with the Yasuda's *Fourteen*.

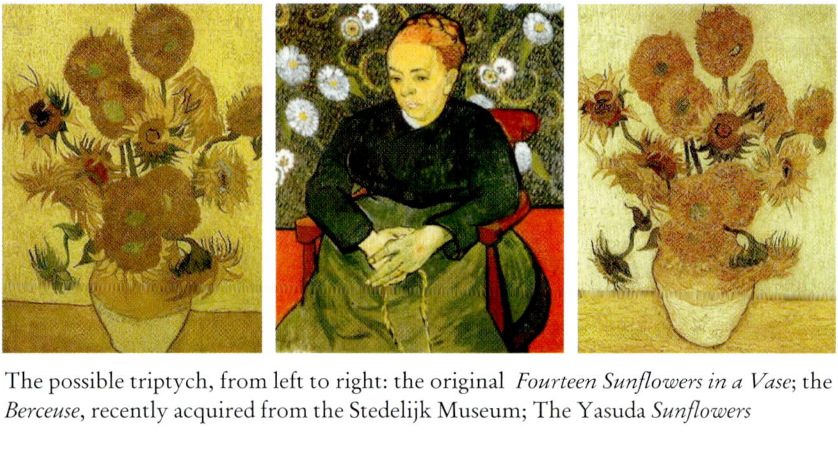

The possible triptych, from left to right: the original *Fourteen Sunflowers in a Vase*; the *Berceuse*, recently acquired from the Stedelijk Museum; The Yasuda *Sunflowers*

Even though not exactly matching Vincent's design, such an exhibit at the opening of the new wing would have been a great honour for the Yasuda, and an enormous crowd puller. But the unwelcome publicity caused by Landais seemed to have ruined the scope for such a grand plan. The press had spread the news about the doubtful authenticity, the art world had taken due note, and the artquake began to register serious levels.

In the ensuing debate, Landais and others who challenged the authenticity of the Yasuda version gave proof of their knowledge and built up their arguments from sound foundations, while those who attributed the painting to van Gogh appeared unable to defend their position convincingly and resorted to dismissing their opponents as 'amateurs'. Transparently inaccurate and false accusations were used against them, not only in the cases of the *Garden at Auvers* and the Yasuda *Sunflowers* but in other cases as well; the defence was weak, evasive, and brutal in its criticism of those who had advanced solid arguments to which it gave no real answers.

The floodgates had really opened early 1997 when, revealing his doubts about the authenticity of certain important paintings, Hulsker had joined the attempt to purify the oeuvre of van Gogh. He appeared publicly on more than one occasion on the side of the 'amateurs', as they were still disparagingly called.

Dr Jan Hulsker is an internationally acknowledged and respected van Gogh expert and scholar whom no one could possibly ignore, and was the first, with Landais, to force curators and directors of museums out of their protective shells into the open, to try to defend their controversial attributions before the hungry press. The Van Gogh Museum seemed to go into a deep crisis over this. Other acknowledged sources joined in the fray.

One important result from all this was, as we read in various prominent newspapers in France, Holland, the U.S.A., and Britain, that the director and curators of the Van Gogh Museum declared that the matter of the *Sunflowers* would be researched in detail and as quickly as possible in order to put everybody's mind at rest. Indeed, the Museum had little option but to appear to be honest and open and, after many promises and after being denounced in the *New York Review of Books*, their new director, Leighton, removed some of the restrictions the Museum had previously enforced on large parts of the family's documentation and certain of the letters, and made them also available to researchers other than the staff of the Museum.

The most welcome proposal was that all three versions of *Fourteen Sunflowers in a Vase*, from Amsterdam, London, and Japan, would be brought together in the National Gallery in London, where international experts could view, discuss, and compare the trio in a public debate and, with the assistance of scientific investigations, could reach a final and, it was to be hoped, unanimous, verdict. The curator of the Van Gogh Museum, however, supported by the director, was reported at one point to be suggesting that we might forever have to live with question marks. Were they hoping the controversy might be interred unsettled?

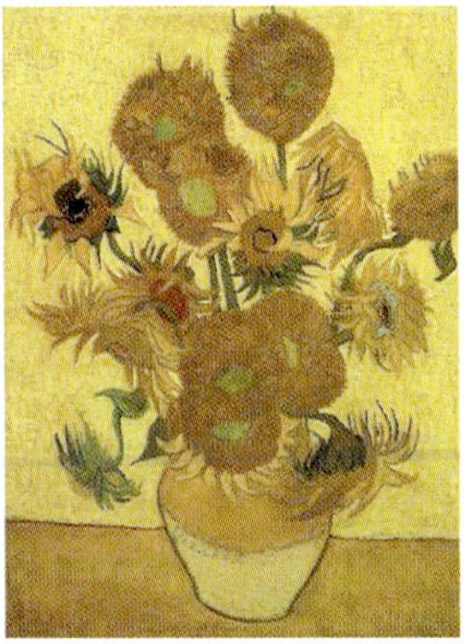

The original, JH 1667
in Amsterdam

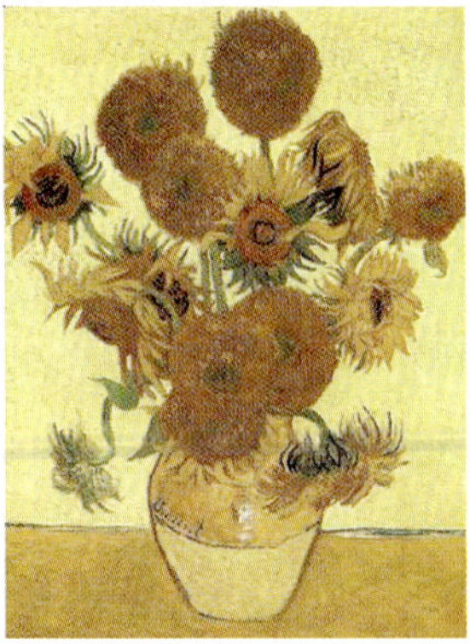

The copy by Vincent
JH 1562, in London

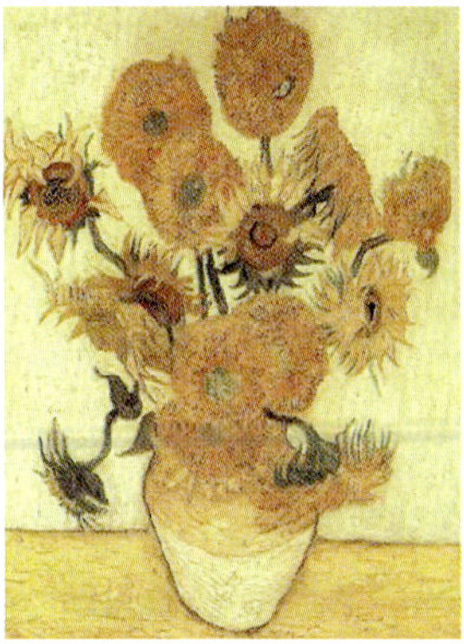

The third version, JH 1666,
"the Yasuda" in Tokyo

Van Heugten, the curator of prints and drawings at the Museum, maintains that the Yasuda version is absolutely genuine. Although listing the characteristics of the painting that are untypical of van Gogh in great detail and very convincingly is precisely what the 'amateurs' were doing, he suggested that they were only studying provenances. He repeated that he sees work by van Gogh on a daily basis and is thus familiar with his 'handwriting' and that, just with the naked eye, he recognises it in the Yasuda *Sunflowers*. He gives no further explanation, offers no definition of the characteristics by which he recognises the 'handwriting'. He does not try to argue that the many features the opposition considers atypical are in fact typical of van Gogh: he simply ignores them. In keeping with the Museum's view that nobody has a right to judge a painting without having seen it, van Tilborgh and van Heugten flew to Japan in September 1997 to have a look at the painting. They returned saying they saw no reason to doubt that it is genuine. Stylistic differences were not mentioned, but 'further research might be necessary'.

Everyone accepts that there are stylistic differences between the Yasuda *Sunflowers* and the other two versions. Leighton has confirmed that differences were already noticed in his time, when it was hanging near the National Gallery's own copy in the early eighties.

In October 1997 the Arthouse film *The Fake Van Goghs** was shown on British television. This film was subsequently also shown, with slight adaptations, on the Continent. In it Tom Hoving, former director of the Metropolitan Museum in New York, calls the Yasuda *Sunflowers* a funny muddy picture although, he said, van Gogh was not a muddy painter. The painting, according to him, is not put together correctly; it does not have that 'snap'. De Robertis explains in detail why he came to the conviction that the Yasuda *Sunflowers* is a fake, both pointing out the shortcomings in the painting and referring to *The Letters* and other documentation which entirely support these views.

The film makers had life-size replicas made of the three versions of *Fourteen Sunflowers in a Vase*. These are shown, in the film, to Alain Tarica, a Paris art dealer with a reputation of being a brilliant 'fake spotter', who is apparently frequently brought in in cases of dispute. In the film he places the three versions side by side, points out a number of features in the Yasuda version that are not typical of van Gogh, and compares these with the actual van Gogh characteristics of the other two versions. Some aspects in the Yasuda version could only apply to artificial flowers and not to real blooms, while Vincent, the lover of nature, would only have painted true to nature. Tarica concludes that without any doubt the Yasuda *Sunflowers* cannot be by the hand of Vincent van Gogh and has been painted by a clumsy copyist.

The Yasuda copy is also of an odd size. Strips of canvas have been added to the original painting, increasing its size by approximately 6cm on all four sides. Even van Heugten and Dorn had to concede, after Landais had pointed this out, that these edges were painted by someone other than van Gogh, and they agreed that they could have been painted by Schuffenecker. Meanwhile, the Yasuda Fire & Marine Insurance Company declined to be interviewed. The film shows a letter from their chairman, Mr Yasuo Goto, which explains that they are not willing to enter the debate about the authenticity of their painting. They say that they are absolutely certain that their painting is a genuine van Gogh and they will not agree to any close study of it by anyone.

---

* Produced at Canalot Studios in London for Third Eye Productions Ltd and Channel Four, it won the 1997/1998 Indie Music and Arts Documentary Award for the best television programme produced by British Independents.

This letter seemed to torpedo the research project confidently announced by the Museum. Leighton's proposal to bring the three versions together in the National Gallery in London for comparison and for close study would be a major step forward, but the Japanese appeared not to support this plan. Had they, after the fiasco of the recent failed sale at auction of the *Garden at Auvers* and after they had seen the curator of the Van Gogh Museum, perhaps formed their own opinion of the Museum's ability to fight off the 'amateurs'? This was an enormous setback for those who wish to see the oeuvre of van Gogh cleaned up, the fakes winnowed from it, and people in authority making or maintaining dubious attributions exposed for their unwillingness to properly consider new evidence. Leighton's plan to bring the three versions together in the National Gallery was not officially cancelled yet but my doubts about this also seemed to have become more justified In any case it was no surprise that the Yasuda *Sunflowers* did not make an appearance at the opening of the new wing.

There is a precedent for bringing paintings together to give art lovers and experts a better opportunity to study the differences between them and to enable them to tell fake from genuine. In 1934, Eberhard Hanfstaengel, the new director of the Munich Art Collections, exhibited the two versions of the *Garden of Daubigny* together in the Kronprinzenpalais. In the end not everybody agreed which was which, but the experts unanimously agreed that the two pictures were not by the same artist. Had a similar agreement on the three versions of the *Fourteen Sunflowers* been possible in 1997, we would have advanced considerably.

The part played by the Schuffeneckers in the whole affair calls for a short explanatory history of the Schuffenecker brothers.

Chapter Eight

The Schuffenecker Brothers

Claude-Emile Schuffenecker (1851–1934) (hereinafter referred to also as just 'Emile') was just over a year older than Vincent (1853–1890). He was an early friend of Paul Gauguin (1848–1903), whom he met in 1872 at the stockbroking firm of Paul Bertin. Schuffenecker and Gauguin were not only colleagues at work, they also shared outside interests as amateur painters. Both decided to leave Bertin's in order to pursue careers as artists.

Schuffenecker also became certified as a teacher in art and drawing, in Paris schools, which provided him with a steady income. His finances enabled him to give Gauguin some material support by buying his paintings from time to time, at low prices. Schuffenecker exhibited in numerous group exhibitions and in the last exhibition of the impressionists. At his only one-man show in 1896 nothing was sold. Gauguin's painting of the Schuffenecker family, painted in 1889, now hanging in the Musée d'Orsay in Paris, depicts Emile as a disillusioned schoolteacher, standing, with his wife and two children nearby.

Emile frequented a circle of artists including Gauguin, Pissarro, Redon, Bernard, and Degas, whose works he acquired from time to time. He had a good eye for identifying talent. He also befriended the critic and art dealer Julien Leclercq. He had a brother, Amédée, who was three years younger. Amédée changed his formal profession from wine dealer to that of art dealer around the time he took over a large collection of paintings from his brother. He could not paint and is now generally believed to have been the 'bad egg' in the family, less than scrupulous in his art dealings. He is not credited with having produced either copies or fakes. At most, it is believed, he may have painted a signature or two. It was Emile who painted both originals and copies.

The price for a van Gogh rose approximately tenfold between shortly after his death in 1890 and the beginning of the next century, and has continued to rise rapidly ever since. After 1900 the brothers, particularly Amédée, from time to time lent paintings to exhibitions, where they became listed in the exhibition catalogues, thus gaining both credibility and a pedigree. Having acquired originals in the past, the brothers created a situation whereby the originals became more and more mixed up with the copies. Both varieties, genuine and fake, were at various times introduced—though not at the same time—into the best known Paris collections of the period.

Amongst many others, two particular instances of the Schuffenecker brothers' fraudulent dealings deserve more detailed mention. These concern *Self-portrait* by Vincent van Gogh, dedicated: *'à mon ami Paul Gauguin'* and *The Garden of Daubigny*.

Both cases were investigated and written up by the journalist Hanspeter Born in *Die Weltwoche* in August 1997. According to this article:

> A Crown witness for the prosecution in both cases would be Judith Gérard, a painter herself, who was the neighbour of Paul Gauguin at the rue Vercingétorix in Paris and who had been much fancied by Gauguin from the time she was thirteen or fourteen years old.
>
> When Gauguin finally left Paris in 1895 he left a painting by van Gogh behind with his neighbour, Judith's stepfather. This painting was a *Self-Portrait* dedicated to Gauguin. This strong painting did not fail to impress the young artist Judith, who then painted a faithful copy of it which she signed: *'d'après Vincent, Judith'*.
>
> In the meantime the art critic and dealer Julien Leclercq occupied the house of Gauguin, next door to Judith, and it was there that she met Julien's regular visitor and friend Emile Schuffenecker. A little later she received a visit from Emile's brother Amédée, who had heard about Judith's copy of the van Gogh *Self-portrait*. Amédée, on that occasion, offered to buy the painting, together with another painting by Judith, for Fr 200. Judith's mother had an annual income of some Fr 1800 so the offer was welcomed and accepted. Amédée mentioned that he planned to take both paintings to Germany.
>
> Many years later, in 1909, when Judith visited a van Gogh exhibition at the art-dealer and photographer Eugène Druet's gallery in Paris—the same dealer who also bought what later became known as the 'Yasuda' *Sunflowers* from Amédée Schuffenecker in 1907 or 1908, she was in for a surprise. What did she see as a first exhibit on the walls but her copy of the van Gogh *Self-portrait*, which she had sold to Amédée. But the painting showed unbelievable alterations. The concentric brush strokes of the background had been disfigured and replaced, without thought or care, with the use of pure white paint, by paper flowers, moonflowers and daisies. Even Vincent's vest and jacket had been given other colours. The only part, which had remained totally untouched, was the face which the 'restorer' had obviously found too difficult to 'improve' on. But there was no doubt that it was her painting. After a scene at the gallery with the owner Druet, who pleaded with her on his knees

to keep quiet about the affair, she left in a fury and with the positive intention of exposing Schuffenecker.

But, later, at home, her husband is supposed to have talked her out of creating a scandal and ruining the pleasure of the buyer, who would be living in the belief that he had bought a genuine van Gogh. A Mr von Mendelssohn-Bartholdy bought the painting

The same buyer bought the *Fourteen Sunflowers in a Vase*, the copy now known as 'the Yasuda', from the same source.

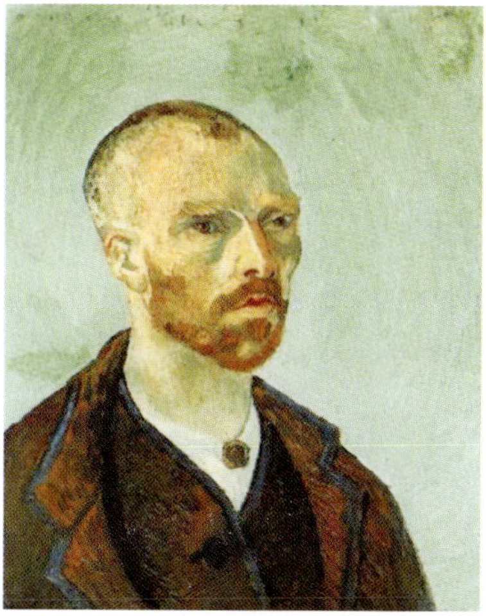

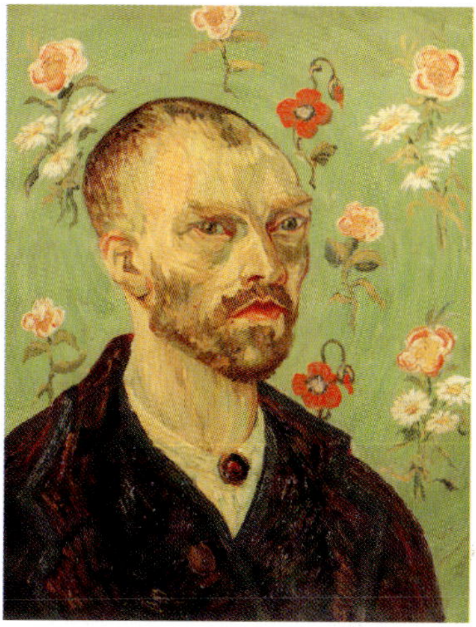

On the left *Self-portrait* by Vincent, dedicated to Gauguin. On the right the copy by Judith Gérard, after serious alterations and originally signed: *'d'aprés Vincent, Judith'*.

Although still attributed to van Gogh in the 1928 de la Faille *catalogue raisonné,* the *Self-portrait* was attributed to Judith Gérard in the 1970 edition. The case exposed Amédée Schuffenecker's deceit.

* * *

The story of *The Garden of Daubigny* is as follows. Landais had given Hanspeter Born a copy of an unpublished manuscript of 1951 by Judith Gérard, and Born wrote about it in the same *Die Weltwoche* article. Judith described how her neighbour Julien Leclercq had also managed to persuade Johanna van Gogh to send him from Amsterdam some of her brother-in-law's best paintings to augment those already in his possession.

Amongst the paintings Judith had seen were what she called:

The Yellow Room (JH177, right),

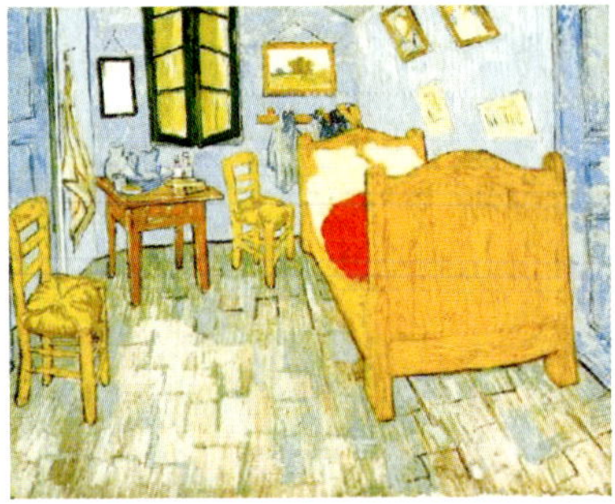

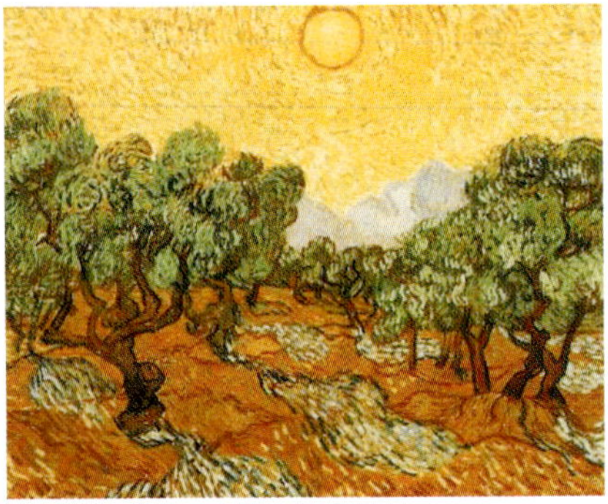

Olive Trees (JH1856, left),

Cypresses (JH1746, right),

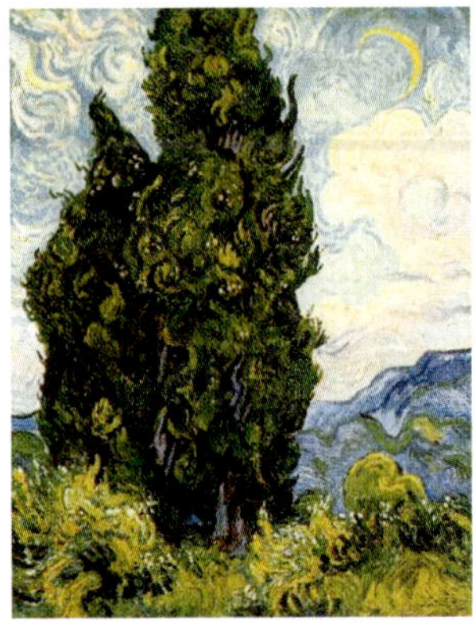

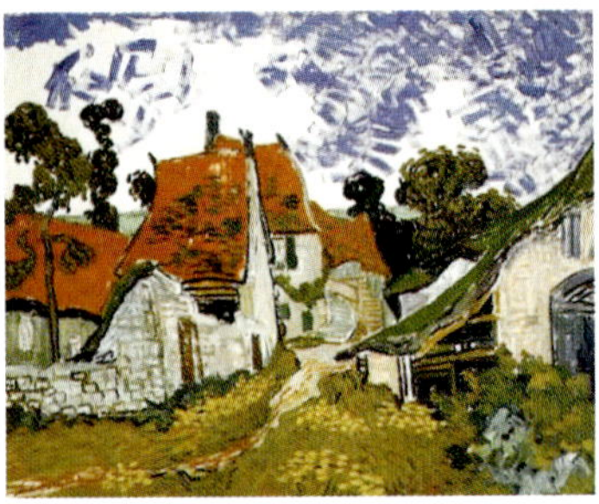

Red Roofs (JH2001, left),

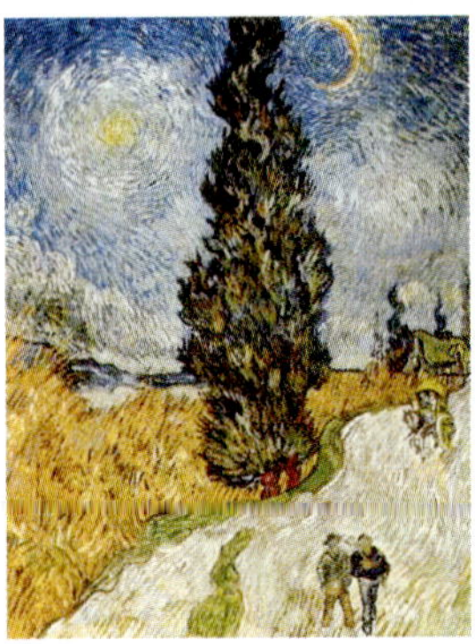

Road with Men, Carriage, Cypress, Star and Crescent Moon (JH1982, left),

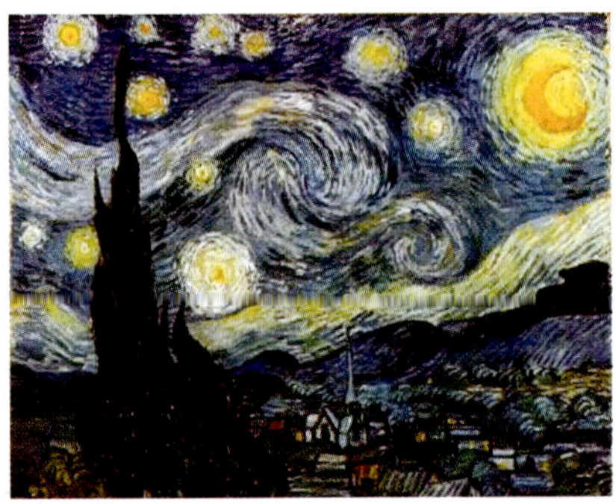

Starry Night (JH1731, right),

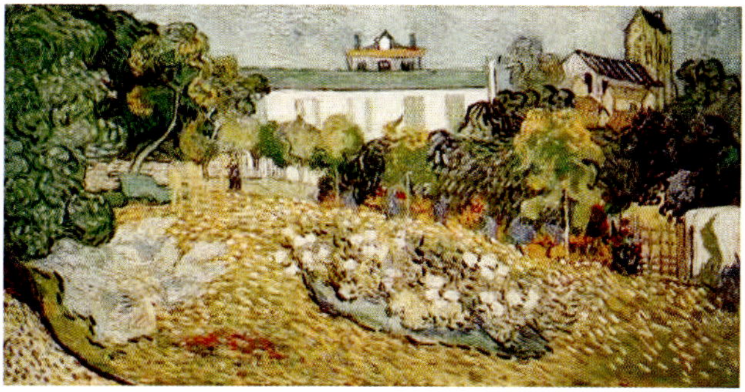

'Garden of Auvers', by which she meant *The Garden of Daubigny* (JH2104, left), the painting which originally had a cat,

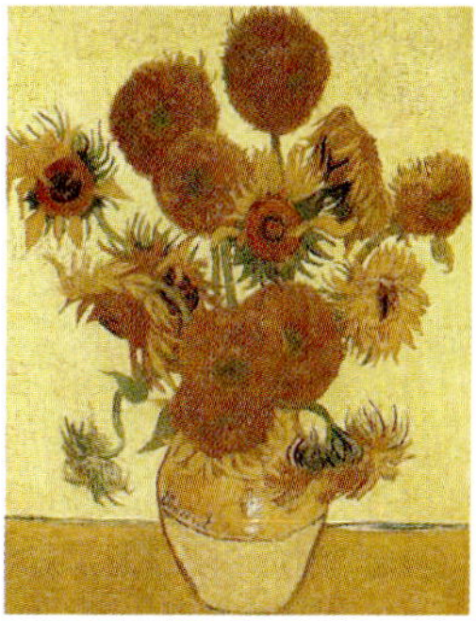

and *Fourteen Sunflowers* (JH1562, left).

The paintings had not been professionally packed. Some had been rolled up with the paint on the inside, which had caused it to flake off in places, and to repair the damage Leclercq had sent for his friend Emile Schuffenecker. According to Judith, Schuffenecker had not been satisfied with just restoring the damaged paintings, he had also started to 'improve' them. When he saw a contour with a sharp edge he had suggested that the painting had not been finished and could not be presented in this form and had rounded the form off. She reported that he called himself 'the cobbler of van Gogh'. He also 'improved' or 'finished' several Cézannes.

On the painting Judith had called the '*Garden of Auvers* (which was in fact *The Garden of Daubigny,* originally with Cat) (JH 2104, above), Schuffenecker had said the cat was badly drawn. He covered the cat by painting some grass over it, but Judith reported that a few years later she had seen the cat reappear after—she had thought—the paint in the area of the added grass had flaked off. The young Judith had seen correctly that Schuffenecker had made the cat disappear, but in thinking that this cat had later reappeared on the same painting, after 'the over-painting had flaked off', she had been mistaken. The painting from which Schuffenecker made the cat disappear, is still without cat (JH2104, F766, illustrated above). It is not difficult to see that the painting has been tampered with, especially where the cat originally was. Leclercq and Schuffenecker had not made the cat disappear for 'aesthetic reasons' at all, nor because it had been 'drawn badly' as they had said: the cat had been removed for purely commercial reasons.

In fact they had produced a new 'van Gogh', another *The Garden of Daubigny with Cat* (JH2105, F777, below) and doctored a pristine provenance to be able to pass the painting off as authentic.

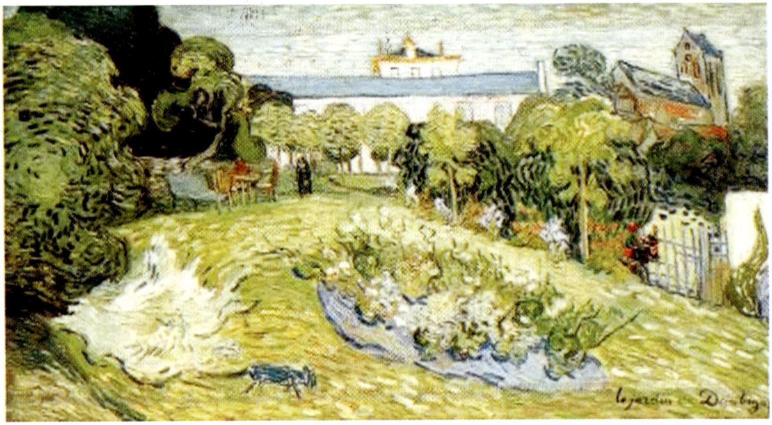

For this trick it was necessary for van Gogh's cat to jump across into the copy by Emile. This copy is the painting Judith had believed to be the one she had originally seen, which she erroneously called *Garden of Auvers,* but which had been in fact the original *The Garden of Daubigny with Cat* from which the cat had been removed. This cat had now, she believed, reappeared. In fact what she saw was the entirely new copy by Emile Schuffenecker of the original painting with cat—and the copy readily confirms that Schuffenecker was no animal painter! The original painting, on which Judith Gérard had seen Schuffenecker working, occupies a special place in van Gogh's oeuvre, as it is probably the last big painting he finished before committing suicide on 27 July 1890.

Shortly after he arrived in Auvers he learned that the widow of the Barbizon painter Charles Daubigny lived in the village. This soon gave him the idea for a large painting of Daubigny's garden. In mid-June he made an early version, a square painting *Corner in Daubigny's Garden* (JH2029, F765, left). On 10 July he started on the large version. On 24 July he wrote his last letter (LT908, 651) to his brother and enclosed a sketch of the painting and also a description of it:

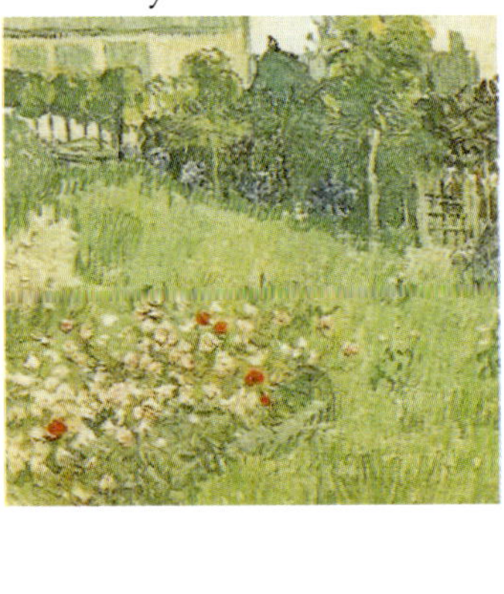

> . . . foreground of grass in green and pink. To the left a green and lilac bush and the stem of a plant with whitish leaves. In the middle a border of roses, to the right a wicket, a wall, and above the wall a hazelnut tree with violet foliage. Then a lilac hedge, a row of rounded yellow lime trees, the house itself in the background, pink, with a roof of bluish tiles. A bench and three chairs, a black figure with a yellow hat and in the foreground a black cat. The sky a pale green.

When Theo visited him on 28 July on his deathbed, Vincent asked his brother to give the painting to Daubigny's widow. He died the following morning.

In her letter of condolence to Theo, dated 12 August 1890, she wrote:

> When I watched your unfortunate brother painting this picture, which he intended to leave to me, I was far from thinking that I would ever become its owner. I thank you, dear Sir, and can assure you that you have all my sympathy in your grief.

But the painting, not even dry when Vincent died and still to be framed before it could be presented to her, never reached her, for she died in December 1890.

Vincent's death had affected Theo to such an extent that he became mentally incapable in October and died on 25 January 1891. Thus the painting became Johanna's property, and she left it in deposit with Tanguy, a dealer in art materials in Paris who also exhibited the odd painting for his clients from time to time. Tanguy died in 1894 and Emile Schuffenecker bought the painting from his widow, together with another van Gogh. Thus Amédée and Emile created an opportunity to produce a version with a cat and colours, following the original, which therefore automatically coincided with Vincent's description in his letter.

Their copied version could now be marketed with the Tanguy provenance and they could still keep the original on which they had made certain alterations such as removing the cat. This mutilated genuine van Gogh ended up in the Museum of Art in Hiroshima. The Schuffenecker copy ended up in the Basle Museum of Art, where Cadorin, then that museum's chief restorer, identified it as a fake, as did Landais. There had already been general agreement that the two paintings were by different hands.

* * *

The undisputed, universally recognised authority on Schuffenecker is Ms Jill-Elyse Grossvogel, in New York. She has studied the life and work of Emile Schuffenecker for 22 years and thus became the world's leading expert on him. She is the author of the *Claude-Emile Schuffenecker Catalogue Raisonné.*

She organised an exhibition of this artist's work in New York in 1980* and was the guest curator for the 1996–1997 *Schuffenecker Retrospective* held in both the Musée de Pont-Aven and the Musée Maurice Denis, Le Prieuré, consisting of 86 works and a fully illustrated and documented exhibition catalogue. This exhibition showed Emile Schuffenecker to be a reasonably talented draughtsman and painter. Pont-Aven, the seaside town in Brittany, was where, in the 1880s, Paul Gauguin, with artists like Emile Bernard, Paul Sérusier, and others, had formed the Pont-Aven Group of painters.

The September 1997 edition of *The Art Newspaper* published an article by Ms Grossvogel documenting the relationship of Emile and his brother Amédée in their involvement as collectors of the new art. The Arthouse film *The Fake Van Goghs* also covers an important interview with her in which she unhesitatingly confirmed that Emile:

> . . . would undoubtedly have had the skill to paint the Yasuda *Sunflowers*;
>
> would have had the opportunity to paint it as he was in possession of the London version for many months, while restoring it;
>
> had had a classical training in painting and had adopted many styles in his work but had never found the recognition he craved;
>
> knew and frequented just about every major artist working in Paris at the time;
>
> knew the work of van Gogh and Cézanne. He very much wanted to, but did not, share the fame of his contemporaries. He collected their work because he greatly admired their skill and vision. His own lack of recognition may have been a motivation to copy work by these contemporaries.

Ms Grossvogel does not suggest that Emile had necessarily originally copied the London *Fourteen Sunflowers in a Vase* as a forgery. He may well have started copying it with the intention of keeping the copy for himself. He did not sign it 'Vincent'. The work was not considered a fake until many years later.

In an interview for the film *The Fake Van Goghs,* van Heugten, then the drawings curator of the Van Gogh Museum, suggested that anyone who knows Claude-Emile Schuffenecker's work could see that he simply

*at the State University of New York at Binghamton Museum and Hammer Gallery

would never have been able to paint the Yasuda *Sunflowers*. According to van Heugten, he did not have the talent.

Leighton, after his appointment as director of the Van Gogh Museum, said much the same: when interviewed by Stefan Koldehoff for an article published on 16 December 1997 in the Kultur section of *Die Tageszeitung*, on the question of Emile Schuffenecker's skill, he replied that his instinct would be to say that "Claude-Emile Schuffenecker was not a sufficiently good artist to have been able to paint the Yasuda *Sunflowers*."

Chapter Nine

The Landais Report

It was becoming clear that *The Diggers* was not the only example of dubious assessments from the Van Gogh Museum, nor the only occasion when assessments were not backed by sustainable arguments.

In the meantime Landais had featured importantly in both the English and Dutch versions of the film with Geraldine Norman, *The Fake van Goghs* and, from what Hulsker had said and from what I had read, I felt more strongly than ever that it was important to get Landais's opinion on *The Diggers*. He lives in Holland, with his wife and two children, and to locate him I approached the office of the journalist Bob Witman, who had originally alerted me, through his February 1997 article in *De Volkskrant*, to Hulsker's appreciation for Landais's knowledge and judgement. Eventually I managed to contact him and, after asking permission, he gave me Landais's telephone number.

Landais did not at first sound very eager to see me but, when I persisted, he relented and agreed to my bringing *The Diggers* to show him. He warned me, however, that he was not in the business of blessing doubtful works.

I went to see him at the end of November 1997. When I unpacked *The Diggers,* he placed the painting in full light. After some fifteen minutes of close observation he shook my hand to congratulate me. During the next two hours he analysed various positive aspects of the painting but also talked about possible obstacles. His early positive reaction and the sensible remarks he had made had impressed me.

When I asked him what he would charge for his research on my painting his answer was unexpectedly generous—as well as realistic. He said that, with the judgement of the Museum against it, the painting would never be formally acceptable as a van Gogh until it became generally accepted that the present team at the Van Gogh Museum was not infallible and, moreover, did not seem to have the right idea of what an expertise on a painting should comprise. Because of this, he said, his work had little value now, as any expertise he might write, however concise and favourable it might be, would still be worthless if the Museum's 'experts' did not concur.

"One day," he continued, "after you and I are dead maybe, and after the conclusions of my studies have been accepted and paintings which I have authenticated can be sold for what they really are, then the owners will appreciate my work and can pay me, or my heirs, for it. Now my work is done free, at my own expense, whether my answer is a 'yes' or a 'no'."

On 9 December I had a further long meeting with him, gave him copies of all the available reports and photographs, and left the painting with him for a number of days. He promised a detailed report, which he hoped to complete in approximately two or three months' time. He browsed through the material I had brought, found what he was looking for, and said that in his opinion the painting was almost certainly a genuine early van Gogh. I thanked him and prepared anxiously to await his final conclusions. When I collected the painting again a few days later he had hung it on a prominent wall, and remarked that if I would prefer a less troublesome painting he would be happy to swap it for any of his.

In February 1998 I received by post the draft of his report, in French. Apart from a thorough analysis of the various aspects of the painting itself it included over 150 quotations from Vincent's letters. A French master at Eton College helped to translate it.

* * *

While studying the painting, Landais had remarked that Cadorin, when restoring the left foot of the foremost digger, had (purposely) left the signature still rather obscure, and he had insisted that he wanted every original part of the painting, including the area of the signature, to be brought back to life as much as possible. Eastaugh had also suggested that it might be useful to have the signature expertly examined for authenticity, and for this the firm Documents in Dispute Ltd had been recommended to me. I had been able to arrange a preliminary discussion with their senior partner, Ms S. Iremonger, who agreed to come and have a look at the painting on 14 February 1998. She too recommended an extra cleaning of the signature area and on 16 February I flew back to Basle—by regular airline this time—to see Cadorin for this purpose.

I was carrying the unframed painting as hand luggage. On the plane I realised that Switzerland is outside the EC and that I would have to go through Customs and Excise. On arrival I told the Customs that I was carrying a painting, which I would be taking back in the evening. I was asked, somewhat sarcastically, "Not a van Gogh, is it?" My heart sank as I replied, "As a matter of fact, it is". The Customs officer smiled amiably and waved me on. Cadorin did his work on the painting expertly and without any problems, and the signature now showed up considerably more clearly. I had no excitement with Customs on my way back.

Ms Iremonger had taken all available documentation to her laboratory on 14 February. She came to study the painting again on 3 March 1998 and submitted an extensive and rather technical report on 9 March. She concluded that: "Based on my observations and on the constraints there is no evidence to suggest that this is not Vincent van Gogh's signature." This sounded as good as it could get.

The final 35-page version in English of the Landais report was available in March 1998. It confirmed that there was no doubt left in Landais's mind that *The Diggers* was an early study by Vincent van Gogh.

Needless to say, I was delighted with these findings. This was, from an up-and-coming Van Gogh expert whom the art establishment could not afford to ignore much longer, an expertise based on a very detailed study and sound observation of the painting. Apart from letting the painting speak for itself, it also contained relevant material he had found in *The Letters* and in other documentation.

The report's text in full, but omitting many quotes from letters and also omitting the appendices, is given in appendix E. I sent copies of the complete report, with six extensive appendices dealing with the reports of Eastaugh and Cadorin, with the Van Gogh Museum expertise, with an account of the Feilchenfeldt and Dorn episode, and with the report from the company Documents in Dispute, to Leighton, Hulsker, van Tilborgh, Ms Tellegen-Hoogendoorn, Dr Op de Coul, Feilchenfeldt, Dorn, Pickvance, van der Wolk, Cadorin, and Eastaugh.

Chapter Ten

What next?

Time had passed since, on the 6 November 1996, *Museums Weekly* had reported that Leighton, the curator for 19th Century European Art at the National Gallery in London, would be appointed director of the Van Gogh Museum with effect from March 1997. It had seemed to me a very fortunate appointment then, as surely he would remember his own earlier assessment and his recommendations to me and, having himself recommended the Eastaugh laboratory, he would value Eastaugh's expert report.

On 9 February 1998, before the Landais report came out but after I knew more or less what it would say, I thought that the time was ripe to write a long letter to Leighton. I had not seen or contacted him since our meeting at the National Gallery on 23 November 1994, more than three years earlier. In the letter I reminded him of our earlier encounter and told him about the setbacks I had endured with the experts—now his subordinates—who, as he told me, must have the final word on *The Diggers*. I mentioned that I had provided van Tilborgh with copies of all the available material on the painting, including the Eastaugh report, all of which should still be at the Museum.

I quoted from recent press reports van Tilborgh's statement that 'amateurs' had thrown doubt on the authenticity of van Gogh paintings "without having a good look at the paintings". He had said, "in a reproduction the so very important impasto gets lost and with that the most important element of the authentic characteristic by which the expert can recognise the correctness of the attribution"—yet had issued his so-called expertise without seeing *The Diggers*, and had later said to me, "Whether I see the painting or not, I shan't change my mind."

I also included the results of the intensive researches by Eastaugh and Cadorin, and I mentioned the Cadorin restoration and his strong recommendation that everybody who had seen the painting before should see it again, but that I had been unable to interest van Tilborgh in looking at it in its restored state. I concluded my six pages by expressing my dissatisfaction with the 'expertise' I had been given and hoping that he would see fit to arrange a proper appraisal of my painting. I also added that I would very much appreciate learning from him whether the three *Fourteen Sunflowers* paintings were indeed coming to London as reported and if so when.

Not having received a reply and fearing that my letter might have got lost, I telephoned him, some five weeks later, on 16 March 1998. He was astonished that I had not yet heard from van Heugten, to whom he said he had given my letter for reply and promised to call me back in the afternoon, which he did two days later. He told me that they would be happy to have another look at the painting but that it would be difficult to arrange this before the re-opening of the Museum in May 1999—it was to be closed in September 1998 for a total refurbishment and for the work involved in linking it to the new wing—the wing financed by the Yasuda gift.

I thanked him for the offer of a second opinion but suggested that a delay of over a year was not very welcome. A doctor had forecast for me a very short life only some 40 years ago, and I felt it was not sensible to arrange an appointment that far ahead. According to Leighton, their main problem was that they did not have any safe storage facilities during the construction period. The only possible solution would perhaps be to leave the painting with them just during daytime. I said I would think this over and I also asked him whether I could see their 1882 van Gogh to look at the canvas. This, he said, might be difficult but he would make enquiries and call me back the following day.

I then asked him when the three versions of the *Fourteen Sunflowers in a Vase* would come to London as he had announced in the press. He answered that this had only been 'a wish' and in reality it would be almost impossible to arrange. He said that the London painting was fragile and had never been lent; they themselves would never agree to lend theirs; and the Japanese painting was too fragile to travel. He also wondered whether there was any need to bring the three versions together. Perhaps the experts could decide on the issue leaving the paintings where they were. In any case no decision had been taken, nor was one likely to be taken in the near future. He did not seem very keen any longer on the idea of bringing the three versions together, even though it had been his idea in the first place. (I now wondered why he had ever suggested it.)

It was a disappointing message. Gone seemed the promise of an early exposure of the Yasuda painting alongside the two paintings of *Fourteen Sunflowers* that are indisputably by van Gogh.

I did not get the promised call on 19 March but did get a fax the next day from the assistant curator of the museum, Ms Marije Vellekoop, confirming that the Museum was prepared to do another study of *The Diggers* but that this would still only be possible 15 months hence, after their reopening in May 1999. I was also told that I could not see their 1882 van Gogh at close quarters as nobody would be available to show me the painting in the week I had suggested.

In an interview on 20 March 1998, published in the cultural supplement of the *NRC-Handelsblad*, a leading newspaper in Holland, Leighton had let it be known that he had given his chief curator, van Tilborgh, a sabbatical year off to enable him to speed up his task of cataloguing the Museum's own collection of van Gogh paintings. The Museum kept on repeating that they were working on a catalogue for their own paintings and that they could not start cataloguing works from outside until that was finished.

Van Tilborgh's sabbatical absence from the museum induced me to write to Leighton on 24 March, acknowledging the fax from Marije Vellekoop but pointing out that it did not mention his suggestion for a possible earlier second study of my painting. I once more expressed my disappointment about the long delay, and enclosed updated material on my painting with the letter. This letter was answered by a fax on 3 April, again from Ms Vellekoop, suggesting that there must have been a misunderstanding about the time when the painting could be researched again. It stressed that when the Museum indicated a time after their reopening, it meant the research on the painting itself. However, a preliminary verdict would be possible within three months of receipt of the documentation and photographs.

I was obviously not interested in another verdict on a photograph without their seeing the painting: I wanted a discussion on the painting with the painting in front of us. I wanted to be able to contrast some of the arguments presented in van Tilborg's 'expertise' with those given by Landais in his. I was also keen for the Museum to provide me with a second expertise while van Tilborgh was still on sabbatical leave, which I hoped meant that someone else would write the report. I decided to wait a little while and then try again to see if Leighton's suggestion of 'day visits' could provide an opportunity for an earlier second study by the Museum.

* * *

Landais had meanwhile become an even more regular contributor about fake van Goghs to many international newspapers and art magazines. His findings had been relayed on radio and television, and Hulsker had again named him on Canadian TV as one of the best experts on van Gogh. But a reputable expert on van Gogh like he, with his controversial but seemingly irrefutable findings, was becoming more and more of an embarrassment to the establishment. The more respect and international repute Landais gained, the graver the embarrassment, especially for the Van Gogh Museum which, understandably, also already seemed a little embarrassed about the gift of some £15 million received from the owners of the disputed *Sunflowers*.

I have long been surprised that the Museum and other interested parties have not taken legal action against Landais and others who have published articles declaring some very important and expensive paintings to be fakes. Their revelations have considerably reduced the value and marketability of these paintings and consequently their owners have suffered damage. Maybe they do not sue because the publicity would be very unwelcome; perhaps they do not take action because of the difficulty of 'plucking feathers from a frog', as we say in Dutch; or is it because the critics are difficult if not impossible to prove wrong?

It would be a great relief for many if Landais could be proved wrong about the Yasuda *Sunflowers,* and a serious attempt was mounted to achieve this. A well known scholar on van Gogh, Ms Bogomila Welsh-Ovcharov of the University of Toronto, was believed to be able to prove that the Yasuda *Sunflowers* was genuine and that Landais was mistaken. Her support for the painting's authenticity was expected to be based on documentary evidence alone.

Although her argument was apparently not supported by visual aspects of the painting, her word would carry greater weight if she had seen the painting herself, and the Yasuda Company invited her to Japan for that purpose. Her article was finally published in the March 1998 issue of the *Burlington Magazine* As expected no mention was made of the characteristics of the painting or of its qualities. The reason for her art-history-based conclusion that 'the Yasuda' is authentic was different, however, from the reasoning given by Dorn.

The Museum's van Heugten hailed the article as proof that his attribution had been vindicated. Leighton in the *NRC-Handelsblad* of 20.3.98 suggested that the public would do better to read articles like that of Welsh-Ovcharov in the *Burlington Magazine,* giving solid foundations for a painting's authenticity, rather than articles by the critics suggesting that important attributions are mistaken. This reaction from the Museum was perceived as their attempt to maintain against all odds its preferred view that the Yasuda *Sunflowers* is authentic.

The flaws in the Welsh-Ovcharov arguments were glossed over by the Van Gogh Museum. Her article also ignores Landais's discovery that the National Gallery's painting is the copy by van Gogh made in January 1889 of his earlier August 1888 original which is in Amsterdam, and not the other way round. The Yasuda *Sunflowers* is thus a copy of the London version, a copy of a copy. Nor was there any reference to any of the arguments in Landais's articles on the non-authenticity of the Yasuda painting.

Ms Welsh-Ovcharov, in her article, delved deeply (and, it can be said, rather boringly) into the correspondence between Vincent, Gauguin, and art dealers, and into sales records. That she had interpreted three letters incorrectly, however—one from Theo, one from Vincent, and one from Gauguin—was not difficult to prove. In an article in the *Daily Telegraph* of 7 March 1998, Geraldine Norman disputed the Welsh-Ovcharov findings and suggested that the balance of evidence remained in favour of the Yasuda *Sunflowers* having been painted by Claude-Emile Schuffenecker. She did not think Ms Welsh-Ovcharov's argument would stand up for very long.

In its May 1998 issue, *Connaissance des Arts* published a detailed response by Landais which provided the evidence for declaring the Yasuda a fake and which exposed the flaws in Welsh-Ovcharov's report. *The Letters* proved that the assumed exchange of a large sunflower painting between Vincent and Gauguin, on which she had based her theory, had never taken place. And in the *Daily Telegraph* of 4 May 1998, Geraldine Norman, after an interview with Landais, further reported where Welsh-Ovcharov was in error.

But the original article in the *Burlington Magazine* had really stirred things up. The brick wall in Amsterdam was crumbling. It became obvious that the Van Gogh Museum had by now realised the flaws in the Welsh-Ovcharov article as well, and all those who had an interest in preserving the attribution of the Yasuda *Sunflowers* to van Gogh had to think again.

The original plan of bringing the three *Sunflower* versions together in the National Gallery in London had been abandoned: was there perhaps a fear that the Yasuda painting might not survive close comparison with the two indubitably genuine versions? Surprisingly, it seemed to be felt that, in lieu, a symposium might suffice to damp down criticism and banish unwelcome doubts on this important issue. This was to be an all-day affair, on 15 May 1998 in the Auditorium of the new Sainsbury Wing of the National Gallery in London. Cameras and tape recorders would be strictly banned.

Among the speakers announced were Welsh-Ovcharov and van Tilborgh and other experts still to be confirmed. Hulsker was not invited and, in the end, no one who contested the attribution of the Yasuda *Sunflowers* to Vincent was invited to speak from the rostrum. Landais was the only known opponent invited, but he was only to participate in one of the panel discussions.

After reading up the precise meaning of the word 'symposium' in my dictionary I was most certainly going to try to get a ticket, even at the price of £30.

When Landais visited the venue the day before the symposium, to inspect the facilities for slide projection, Ms Katharine Adler, Head of the Education Department of the National Gallery and official organiser of the symposium, apparently told him, clearly in reference to his rebuttal of the Welsh-Ovcharov theory, "You have convinced us".

* * *

If there had been a conclusion that the Yasuda painting was not—or even perhaps not—by van Gogh, it would not have been the only time that some art experts have had red faces. For instance, the February 1999 issue of *The Week* reported that the brilliant con man John Drewe had for years been persuading leading art dealers and auction houses to accept paintings by such modern masters as Graham Sutherland, Marc Chagall, Alberto Giacometti, and Ben Nicholson.

What was particularly embarrassing for those involved in this particular case was that the paintings were such poor copies, mostly amateurish. One dealer told the *Guardian*, "some paintings contained so many errors that it was a joke". They had been painted by an impoverished artist, John Myatt, who had placed an advertisement in the satirical magazine *Private Eye* offering to paint 'genuine fakes' at £150 each. Drewe commissioned him to paint hundreds of them. So how did Drewe get away with it?

His genius, said Amelia Gentleman in the *Guardian*, was to convince listeners that he was a true professional. He began by donating £20,000 to the Tate Gallery and by writing his own reference for the Victoria & Albert Museum in London in order to gain access to their archives. He then doctored the catalogues in these archives to include photographs of the fake paintings. These records, as David Williams noted in the *Daily Mail*, are "the art world's equivalent of holy writ" so, once Drewe's fakes appeared in them, even sophisticated Bond Street dealers were persuaded of their authenticity, despite their poor quality. "The implications are horrendous", Jonathan Searle of the Organised Crime Squad told *The Times*. The trial lasted six months. Drewe was sent to prison.

The case of Han van Meegeren in Holland will also be remembered. His masterly 'Vermeers' fooled collectors and experts alike. He signed them 'Vermeer' and successfully sold them under that name, including one to Reichsmarschall Hermann Goering, which caused him to be accused of having collaborated with the enemy by selling them a genuine Vermeer. To get this charge reduced to the less serious one of faking he had to prove that he had sold fakes painted by himself. He was made to paint more while in prison before the experts would believe even him.

Rembrandt's oeuvre has also had to be scrutinised, with the emergence of some embarrassingly opposing opinions.

Anybody who buys art on the basis of an attribution only, without properly observing the painting, almost deserves to be taken for a ride. Sadly, the appreciation of art is often no longer a matter of believing and trusting one's own eyes and intuition: buyers now often rely not on the quality of the work but on the prestige of the alleged artist, or of the provenance, and these now seem to dictate the price.

Some forgeries are so good that their purchasers should perhaps not develop too much of a complex about their mistake but just swallow the consequences. In many cases, however, such as with many of the currently disputed paintings still attributed to van Gogh, proper observation of the painting makes the forgery more obvious than was the case with some van Meegeren fakes or certain Rembrandts. It is believed by certain independent resarchers that some attributions to van Gogh only survive because of the prestigious names behind the attributions and provenances.

That hitherto acknowledged experts on van Gogh have also had to admit to having made grave errors in their attributions to him and later had to rescind them is well known. The 'Otto Wacker scandal' comes to mind.

A Berlin art dealer by the name of Otto Wacker apparently acquired some thirty previously unknown van Gogh paintings in 1927 with a provenance giving as owner the family of a so-called Russian aristocrat wishing to remain anonymous—the story went that, living in Switzerland, he feared reprisals against his family if it became known that these paintings had been removed from the Soviet Union. The paintings had been declared genuine by some of the most eminent experts of the time, such as the German art historian and van Gogh expert Julius Meier-Graefe, the Dutch art collector H.P. Bremmer, who was instrumental in helping to build the Kröller-Müller collection, and de la Faille, who included these paintings in his 1928 *catalogue raisonné.*

In 1928 some of these paintings were made available to a loan exhibition in the Paul Cassirer Gallery in Berlin of which Walter Feilchenfeldt senior had become one of the directors/partners after the suicide of Paul Cassirer. (This exhibition was also the launching pad for de la Faille's first catalogue.) In an interview shown in the Arthouse film *The Fake Van Goghs,* his widow, the late Marianne Feilchenfeldt, who at that time still lived with her son Walter Feilchenfeldt junior in Zürich, said that her husband had not bought any of these paintings because he did not like them. He had felt that they did not posses the usual van Gogh colouring or zest. When the last four paintings arrived at the Cassirer Gallery on loan from the Otto Wacker Gallery, one of the Cassirer directors, Ms Grete Ring, suspected immediately that they were forgeries. She called for Feilchenfeldt, who agreed. It was not only the last four, however, which were fakes. The press learned about the matter and an artquake shook Berlin and the art world.

One art dealer who had purchased a number of the Otto Wacker paintings demanded that his purchases be annulled, but it was years before the early attributions were finally denounced in a much publicised court case in Berlin, which became known as the 'Otto Wacker Scandal'. Feilchenfeldt's widow attended the case and reported that it was amazing how well known experts on van Gogh and on other painters continually kept changing their minds during the proceedings. Finally, technical experts from the Berlin National Gallery were supposed to have been able to prove with Xray and laboratory tests that the paintings were forgeries. Scientific research proved that they had been painted recently and could not therefore have been by van Gogh. When the police searched the studio of Leonard Wacker, Otto Wacker's brother, in Düsseldorf, they were reported to have found a newly painted copy of a van Gogh, the paint still wet.

On 19 April 1932 Otto Wacker received a prison sentence and a fine, though he never admitted guilt. Thirty-three paintings were officially declared forgeries and de la Faille, admitting he had made a mistake in listing the Otto Wacker paintings in his 1928 catalogue, had already published *Les Faux van Gogh* in 1929 declaring not only these thirty-three Otto Wacker paintings, but in all some one hundred and twenty-eight works to be forgeries. Even van Gogh expert Julius Meier-Graefe, after having hung on as long as possible, finally had to admit to having been wrong.

Everyone now agrees that the Otto Wacker paintings were not by van Gogh, and most of them have now disappeared, both physically and from the catalogues. This particular artquake has been laid to rest, but it took quite a number of years to do so.

The whole affair, instead of being detrimental to the value of van Gogh paintings, has probably substantially boosted his reputation and stimulated the steady increase in price for his work—scandals often do. People seem to enjoy being shocked and are willing to pay for it, as Damien Hirst, Tracey Emin, and many others have discovered. In 1970, some forty years later, the editors of the revised 1970 de la Faille *catalogue raisonné* felt it appropriate still to list the Otto Wacker forgeries in a 'Rejected Works' chapter, rather than to leave it to any lesser publication to remind us that they ever existed.

It is to be hoped that those of today's authorities who still support unjustified, or criticise correct, attributions may have the courage similarly to admit any mistakes they now feel they could have made. I wondered whether the van Gogh Symposium on 15 May 1998 might be the catalyst for this much desired development. My hopes proved naïve.

Chapter Eleven

The Van Gogh Symposium

The Symposium was held on 15 May 1998 in the beautiful auditorium of the new Sainsbury Wing of the National Gallery in London. This impressive venue could hold, at a guess, some 500–600 people but was only about half occupied on this occasion. On the stage was a large projection screen which could be operated from the speakers' rostrum. A boardroom table large enough to seat some twelve to sixteen people had also been placed on the stage.

The panel was seated at this table. The chair was taken by Ms Katharine Adler (the Gallery's organiser of the Symposium) in the morning and by Neil MacGregor, director of the National Gallery, in the afternoon. John Leighton, ex-curator of the National Gallery in London, now director of the Van Gogh Museum in Amsterdam, was on the panel in the morning but not in the afternoon. Benoit Landais was on the panel in the afternoon.

The programme circulated with the booking forms had promised lectures by Professor Richard Thomson, University of Edinburgh, Professor Bogomila Welsh-Ovcharov, University of Toronto (promoted for the occasion?), and Mr van Tilborgh of the Van Gogh Museum. On the day, however, there was no mention of van Tilborgh on the programme; Dr Dorn was to speak; and Professor Ronald Pickvance was to participate in the panel discussions.

As, surprisingly for such an important scholarly event, no official record has been published, I give here my personal version from notes I made at the time.

* * *

The proceedings opened with a word of welcome by Neil MacGregor, followed by an introduction by John Leighton. The gist of their messages was that considerably more research would be required to arrive at final conclusions regarding currently outstanding questions on the oeuvre of van Gogh. There was doubt as to what might be learnt from further research and, equally, as to what was likely to remain contentious for a long time. By implication, therefore, there was a long way to go and no final conclusions were imminent. It seemed like an attempt to delay matters at least until 2002. If this was indeed the intention, the organisers certainly succeeded.

The first speaker was Professor Thomson from Edinburgh. His lecture was entitled *Vincent and Theo Van Gogh.* He started by telling us that he had been unable to understand why he, not being an expert on the issue for which the symposium was being held, had been asked to give a lecture. He had had to think hard what to talk about to us. However, being involved with an event to do with Vincent's brother Theo for which he had prepared a speech, he had decided to use that for this occasion (smiles all round.). He gave an interesting lecture but it was entirely irrelevant to the Yasuda *Sunflowers* or any other aspect of the debate.

The second speaker was Dr Dorn, speaking to the title *Symbolic means, decorative ends: Van Gogh's decorative cycles.* Unfortunately he was very hard to understand, as he mumbled throughout, but in the event this did not matter much as his lecture in my opinion was 'old hat'. He missed this ideal opportunity to justify his information that enabled Christie's to change the provenance for the Yasuda *Sunflowers* from Schuffenecker to Theo van Gogh as first owner in their auction catalogue in 1987, a subject of which he steered well clear. Nor did he say anything about Pickvance's rebuttal of his mistaken theory of the provenance. Instead, at the *Yasuda Sunflowers Van Gogh Symposium,* he talked about matters totally irrelevant to the burning questions of the day. (Pickvance, it now turned out from fruitless appeals over the public address system, had not turned up to take his place on the panel.)

After a break for coffee the proceedings continued with a third lecture, entitled *In search of Van Gogh—1. The artist's letters,* by Leo Jansen and Hans Luijten, two researchers on part-time secondment to the Van Gogh Museum to research *The Letters* with a view to producing a completely revised publication of all the known letters. They told us that the chronological order was to be adjusted in the light of new knowledge; previously unpublished letters were to be included and interpretations updated; and that this work, which started a few years ago, would take a few more years to complete. A most interesting lecture but also largely irrelevant to the Yasuda attribution problem.

The lectures in the morning session had overrun their time and had eaten away most of the hour (12–1p.m.) set aside for the panel discussions. As a result only one other member of the public and I were able to put our questions to the panel before lunch. I told the audience that a while ago I had read in the press about a plan to bring the three versions of *Fourteen Sunflowers in a Vase* together in the National Gallery in London, our present venue, so that the world's experts would have a chance to compare the three paintings and bring clarity to the present most unpleasant situation in which one of them is being branded a fake. I had thought this an excellent idea and I had been disappointed that it had been abandoned in favour of just a symposium on the issue. I had now come to the one-day Symposium but was beginning to wonder if I had come to the right place, since half the day was gone but the plight of the Yasuda painting had not even been mentioned.

There was audible support from the audience, who must have felt the same, but Ms Adler gave me short shrift, simply saying that the *Sunflowers* would be discussed in the afternoon.

The afternoon session started with Neil MacGregor in the chair, telling us, with special reference to my question before lunch, that the main reason why the plan to bring the three paintings together in the National Gallery had not been realised was because, on reflection, it had been felt that the National Gallery would not have been the proper venue, the Amsterdam Museum was far more appropriate. The plan had not been abandoned, however, and it was still hoped to achieve it although, because of other commitments, probably not before 2002—another four years' delay.

The first lecture of the afternoon session, the fourth of the symposium, was given by Ms Welsh-Ovcharov and was entitled *Van Gogh's Sunflowers*. Her lecture was little more than a verbal repeat of her recent article in the *Burlington Magazine*. It was embellished with dozens of slides on the big screen, mainly of sunflowers, for which she had to push buttons on the rostrum which did not always produce the pictures she meant to show. Hard though it is to believe, she stuck to her already published theory on the Yasuda *Sunflowers*. She did not even mention the detailed criticisms, published in the *Daily Telegraph* by Geraldine Norman and in the *Connaissance des Arts* by Landais, of her unsupported assumptions. Some art historians seem at times to be on a different planet from the rest of us. There was no opportunity for questions or a discussion immediately following this lecture.

The fifth lecture, by Richard Kendal, Tameside, was called *I keep thinking about Degas... Van Gogh and the 'small lawyer'*. It was interesting enough in itself but, again, irrelevant to the ostensible purpose of the Symposium. It brought no satisfaction to those who had come to hear the Yasuda painting discussed, though it did bring us to teatime. The organisers had now successfully got three-quarters of the way through the day without the real issue being touched on.

The sixth and final lecture, *In search of Van Gogh—2. The Van Gogh research project at the Van Gogh Museum*, was given by Mr van Heugten, curator of drawings and prints at the Van Gogh Museum. He explained at length that the work of cataloguing the drawings in the museum's collection was well advanced. The first part of the catalogue on the drawings had been published in two volumes, and the final part would appear shortly; the first of three planned sections of the catalogue on the paintings would follow. To complete the entire catalogue for the Museum's own collection of the oeuvre would take time, but it was hoped that it would be finished by 2001. Only after that would works outside the Museum's own collection be studied and catalogued.

Leighton has stated that the Museum has a clear policy with regard to publicising their opinion on works that belong to other institutions or private owners. The rule is that unless they have the owner's permission to do otherwise they keep their opinions to themselves, though he has recently said that this does not apply to compiling a *catalogue raisonné*.

To illustrate that the Museum's experts were not out to keep every work at the Van Gogh Foundation in the oeuvre at all costs, van Heugten projected a painting on the screen which he said was no longer considered authentic. At this point he was interrupted by Landais insisting that the painting in question was in fact authentic.

The van Heugten talk also overran its time without discussing the authenticity of the Yasuda *Sunflowers*, at the expense of the afternoon panel discussion, which started 45 minutes late for its allotted hour. (A large part of the audience now appeared to be asleep.) The chairman asked first for questions on Kendal's talk on Degas and then, finally, with officially only fifteen minutes or so to go, we got to the subject most of us had come for, 'the Yasuda'.

Leo Jansen, one of the two researchers, was asked what *The Letters* revealed about the *Sunflowers*, and he replied that Luijten and he had not reached that stage yet.

Another question gave Landais the chance to point out aspects of the painting uncharacteristic of van Gogh. A large image was projected onto the screen and he offered his analysis in detail. It would have been difficult to contest the points he made and nobody tried. He expressed his firm opinion that we were looking at an image of a painting by Claude-Emile Schuffenecker and not by Vincent van Gogh. Van Tilborgh asked whether he had found any features typical of Schuffenecker in the painting, and Landais replied that indeed he had and proceeded to point them out.

It was a pity, however, that his mastery of English was insufficient to do full justice to his expert knowledge of the subject that day at the National Gallery. Nevertheless, he managed to make his points well enough. He had also distributed his very detailed booklet entitled *Pour le rejet de la thèse d'un échange avec Gauguin d'une toile de Tournesols arlésiens de Vincent et pour l'attribution à Claude Emile Schuffenecker de la copie, aujourd'hui au Japon, de la toile de 14 Tournesols de la National Gallery,* which sets out the evidence why Welsh-Ovcharov was wrong and that 'the Yasuda' is a copy of a copy and not a copy of the original. (His booklet containing the revelations unwelcome to the organisers was ignored by all the day's speakers.)

Geraldine Norman was kindly given an opportunity to read out an essay by Mr Antonio de Robertis, the man who was first to publicise his opinion that the Yasuda *Sunflowers* is a fake. The language barrier prevented Mr de Robertis from being able to speak for himself and this could not but reduce the force and impact of his arguments. However, they were loud and clear for those who wanted to hear them, although perhaps not sufficiently so for those who preferred to ignore them. Van Tilborgh was invited to repudiate the arguments, but he seemed nervous and declined to do so, and no one else offered to debate them.

Van Tilborgh was also asked about the provenance for 'the Yasuda'. By now pale and nervous, he replied that, as five or six different provenances had been mentioned at various times by various sources, time would be needed to sort these out. I have never heard such five or six different provenances suggested before and he must have been referring to the five or six different attempts to mutate the original de la Faille provenance of 1928 giving Schuffenecker as first owner to one suggesting that the first owners had been Theo and Johanna.

There were murmurs of dissent from the audience and, with some difficulty, I got another chance to speak. I thanked the chairman for what he had told us at the opening of the afternoon session. The anticipated delay was regrettable and although it would still be very fruitful to see all three versions of the *Fourteen Sunflowers in a Vase* together for a thorough comparison, I felt he had been overoptimistic to suggest that this was still possible. I referred to the letter from Mr Yasuo Goto, chairman of the Yasuda Fire and Marine Insurance Company, shown in the Arthouse film, *The Fake van Goghs*, in which it is clearly stated that Yasuda would not participate in any further research on the authenticity of their painting, which they firmly believe to be genuine. Also, I continued, I had heard the director of the Van Gogh Museum saying that the Yasuda painting was too fragile to travel and could not leave Japan.

The chairman retorted, "If you have heard that from the director of the Van Gogh Museum you should speak to him directly, not to me." I said that I would be delighted to do so, whereupon Leighton, sitting a few rows in front of me, stood up, turned towards me, and said words to the effect of, "Where have you read that? I never said that, and who are you anyway?"

I answered, "I have not read it anywhere, I heard it directly from you. My name is Bouwe Jans, and we have corresponded and it was when we were speaking on the phone quite recently that you told me what I have just said." He blushed and said, "Oh yes, I remember", making no attempt to deny it. Then he sat down again, saying something like 'Yasuda have not been asked yet'.

Since then it has been announced that an exhibition entitled *Van Gogh and Gauguin: The Studio of the South*, is to be organised by the Van Gogh Museum. It is scheduled to open in the Art Institute of Chicago in September 2001, after which it will move to the Van Gogh Museum, very likely in their new 'Yasuda wing', in February 2002. This is the exhibition now mentioned as a possible venue for bringing all three versions of the *Sunflowers* together.

* * *

The whole performance at the Symposium had left me flabbergasted. It seemed to have been a trick in broad daylight, and it had filled me with a desire to protest. The organisers seemed never to have had the slightest intention of tackling, let alone trying to reach a conclusion on, the authenticity of 'the Yasuda'. They had very successfully diverted the proceedings from this subject by arranging as many time-wasting irrelevant lectures as possible and allowing them to overrun the time earmarked for public debate.

I don't think that there is really much doubt left in the mind of anyone knowledgeable that the Yasuda *Sunflowers* is not by van Gogh—people in the business cannot be that blind. For some, it now seems to be a matter trying to save face. I myself have tried to remain impartial as long as possible, but after hearing the evidence before and during the Symposium, there is no longer much doubt in my own mind on the point.

The Symposium received widespread international press reports with headlines such as: "Authenticity of Sunflowers remains a riddle", by Jhim Lamoree in *Het Parool*, 16 May 1998; "No clarity on Sunflowers authenticity till 2001", by J. Wesseling in *NRC-Handelsblad*, 16 May 1998; "Le doute s'installe", in *Le Figaro*, 18 May 1998; "Sunflowers authenticity will remain an argument till 2002", by Bob Witman in *De Volkskrant*, 16 May 1998; "Christie's faces lawsuit over £24 million Sunflowers", in the *Guardian*, 16 May 1998, and others.

It obviously does take time to get rid of fakes, even after they have been irrefutably exposed, and one may wonder how long it will take to rid the van Gogh oeuvre of the Yasuda *Fourteen Sunflowers.*

* * *

Meanwhile, I still had *The Diggers* 'on my plate', and I still had the offer of a second expertise. Ten days before the Symposium, on 5 May 1998, I had written to Leighton thanking him for the offer and enclosing updated documentation on the painting. I had also confirmed that I could bring the painting in the morning, as he had originally suggested, and collect it in the evening to solve their security problem during building operations. I was hoping to get this second opinion as soon as possible.

While waiting for a reply, however, I received great news from Dr Jan Hulsker in British Columbia.On 21 May 1998, I received a fax from him which read:

> I don't have to tell you that I am, because of one thing and another, absolutely convinced that your painting is an early work by Vincent.
>
> [Ik hoef U niet te zeggen dat ik door een en ander volkomen overtuigd ben van het feit dat uw schilderij een vroeg werk van Vincent is.]

When I wrote to him, I had sent him the best photograph of *The Diggers* I could find and all the reports, and also asked if I could show him the painting one day. He had replied that it would be unlikely that he and his wife would be coming to Europe in the foreseeable future, so I had already written that I was quite willing to bring it to him in Victoria. Other quotes from his fax were:

> I hope that the detailed studies made by Landais and you will also convince the so-called real "experts" that you have made, with your find, a real "discovery".
>
> Personally I still have a little difficulty about the exact date which Benoit Landais attaches to the painting, but that is a side-issue, and perhaps, after a little further study, I will also on that point have to agree with him.
>
> Now in connection with the question of showing me the painting, I would of course not have the slightest objection to that. As I think I already wrote to you earlier, it would mean a considerable expense for you.
>
> Therefore you will have to decide for yourself, you are most welcome here. It is unlikely that I will come to Europe this year, also because my wife's health would hardly permit such a long and tiring journey.

I decided to plan a trip to Canada to show him the painting as soon as possible after it had been re-examined by the Museum. Meanwhile his opinion, even if only based on a photograph—as was the first expertise—should make an impression in Amsterdam.

Chapter Twelve

The Second Expertise

My letter of 5 May 1998 to Leighton at the Museum produced a faxed reply on 6 June, not from Leighton, but from van Heugten, inviting me to fix a mutually convenient date to bring the painting to the Museum for a day. I telephoned him immediately and we arranged provisionally that I would bring it on 17 June. He would check that his experts would be available on that day and if I did not hear from him it would mean that the date was confirmed. (I wondered whether Ms Peres, the conservator, might now get a good look at the painting on this occasion.) I did not hear further and on 16 June I crossed the Channel again with *The Diggers* and drove to Amsterdam.

At 9 a.m. the following morning I was at the Museum offices punctually and after checking in at the reception I was directed round to a protected side entrance of the museum to offload the painting from my car. It was signed for at the concierge's office by the registrar, Ms Noordermeer, and I was told that I could collect it at 5 p.m. When I returned at that time, I had to wait until, eventually, the painting was brought down by a porter at approximately 6 p.m. I signed for it and was told that I would receive a letter in due course.

A few days later the letter arrived and, to my surprise, it was from none other than van Tilborgh again, though he had not signed it. The letter was in Dutch and it translates as follows:

Amsterdam,
22nd June 1998
Corr.Nr.: EU51.1.98/eh
In connection with: expertise

Dear Mr Jans,

With reference to the conditions as contained in the contract of 12th May 1995 and my letter of 23rd March 1995 I can inform you as follows:

After having carefully studied the painting as well as the documentation sent, we are of the opinion that the work cannot be attributed to the artist Vincent van Gogh.

The painting differs entirely from other works of the Dutch period of Van Gogh on the points mentioned below. We have looked at the painting with the naked eye as well as with the microscope and under infrared light.

The weave pattern of the canvas and the colour of the ground (grey) do not exist in the Dutch work of Van Gogh. Also, the gay colours used for the sky in this painting cannot be found back in other early works of Van Gogh.

Furthermore it is very unlikely that the artist at that time used cadmium yellow, as was shown from a pigment analysis of a sample taken from the sun. This pigment did exist already but was very expensive and as far as we know was not used by Van Gogh in his Dutch years.

The greatest difference is in the brush strokes and the absence of any impasto. With Van Gogh the brush strokes are usually clearly recognisable, while in your painting this is only very exceptionally the case.

The figures have been drawn in with dark contour lines which function at the same time as a preparatory study. Nothing in this drawing resembles the characteristic drawing style of Van Gogh.

The signature is also not convincing. This has been scraped with a sharp instrument in very dry paint. Van Gogh did sign a few times with the back of a paintbrush in wet paint, but with paintings which were already completely dry he did not scrape his name in the paint surface but placed it with paint.

Hoping to have informed you sufficiently with this, I remain,

Yours sincerely,

[for] Louis van Tilborgh, Head Curator.

The unfamiliar signature looked as if it could be that of van Heugten.

On carefully analysing the contents I concluded that the arguments used, although partly different from those in his first expertise of 8 January 1996, were equally inconsequential and appeared to be purely an attempt not to conflict too much with the first expertise. They seemed to be based on the premise that an expert never makes mistakes.

Yet van Tilborgh was an art historian. Had he also been an expert in painting he would have analysed the aesthetic aspects of the picture. His persistent unwillingness to see anything positive at all in the painting except, as he had said, very occasionally the brush strokes, and his refusal either to admit or to refute the clearly positive aspects pointed out by other experts, as well as in Vincent's letters, were now beginning to have an impact on me. I was getting tired.

* * *

As van Tilborgh's letter had dealt with a number of technical arguments, I sent a copy of his latest opinion to Eastaugh, who had originally been recommended to me as the expert in this field by Leighton. I quote his response in full:

3rd February, 1999   our ref.: 983 12.2

Dear Mr Jans,

re: Two Diggers in a Field, thought to be by Vincent van Gogh.

I have now had the opportunity to study in some detail the comments sent to you by Louis van Tilborgh of the Van Gogh Museum, Amsterdam in his letter dated 22nd June 1998. On the basis of these I would make the following points:

1) Regarding the weave pattern of the canvas, it is difficult to know whether this is atypical or not since, as far as can be told, no detailed studies of canvas weave in earlier paintings by Van Gogh appear to have been published, or even, for that matter, those of the Hague School of the period.[1] At the same time, since such weaves have certainly been found on roughly contemporaneous (actually slightly earlier) canvases in France,[2] it would surely seem unreasonable to discount The Diggers on such a basis as this.

2) The ground of the painting is not grey, being in fact based on a conventional lead white–oil composition. The current surface appearance is likely to be due to other effects which have altered the way it now looks, of which there are several possibilities. Firstly, there has probably been a build-up of dirt on the unpainted areas of the ground over time which may become trapped in the surface, causing it to look grey. Secondly, it is not uncommon for the outer surface of a lead white-based ground to discolour through reaction with sulphur in the atmosphere, which causes a chemical reaction to take place and brownish-black lead sulphide to be formed.[3] Thirdly, it seems probable that an egg-white varnish was used on the painting—this was noted by the restorer (Dr Cadorin); egg-white varnishes were not uncommon in the later nineteenth century and have been specifically associated with Van Gogh.

3) Some additional comments may be in order regarding the use of egg-white varnishes by Van Gogh. According to Peres,[4] Van Gogh probably encountered these fairly early on in his career, with reference in letters of 1883 and 1885; moreover, the use of these varnishes has been further specifically linked to the Hague School.[5]

4) The question of Van Gogh's possible use of cadmium yellow in the earlier

1880s is an interesting one and there are several points to be made here. Firstly, the limited facts available on usage of this pigment by Van Gogh encompass the letters[6] and published analyses on a handful of paintings (these latter exclusively from the period 1886–8);[7] this information shows that he was certainly using the pigment by 1886–7 and, because of the paucity of data, it may only be the lack of analyses on earlier works that hides the occurrence of cadmium yellow.

This pigment was certainly more expensive than, say, chrome yellow, but this fact probably applied throughout the 1880s (i.e., it did not apparently get substantially cheaper in this time, and in fact would be employed to only a limited extent by artists until wider industrial use around 1917 reduced the cost); therefore the decision to use cadmium yellow would probably be based on a desire to achieve the particular colour it afforded, as seems to be the case with Monet for example. We might also suggest that cadmium yellow could have been a witting or unwitting substitute for Naples Yellow, a pigment mentioned in the list included in a letter of 1882.[8] Moreover, this probably also relates to the question of the seemingly 'gay' colours; specific pigments might have been chosen to depict the (apparently) unusual pictorial matter of this painting.

The subjective issues of brushwork, drawing style and relative use of impasto in your painting are rather outside the scope of my technical analysis and I also rather think that the matter of the signature has probably been adequately covered by my previous reports and the investigation of it by Sue Iremonger of 'Documents in Dispute'. Consequently, in the light of my research so far and the comments above I still have no technical objections to the proposed attribution of the Two Diggers in a Field to Van Gogh.

Yours sincerely,

Dr Nicholas Eastaugh

This letter was in effect an expertise on the experts of the Van Gogh Museum and threw considerable doubt on their technical competence.

It is noteworthy (see 3 above) that he also cited a study by Ms Peres of the Van Gogh Museum 'on egg-white coatings', edited by van Tilborgh, to illustrate the invalidity of one of the latter's own arguments.

At some future date I might make a serious complaint about this second 'expertise' to Leighton: when I complained about the inadequacy of the first, I was rewarded with a second, but this was signed on behalf of the author of the first one, in whom I had now lost confidence.

---

1. Grimm, R. Materiell und Technik der Haager Malerschule. In: Althöfer, H. ed. *Das 19 Jahrhundert und die Restaurierung.* Munich: Callwey, 1987: 217–21.

2. Vanderlip de Carbonnel, K. A study of French painting canvases. *JAIC* 1980; 20(1): 3–20; Bomford, D., Kirby, J., Leighton, J., Roy, A. *Impressionism: Art in the making.* London: National Gallery and Yale University Press, 1991: 144.
3. Carlyle, L., Townsend, J. An investigation of lead sulphide darkening of nineteenth century painting materials. *Dirt and Pictures Separated.* London: UKIC, 1990: 40-43 [conference proceedings].
4. Peres,C. *On Egg-White Coatings, a Closer Look. Technical and Art-Historical Studies on Works by van Gogh and Gauguin.* Cahier Vincent 3 Peres. Hoyle M., van Tilborgh, L., eds. Zwolle: Waanders Publishers, 1991: 39-43.
5. Roelofs, Willem E. jr. *De praktijk van het schilderen.* Amsterdam, 1919. Roelofs was the son of and taught painting by Willem Roelofs (1822–1897), a member of the Hague School. Roelofs mentions Anton Mauve, van Gogh's early teacher.
6. Van Gogh, V. *The Complete Letters of Vincent van Gogh.* 3 vols. Boston/Toronto/ London: Bulfinch Press/Little, Brown, 1958/1991: 429 [#222, 5 August 1882, includes a list of pigments].
7. Leighton,J., Reeve, A., Roy, A., White, R. *Vincent van Gogh's A Cornfield with Cypresses.* National Gallery Technical Bulletin 11. London: National Gallery, 1987: 42-60; Jirat-Wasiutynski, V., Travers Newton, H., Farrell, E., Newman, R. *Vincent van Gogh's Self-portrait dedicated to Paul Gauguin. An Historical and Technical Study.* Cambridge, Mass: Center for Conservation and Technical Studies, Harvard University Art Museums, 1984; *A Closer Look, Technical and Art-Historical Studies on Works by van Gogh and Gauguin.* Cahier Vincent 3. Peres, C., Hoyle,M., van Tilborgh, L., eds. Zwolle: Waanders Publishers, 1991 [gives analyses for *The Pink Orchard, Peach Trees in Blossom* and *The White Orchard*]; Fiedler, I., Bayard, M. Cadmium Yellows, Oranges and Reds. In: Feller, R.L., ed. *Artists' Pigments. A Handbook of their History and Characteristics.* Washington DC: National Gallery of Art, Washington and CUP, 1986: 65-108 [gives identification of cadmium yellow in van Gogh's *Self-Portrait* of 1886–87 and *Still Life with Fruit* c. 1887, both in the Art Institute of Chicago].
8. Van Gogh, V. *The Complete Letters of Vincent van Gogh* [#222] (5 August 1882) op.cit. 429; Wainwright, I.N.M., Taylor, J., Harley, R.D. Lead Antimonate Yellow. In: Feller, R.L., ed. *Artists' Pigments. A Handbook of their History and Characteristics.* Washington: National Gallery of Art and CUP, 1986: 219-254 [comment that after 1850 cadmium yellow was used as a substitute for Naples Yellow].

Chapter Thirteen

The visit to Dr Jan Hulsker

After I had collected the painting from the Museum on the evening of 17 June 1998, I felt rather depressed about the fact that I had not even been given the chance to discuss it with anyone. Having brought it all the way from England, by appointment, I had expected better.

After leaving the Museum I had telephoned Landais and asked him if I could drop by to see him, as I needed cheering up. He seemed pleased to see me. He was not surprised to hear my story, he had heard about similar cases.

We discussed my plan to visit Jan Hulsker and I suggested he should join me on the trip. Apparently he was in reasonably regular contact with Hulsker and this would be an opportunity for them to discuss other points together, as well as my painting. We rang Hulsker and he sounded delighted at the prospect. The next morning, we were fortunate to be able to book two cheap return flights to Canada, leaving on 26 June.

I left by road, with the painting, for home in the U.K., intending to go via the travel agent's office, somewhere to the east of Utrecht, to collect the tickets. I was hardly past Amsterdam, however, when Landais called me on my mobile to tell me that his passport had expired and he had already found out it would be impossible to get it renewed in time. *The Diggers* and I would have to go without him.

I now had a wheeled crate made for the painting, so that it could travel in the baggage hold safely. I was booked on an early flight from Heathrow to Amsterdam to connect with an onward flight to Frankfurt. Landais had arranged to meet me at Schiphol, but my flight was considerably delayed. As my luggage was not booked through, I would have to check it in again.

At Schiphol my crate was nowhere to be seen. I reported it missing and rushed with Landais to Lufthansa to tell them that I could not make the flight. However, very fortunately, their flight was also delayed which still gave me a chance to sort things out. It emerged that the crate had been left behind at Heathrow and while it would come on a later flight it would not be in time to accompany me and would have to be put on an afternoon KLM flight for Vancouver. After signing many documents and giving an exact description and the measurements of the crate, I was just able to get to my delayed Frankfurt flight in time to board with my remaining luggage in hand. Landais was kind enough to stay behind at Schiphol until he could find out on what flight and at what time the painting would arrive in Vancouver and let Hulsker know. In the event my next flight was further delayed and reached Frankfurt only fifteen minutes before the official departure time of the onward flight to Vancouver. I was not the only passenger on this leg scheduled to catch the Vancouver flight, however, and special arrangements were made to get us through as quickly as possible at Frankfurt. In the end only those with nothing but hand luggage made it. I was by now more than a little nervous.

Before leaving England I had checked with Customs and found that no special permits were required for Canada, but the painting would have to clear Customs in Vancouver, the first point of landing in Canada. On arrival at Vancouver I found that *The Diggers* now would not arrive until around 17.00 hrs the next day, only just over 24 hours before I was due to catch my return flight from Vancouver back to the U.K. It had been arranged that the painting, after arrival in Vancouver, would be transferred to the last flight to Victoria that same Saturday evening, which was scheduled to leave approximately one hour after arrival of the KLM flight. If all went well the crate would arrive in Victoria at about 19.00 hrs. However, I had not been able to book a flight back to Vancouver, which meant having to leave Victoria on the Sunday at 13.00 hrs to catch a ferry at 14.00 hrs to Vancouver. Things were therefore getting a little tight.

The airline representative had assured me that they could get the crate through Customs and onto the internal flight to Victoria within the hour. When I checked with Customs, however, they were not so sure and I was handed over to the Chief Customs Officer, a very kind lady who to my great relief listened carefully and promised to look after the matter personally. However, as I turned away she called after me, "You did sign and give the airline the customs form, did you?" The airline had forgotten to mention the most essential part of the procedure, and I had to return to their office and complete the form.

At Victoria I had expected to be met by Hulsker but he wasn't there.

While waiting I got talking with the freight officer and told him about the crate which was supposed to arrive the following evening. He thought it would never be able to be cleared and put on the Victoria plane in an hour, but if it did arrive, he would send it immediately by car to Hulsker's home. I left an address and telephone number. Keeping my fingers crossed was beginning to hurt.

After a time I telephoned a very surprised Hulsker, who, after hearing about the missing painting from Landais by phone, had expected me to arrive a day later, with my crate. I took a taxi to his home, arriving about nine in the evening local time (six the following morning 'my time') to meet him and his charming wife Chris. After they had made me welcome, we discussed possible emergency procedures, but after considering the worst scenario we decided to talk about more interesting things and let events take their course.

The Hulskers' comfortable home is surrounded by its own beautifully kept, secluded garden with mature trees, in which I was able to relax the next day until they kindly took me on a tour by car of Victoria, a beautiful city with well laid-out suburbs. It is almost entirely surrounded by water, with views of nearby islands and distant coastlines—should the painting not turn up it would be no hardship to come back another time. Meanwhile, what more could I want than to hear the story of Jan Hulsker's life's work and study of Vincent van Gogh, and to be shown interesting bits and pieces from his extensive library on this and related subjects. I felt very fortunate to be able to spend time with the most internationally renowned and respected authority on van Gogh.

Not only is his knowledge on van Gogh legendary, he is also a very nice man, and although he agrees that the Yasuda *Sunflowers* is not by van Gogh he has no desire to make a noise about it—he would rather avoid quarrels and making enemies. Although he believes that in the long run it will be in the establishment's best interest to be more open, their attitude discourages him from speaking openly about all he knows. He does not wish to be in the forefront of sorting it all out, preferring to leave that to others such as Landais—a wise stance for a man of his age and in his position perhaps. (When we discussed the two expertises by van Tilborgh, he merely commented that he knew of a number of similar misjudgements by that gentleman on other paintings by van Gogh.)

We called at the airport on our way out to dinner, not expecting to do more than tell the freight office that we were not at home and make alternative delivery arrangements if and when the painting arrived, but as I made for the freight counter I saw my crate through the open door of a small office and I was able to walk back to the car with it. Back home after an excellent dinner and in great spirits, we opened the crate and hung *The Diggers* in a good position on a wall in Hulskers' lounge.

When I got up the following morning Hulsker was 'dug in' to the *Two Diggers*. There was little doubt that he was very pleased with what he saw. Later, in the garden, we discussed future plans for the painting. After all, as Vincent had possibly mentioned it in one breath with *The Tower in Nuenen*, *The Potato Eaters,* and *The Cottage,* some important museum might be interested in it, and Hulsker very kindly offered to assist by writing to museums and also offering to discuss the painting with them.

The Hulskers took me to the ferry, which took me from Victoria to Vancouver on a spectacularly beautiful trip. My return flight to London was uneventful, even restful. The trip to Victoria had pleasantly overshadowed the disappointing second expertise.

Hulsker had not forgotten *The Diggers* and as promised, sent me further news. During July and August 1998 he had done some more research. Early in September he kindly sent me what he himself called a *studietje*, 'a little study'. The translation from Hulsker's original text in Dutch reads as follows:

> The painting *Two Diggers in the Afternoon Sun*
> and Millet's *Les Bêcheurs (The Diggers)*
>
> There can be no doubt in my mind that Vincent van Gogh, when he painted the *Two Diggers in the Afternoon Sun* (which is what I will call the painting in this report) was strongly influenced by Millet. To see how strong this influence of the person and the work of Jean-François Millet (1814–1875) had been on Vincent, one has to go back far in his exchange of letters with his brother Theo.
>
> The first time we encounter the name of Millet in that correspondence was in September 1873—therefore still before Millet's death—when the then twenty-year-old Vincent was working in London at the firm of Goupil & Co. Theo was working for the same firm at the branch in The Hague. The end of this letter (LT 11) reads:
>
> "Thanks for what you wrote to me about the paintings. That painting by Millet must have been rich."
>
> Four months later, in January 1874, he wrote to Theo:
>
> "Yes that painting by Millet, *L'Angélus du Soir*, that is it, that is rich." (LT 13)
>
> Of this canvas, which was already famous then, he was to draw a copy in October 1880 which is now in the Kröller-Müller Museum.
>
> In June 1874, shortly after he had been transferred to a branch of the

firm in Paris, he wrote that he had attended an auction sale of drawings by Millet:

"When I entered the sale-room of Hotel Drouot, where they were on display, I felt something like: 'Take off your shoes, because the spot where you are standing is holy ground'." (LT 29)

At the end of letter 30 he gave a summary of the prints which he himself had hanging on his walls, some twenty of them. Amongst those were four by Millet, the series of four etchings entitled *Les Heures de la Journée*.

In letter 42 of 11th October 1875 he tells of having visited the Musée du Luxembourg with a friend. Amongst the paintings he had pointed out as those that appealed to him most was also a Millet, *L'Eglise de Gréville*.

On 28th March 1876 follows an even more important announcement: he had looked at paintings at the art gallery Durand-Ruel and there one could get many etchings by Millet and others for as little as one franc each. He wrote to Theo:

"This is tempting, I could not resist a few by Millet, I bought the last three available ones of the *Angélus du Soir*, and of course my brother receives one of these on this occasion." (LT 58)

Some time passes before a special interest in Millet shows up again in Vincent's letters, but all the more instructive is a letter from March 1878. Vincent has in the meantime started to make preparations for a study in theology and is living in the house of his uncle Jan in Amsterdam. During a visit to his other uncle in Amsterdam, the art dealer Cornelis Marinus, he has been browsing through a complete year of publications of the magazine *L'Art*, and he mentions to Theo:

"I was especially impressed by woodcuts after drawings by Millet, amongst others *La Chûte des Feuilles*, *La Noche* [Nuit] *des Corbeaux*, *Ânes dans un Marécage* (effet de brume), *Les Bûcherons*, *Ménagère Balayant sa Maison*, *Cour de Ferme* (effet de nuit), etc." (LT 119)

However, much more important is what he writes, two weeks later, as an older brother to Theo:

"Have you ever seen an etching by Millet himself, a man who shovels manure into a wheelbarrow, on a day like today, early springtime, and also remember that he has made an etching *Les Bêcheurs* (The Diggers), and if you ever see one of those you won't lightly forget them." (LT 120)

In any case Vincent never forgot that etching with the two diggers; even in 1889, a year before his death, he made a copy in oils of the large canvas Millet had painted of this subject.

In 1879 and 1880, after Vincent had been working in the Borinage, Belgium, as lay preacher for a while and after he had decided to become an artist, he started making copies of prints again, this time with professional intent. On 20th August 1880 he wrote Theo (in French) as follows:

"You should know that I am working on sketching large drawings after Millet, and that I already have made *Les Heures de la Journée*, as well as *Le Semeur*." [*The Sower*], (LT 134)

He asked Theo to lend him *Les Travaux des Champs* and if possible also other prints after or by Millet, Breton, Feyen Perrin, and others. From Millet he would like to have (and this is of particularly great interest, especially for this little study) *Les Bêcheurs* of which he therefore did not have a print or photograph at that moment. We know already that he knew this work from a reproduction of it in the magazine *Les Arts*, as mentioned above, and that he had noted in letter 120 that Millet had made an etching of this subject. Now, in letter 135 of 7 September he even went as far as urging Theo to try and buy a copy of that etching, even though he knew that they were rare:

"Because I already have twenty sheets after Millet, you will understand, that, if you could still get me more, I would make those with great enthusiasm, because I am trying to study that Master seriously. I know that the large etching of *The Diggers* is rare, but I nevertheless keep looking out for it and please tell me for how much you could still get one" (this was also written in French).

It seems that this was not very easy for Theo, but we do read in letter 137, written from Brussels on 15th October 1880, that Vincent had made a pen drawing after Millet's *Le Bûcheron* ("the woodcut you sent me").

On 1st November 1880 however, he was finally able to write:

"Have drawn *Les Bêcheurs* after Millet, from a photograph of Braun, which I found at Schmidt's and which he lent me along with the one of *L'Angélus du Soir*. I have sent both these drawings to father so that he can see that I am doing something". (Schmidt was temporarily in charge in the branch of Goupil & Co. in Brussels.)

Therefore, Vincent, because of the tenacity which has always typified him, had got what he wanted even though Theo had not been able to help him this time.

The copy he had made came into the possession of his father, and when his father died in 1885 it passed to his mother. But as we know of two copies of *Les Bêcheurs* (*The Diggers*) he must, in 1880, have tried twice to make a good drawing of it.

We know that the one now in the collection of the Kröller-Müller Museum, is F 829. The other, F 828, is known to have been auctioned in April 1978 by Sotheby's in New York.*

The earliest known owner of F829 was the collector and adviser to Mrs Kröller-Müller, H.P. Bremmer; of F828 it was J. Hidde Nijland (Dordrecht), also a collector, but who brought early drawings by Vincent together on a much larger scale than Bremmer.

For a considerable time after making those two copies in 1880, in Vincent's time in Brussels we do not read much anymore about Millet in his letters. However, he had not lost sight of him because, when he had made the now very well known nude drawing of Sien, entitled *Sorrow*, he remarked in his letter 186:

---

* Author's note: for reproductions of these pictures see page 13.

"I do not have the pretension of course to think that I could say, with one single outline, as much as Millet can."

His respect for Millet had recently been rekindled again because he had acquainted himself with Millet's biography by A. Sensier, which was published in 1881.

"Hey, Theo, that Millet, he was really someone, I have on loan from De Bock a great work by Sensier. It interests me so much that it makes me wake up at night, light up a lamp and keep on reading." (LT180)

At the end of June 1882 his companion was in hospital in Leiden expecting another baby and Vincent used those days to move home, from the address in The Hague, Schenkweg 138, to a larger floor in the house next door, Schenkweg 136.

When 'furnishing' the new apartment he made certain that the living room would be adorned with prints on the walls ("all very nice ones" he wrote in his letter 213 of 6th July 1882) and amongst those prints were two by Millet, *Le Semeur* [*The Sower*] and —*Les Bêcheurs* [*The Diggers*].

This means that, if the painting *Two Diggers in the Afternoon Sun* had been painted around that time, as suggested, Vincent must have had a reproduction of Millet's drawing daily in front of his eyes. It was not his own drawing from 1880, of which he must have kept one copy in a file. It must have been the etching by Millet of *Les Bêcheurs,* sent to him by Theo along with many other prints, but the image would have remained the same and would continue to inspire him for many years to come.

Jan Hulsker,
September 1998.

P.S. In the above I have used, as much as possible, only documentary evidence. It can all be found in the catalogue of de la Faille, ed. 1970, in the catalogues of the Kröller-Müller Museum at Otterlo, the book *Van Gogh & Millet* (1989), edited by Louis van Tilborgh and Sjraar van Heugten of the Van Gogh Museum, and especially of course in Vincent's own letters (reproductions enclosed).

Chapter Fourteen

The Millet-Van Gogh Exhibition

In July and August 1998 the press continued to report extensively on the fake van Goghs. Important articles appeared in *Le Journal des Arts*, the *Sunday Times*, the prestigious *Art Newspaper*, the *Herald Tribune,* and in publications in France and Holland.

Benoit Landais had, over a period of years, been exchanging information on, and possible interpretations of, mountains of documents with Jan Hulsker and other independent scholars. After careful studies of paintings they had also been comparing notes on their discoveries in detail, to the extent of analysing the precise meanings of words and the significance of the placing of commas and other aspects to arrive at the correct interpretation of sentences in *The Letters*. In general they agreed on their conclusions, and the body of evidence against some previously accepted authentications had been growing to substantial proportions. Because of all the new revelations and publications the global artquakes rumbled on with continued intensity.

One can imagine that this situation called for a new strategy from the major museums, in the face of a tide of unwelcome news, to defend their collections against further attack. Should they retire behind their fortress walls, pull up the drawbridges, and prepare metaphorical boiling oil to pour on the heads of their critics?

The link between the Van Gogh Museum in Amsterdam and the National Gallery in London had naturally grown closer of late, because of the Yasuda *Sunflowers,* which had been on show in the National Gallery for a number of years, and because Leighton, the Gallery's former curator of 19th century European art, was now director of the Van Gogh Museum in Amsterdam. Was the unproductive Van Gogh Symposium (May 1998, Chapter 12) evidence of co-operation between London and Amsterdam to defuse a threat to 'the Yasuda'?—it certainly succeeded in damping down the controversy for a while.

Landais had at the end of 1997 published his doubts about a number of important paintings attributed to van Gogh in various museums, such as the New York Metropolitan Museum of Art's *L'Arlésienne* and the Amsterdam Van Gogh Museum's *Garden of the Asylum*, a donation from the Gachet collection. Perhaps the greatest stir, however, was caused by the doubts he expressed about other paintings from the collection of Dr Gachet, such as the copy of the *Portrait of Dr Gachet* and others now owned by the Paris Musée d'Orsay. In an interview with *Le Figaro*, the director of the Musée d'Orsay, Henri Loyrette, announced that to put an end to the rumours following the publication of the article by Landais in *Connaissance des Arts* he had decided to organise an *exposition-dossier*, a study exhibition, of the Gachet donations, and he promised that a clear light would be shed on the affair [*toute la lumière sera faite*]. All would be revealed. Exhibits would be thoroughly examined scientifically prior to the exhibition, to 'clear up any doubts about their authenticity'. The exhibition was to run around the same time as a Millet–Van Gogh exhibition in the Musée d'Orsay, Paris in the autumn of 1998—a repeat of that held ten years earlier in the Vincent van Gogh Museum in Amsterdam.

In the event, the difficulties the experts had with the authenticities of some of the Gachet donations led to the exhibition being postponed to January 1999 (see Chapter 15). Before it opened, however, as a new twist it was announced that after Paris the exhibition would move to the New York Metropolitan Museum and thereafter to the Amsterdam Van Gogh Museum. As will appear in the next chapter, however, the Van Gogh Museum's enthusiasm to co-operate in the project seemed to have waned a little when its turn came, and it gave the exhibition reduced space and publicity compared with Paris and New York.

It is tempting to speculate that these three powerful museums, with the support of the scientific laboratories of the Musées de France, were joining forces against the unwelcome disturbance of their peaceful and profitable existence by obstreperous critics and hoping jointly to defend the status quo of their collections and to resist aspersions on attributions they had confirmed and supported in the past. Yet none of this would have been necessary if the museum managements had been prepared to allow open and honest discussion of the points their critics were raising.

* * *

Be these things as they may, the Millet–Van Gogh exhibition went ahead on schedule at the Musée d'Orsay from September 1998 to January 1999. Van Tilborgh, who had been curator of the Van Gogh Museum during the earlier exhibition in Amsterdam, was guest curator for this anniversary repeat in Paris.

This exhibition was another chance to see the similarities in colour and sentiment between *The Diggers*—undoubtedly inspired by Millet's work—and Millet's own paintings such as *Farmer Spreading Manure,* and his famous *L'Angélus,* which hint at a comparable atmosphere.

For this exhibition, van Tilborgh introduced two additional paintings ostensibly by van Gogh. One of these, *Wheatfield with Sheaves*, a gift from Yad Hanadiv to the Israël Museum in Jerusalem, was apparently considered a masterpiece; it came foremost in the press release and was therefore reproduced by many French newspapers. Reaching the Museum by the *Métro*, one could hardly miss a huge projection of it on a wall in the hall of the station.

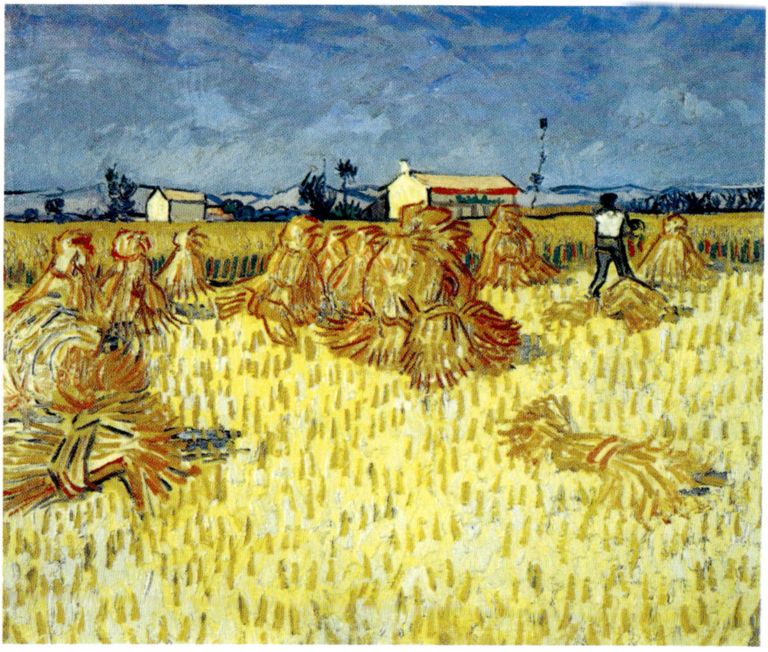

Wheatfield with Sheaves (JH1481, F558), 50 × 60 cm,
Israel Museum, Jerusalem. Cat. no. 16

But despite the acclaim it is an inferior painting. There is no perspective in the harvested area of the wheatfield, and the figure seems not to know what it should be doing and to have decided to try goose-stepping out of the painting. Some sheaves resemble bundles of shoelaces, and so on.

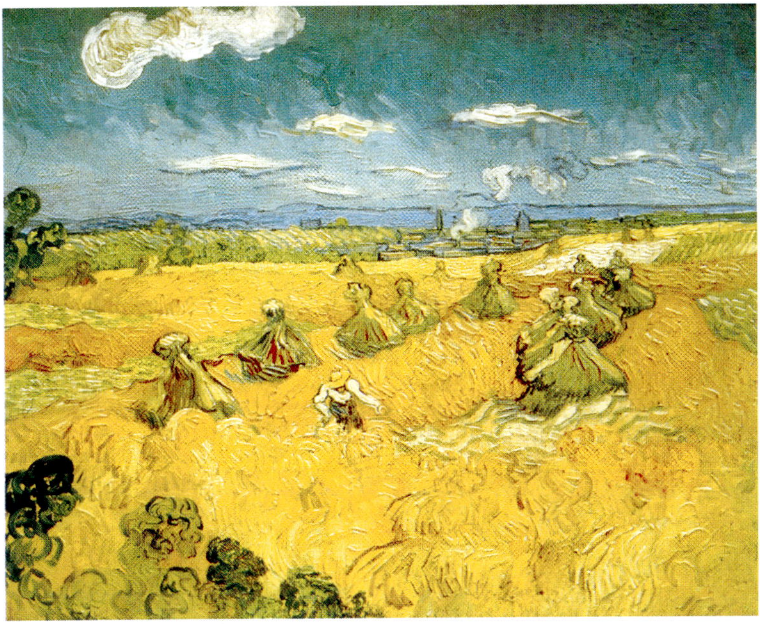

Wheatfield with Sheaves and Mower (JH1479, F 559), 73 × 93 cm
The Toledo Museum of Art, Ohio, Cat. No. 23

The other, also mentioned in the press release, was *Wheatfield with Sheaves and Mower*, owned by the Toledo, Ohio, Museum of Art.

In November 1998, during the exhibition, *Le Monde* published an article by Landais exposing both these paintings (cat. nos 16 and 23), the one purporting to have been painted in Arles, the other allegedly in either Saint-Rémy or Auvers, as forgeries. Nobody tried to refute this bombshell outright, but van Tilborgh had established himself as a specialist on the relation between Millet and van Gogh, and Dorn, once more, came to his support, agreeing with him on the authenticity of these two harvest scenes.

Landais had focused primarily on the style of the paintings and so far as I know no one has yet attempted publicly to dispute his arguments. In addition to attacking their aesthetic qualities, however, Landais had also advanced strong evidence against their authenticity from *The Letters*. Vincent, in a letter to Emile Bernard, written at the end of his series of harvest scenes of the summer 1888, said that he had made '*sept études de blé*' [seven studies of cornfields].These seven, which he said he had painted *vite, vite, et pressé* [in a great hurry and against the clock], were of course in addition to an earlier eighth harvest scene, the *Harvest at La Crau*, JH1440, F412. According to van Tilborgh's catalogue for this exhibition there would now have to be ten authentic harvest scenes in the series. When Hulsker then sent the Van Gogh Museum his study on the harvest series, which shared the views of Landais, the tremors really began to be felt and the 'quake advanced a couple of notches up the Richter scale.

Dorn was the first to respond. The quality of the paintings was not a suitable battleground from which to defend his and van Tilborgh's views, so he turned his attention to the documentary evidence. He needed to be able to disqualify Vincent's own written word which said that he had painted only a maximum of seven (plus one) harvest scenes. To make room for extra harvest scenes there was only one solution, which was to throw doubt on the dates of Vincent's visits to Saintes-Maries. It had to be argued that Vincent had continued painting harvest scenes instead of visiting Saintes-Maries when he had said he did. Vincent had written, "*je refile aux Saintes-Maries*" [I'm going to slip over to Saintes-Maries *again*], which confirms that he had already been there before, in which case he would not have had time to paint two extra harvest scenes. Dorn now suggested that '*refiler*', which unquestionably means 'to go again', did not mean that in this case, but meant just 'go', and thus that Vincent had *not* been there before and so he *would* have had time to paint extra harvest scenes in Arles instead. This interpretation was hardly convincing—he would have done better to have debated the issues, especially the painterly qualities in the disputed works, with Landais, and to have obtained expert French opinion on the verb *refiler*.

* * *

Hulsker has made a special study of the authenticity of the harvest scenes Vincent painted in 1888 and has, on the basis of both documentary evidence and for stylistic reasons, come to the conclusion that catalogue no. 23 is definitely not a work by van Gogh and—here he displays typical

Hulsker caution—that the authenticity of Catalogue no. 16 is at best highly suspect. If, forewarned, one studies the paintings closely it is difficult not to agree with him and Landais.

At the exhibition Cat. no.16 hung (as below) next to cat. no.17, a beautiful authentic van Gogh, *Wheat Field with Sheaves* (JH1480, F561), 53 × 64 cm, owned by the Honolulu Academy of Arts.

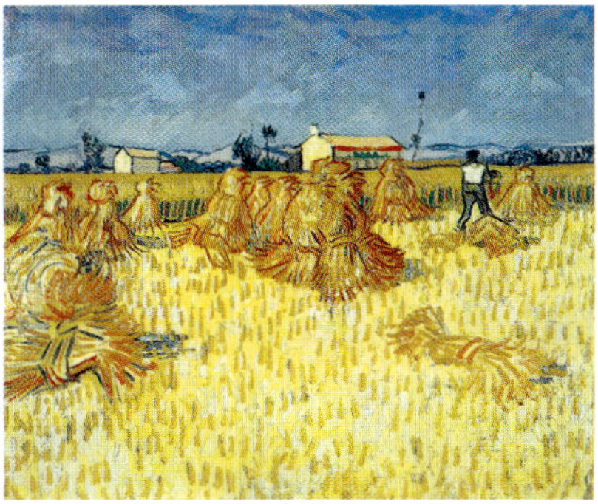

Cat. no. 16

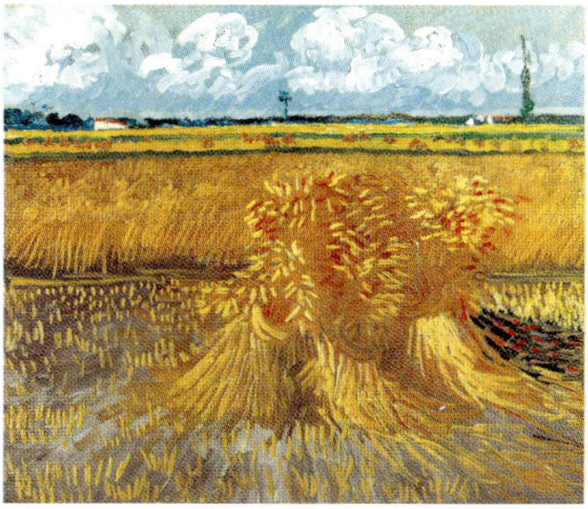

Cat. no. 17

This exhibition was another demonstration that the general art-loving public tends not to question what museum catalogues tell them. Visitors, including journalists, in the impressive atmosphere of the Musée d'Orsay and unaware of the underlying doubts, seemed to accept both attributions to van Gogh, though the lack of perspective in the foreground and the lifeless sheaves in no.16 should have been a give-away. No.23 hung close by, to the right of no.17, making the latter resemble a rose between two thorns.

Years ago an art historian wrote that with art on show 'anything goes'. He was surely an excellent prophet.

Chapter Fifteen

A Provocative Exhibition

Benoit Landais—a son of Hubert Landais, a former director of the Musées de France, including the Louvre—published his momentous article about Dr Gachet and his in-house team of painters who copied numerous works from several painters, among them van Gogh, in *Connaissance des Arts* in 1997. The article also related how, after Gachet's death, a number of these paintings had been sold on the market, and some sold and some donated, by his son Paul Gachet to museums, including the Louvre, as genuine works by van Gogh. When the Musée d'Orsay opened in 1986, most of the purchases and donations from the Gachet collection were transferred there from the Jeu de Paume Gallery of the Louvre.

The *Connaissance des Arts* article set off a violent artquake, reverberating from its epicentre in Paris all the way to Amsterdam and beyond. It had prompted the announcement of an *exposition-dossier* of the Gachet donations, which would be the answer to Landais and would silence the rumours he had started. To add impact, the Metropolitan Museum of Art and the Van Gogh Museum subsequently decided to participate in the project, thus giving it greater international exposure and, one might feel, acting as a rescue force to preserve the attributions under attack.

The eagerly awaited exhibition, entitled *Un Ami de Cézanne et Van Gogh, Le Docteur Gachet,* originally planned for the autumn of 1998, finally opened in the Grand Palais in Paris on 28th January 1999. The catalogue for the exhibition did not appear until a few hours before the opening.

The organising committee consisted of Ms Irène Bizot, administrator of the *Réunion des Musées Nationaux*, Henri Loyrette, director of the Musée d'Orsay, John Leighton, director of the Van Gogh Museum in Amsterdam, and Philippe de Montebello, director of the Metropolitan Museum of Art in New York. Not only would the exhibition visit all three countries but the three museums were apparently also accepting joint responsibility for the organisation and presentation.

In the *Directors' Foreword* in the catalogue, the three directors jointly signed a text containing some rather strange statements. There was no longer any mention of the true original reason for the exhibition—to silence Landais—as had been reported in *Le Figaro* from the interview with Loyrette before the Metropolitan and Van Gogh Museum had joined the project, nor of Loyrette's promise that 'everything would be revealed'. Instead, the three directors now proclaimed: "A half century after the first gift in 1949 seems the right time to pay homage both to Dr Gachet and to the artists he loved." Their foreword contained further rather vague information. In 1949, which they called the year of the first gift, Dr Gachet had already been dead some forty years, as he died in 1909. But before he died he had donated an artist's proof of *The Man with the Pipe*, the only etching attributed to Vincent van Gogh, to the Stedelijk Museum in Amsterdam in 1905.

Dr Gachet's son, Paul Gachet junior, had by 1949 already been selling 'van Goghs' and other paintings and antiques for some time from the collection inherited from his father. His sister Marguerite died in 1949, and all other witnesses who might have known how and when the suspected copies and fakes got into the original Gachet collection were also dead by then. Thus the path was clear for him to continue the sales to interested parties and to negotiate with museums their acceptance of donations, as well as sales on preferential conditions, of both masterpieces and fakes.

The *Foreword* also stated that substantial attention had been paid to finding and demonstrating proof of authenticity, by scientific research, for many items in the collection. The exhibition in Paris—but not the later one in Amsterdam—included a considerable number of exhibits from this scientific research, though none of these could, of course, provide any positive proof of authenticity.* The results of the scientific research had been keenly awaited before the opening of the exhibition, and at least some revelations about mistaken attributions in the past had been widely expected. It did not seem possible that none at all of the earlier mistakes, some of which seemed abundantly obvious, would be admitted, yet not a single one was changed. The organisers had unexpectedly decided—feeling, perhaps, that the Gachet benefactors did not deserve to go down in history as forgers—to maintain all the original attributions, even without supplying any new supporting evidence of authenticity.

* When suspected 'fakes' are created close to the time the originals were painted, scientific research is unlikely to come up with great surprises. This was and is the case for *The Diggers*, in exactly the same way as it applied to the paintings from the Gachet collection.

This was a remarkable decision indeed, implying that it was of little concern that, instead, Vincent van Gogh should go down in history as the painter of a number of inferior works by copyists. It did, of course, also imply that the two other museums involved in the project tacitly supported the 'authenticity' of all the Musée d'Orsay's van Goghs donated by the Gachets and *vice versa*.

The press had already begun to question the value and the quality of the results of the research even before the opening of the exhibition. After it had opened, and details of the research had been published in the catalogue, a general conclusion that the exhibition and the scientific research had not proved anything of interest soon emerged. Doubts would remain. The plot had only thickened.

* * *

A short history of the origins of the Gachet collection

In May 1890, seventy days before his death by suicide, Vincent moved to Auvers-sur-Oise, where Dr Paul Ferdinand Gachet (1828–1909) had bought a house in 1872. Cézanne and Pissarro and other well-known artists had also lived in Auvers or visited him there. Dr Gachet's medical practice was in Paris, not Auvers. His daughter Marguerite (1869–1949) was born in Paris and his son Paul Louis-Lucien (1873–1962) in Auvers. His wife Blanche died in 1875.

Vincent first arrived in Auvers-sur-Oise on 20 May 1890. Sixty-eight days later he wounded himself with a pistol shot near the heart and died from the wound two days later, on 29 July 1890, at thirty-seven years of age.

While in Auvers, Vincent lived at the Auberge Ravoux, in the centre of the village. Dr Gachet's home was a shortish walk away on the outskirts. Vincent visited it a number of times and made a few paintings there. But he was certainly not a daily house guest. (Dr Gachet was away at least four days a week in Paris, and Vincent's letters on the extent of their association are explicit.)

During his sixty-eight days in Auvers, according to the works attributed to him by de la Faille, Vincent produced some eighty-two oil paintings, some four or five watercolours, over fifty drawings in pencil, chalk, and pen, and one etching. This would surely have been an impossible task, even for an artist as prolific as he. That alone must raise doubts about the authenticity of some of the paintings listed by de la Faille, quite apart from other reasons, of which there are plenty.

Gachet himself was a keen amateur painter, painting under the name of Paul van Rijssel (Rijssel being the Dutch name for Lille, his home town). His son Paul, after some studies in agronomy, never took up any paid employment. The only titles he gave himself were 'artist-painter' and 'friend of van Gogh'. He painted under the name of Louis van Rijssel. He was only just seventeen when Vincent died.

A longstanding guest in the Gachets' home was a Mlle Blanche Derousse (1873–1911), the eldest daughter of an old friend. She was quite a prolific and talented artist. She also was only just seventeen at the time of Vincent's death, and when she herself died, at the age of only thirty-eight, many of her paintings and etchings formed part of the Gachet collection. She was undoubtedly the most gifted of Dr Gachet's 'pupils'.

These three—Dr Gachet, his son Paul, and Blanche Derousse—happily painted both original works as well as copies of works by other painters such as Cézanne, Jordaens, van Gogh, Sisley, Renoir, Armand, Guillaumin, and others. They also made copies of their own works. This 1999 exhibition of the Gachet collection showed a multitude of examples of the sizeable output of their tripartite studio.

After Vincent's death, Gachet amassed what purported to be a large collection of works, not only by Vincent but also by other famous artists as well as works he himself, his son, and Blanche Derousse had painted. He also commissioned Blanche to make copies of paintings by famous artists for the purpose of a catalogue that he intended to produce, though this never materialised.

Many of the watercolour copies by Blanche Derousse are dated some ten or more years after Vincent's death, well before the death of Dr Gachet and, even more importantly, well before a number of important oil paintings, currently still attributed to van Gogh, had been seen by anyone outside the Gachet household. Many of these were in the 1999 exhibition in Paris.

After Dr Gachet's death in January 1909, his collection passed to his son and daughter. The heirs were very secretive about the collection and very selective about whom they allowed into the house. After his father's death, Paul Gachet junior, not having a profession or gainful employment, seems to have existed by the sale of paintings, including 'van Goghs' and antiques from his father's collection, to various buyers, including the Louvre.

He had managed, by means of correspondence or otherwise to get a number of items from the collection into the 1928 de la Faille *catalogue raisonné* as the work of van Gogh solely on the strength of his own assurances that they were genuine. In this way he obtained formal attributions not only for genuine paintings by Vincent, but also for what are believed to be copies by others. In all cases Dr Gachet senior was recorded in the de la Faille provenances as the first owner.

According to de la Faille, of the works attributed to van Gogh from his period in Auvers alone, some twelve oils and some ten drawings, and the one and only etching, are supposed to have been given to or acquired by Dr Gachet.

Van Tilborgh has been quoted as suggesting, in an interview, that Dr Gachet was also the first recorded owner of some eighteen paintings by van Gogh painted in previous periods, in Paris, Arles, and Saint-Rémy. In all, therefore, Dr Gachet is supposed to have ended up with at least thirty oil paintings formally attributed to van Gogh—this after an acquaintanceship of less than seventy days, during the majority of which Vincent and he were not even in the same town. And these formed only part of the considerable number of works of art and other items in the inheritance, of which, after his sister died in 1949, only Paul junior knew the real provenance.

One may suspect that on the back of the prestige earned by the donation of, for example, a genuine van Gogh self-portrait to the Louvre, he would also have been able to pass off some fakes as genuine.

One very ugly painting, *The Cows*, ended up attributed to Vincent in the Musée des Beaux Arts in Dr Gachet's home town of Lille, as a gift from Paul Gachet in 1950. The last Gachet donation was in 1954: six paintings to the Louvre and *The Garden of the Asylum* to Holland, where it now is in the collection of the Vincent van Gogh Foundation in Amsterdam.

Contrary to general belief, however, the most important part of Dr Gachet's collection was sold by his son to dealers and collectors and museums, and the donations formed only a small part of the whole.

Gachet junior was successful in getting not only his genuine van Goghs into de la Faille's 1928 catalogue but also others, about which de la Faille harboured doubts. These inclusions are likely to have contributed favourably to Gachet's ability to achieve the numerous sales he did make. Yet the question of how many of all these works from the Gachet collection attributed to Vincent van Gogh were in fact genuine still remains. There are records of two gifts to by Vincent to Dr Gachet and his family, but none of any purchases by Gachet before or after Vincent's death.

* * *

Landais states for instance that he has evidence that the first Van Gogh forgery: *Two Children*, JH 2051, appeared in the Gachet collection as early as 1893.

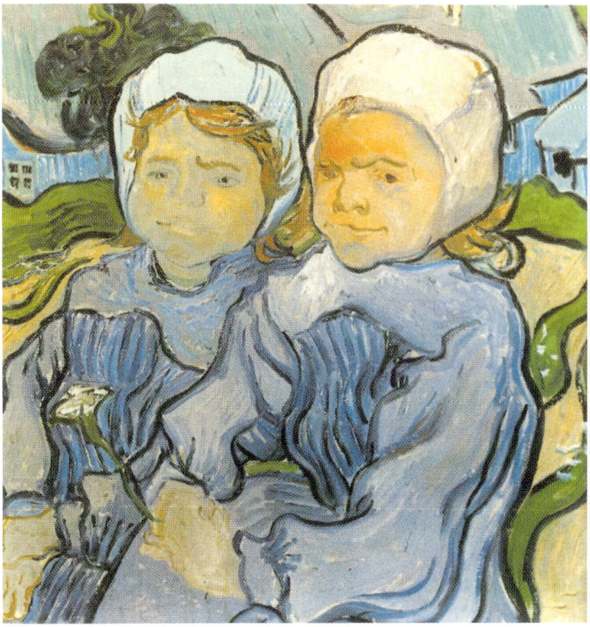

Two Children
(JH 2051, F 783),
51.5 × 51.5 cm
Musée d'Orsay

He has set out other conclusions in his 1999 book *L'Affaire Gachet*, published in French during the exhibition in Paris.

A painting called *Rosiers en Fleurs* [*Roses in Bloom*] (JH1679, F580 right) 33 × 42 cm, for instance, says Landais, has vegetation of a kind never painted like this by van Gogh. He goes on to point out that the colour explodes and the rhythm is ruptured. "It was painted", he concludes, "by someone under different influences than those of Vincent."

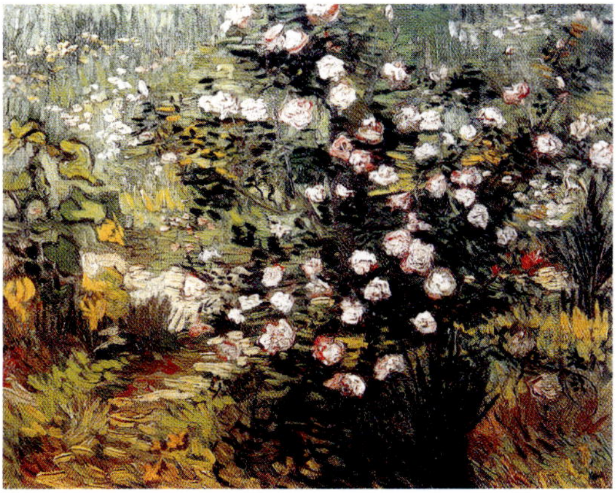

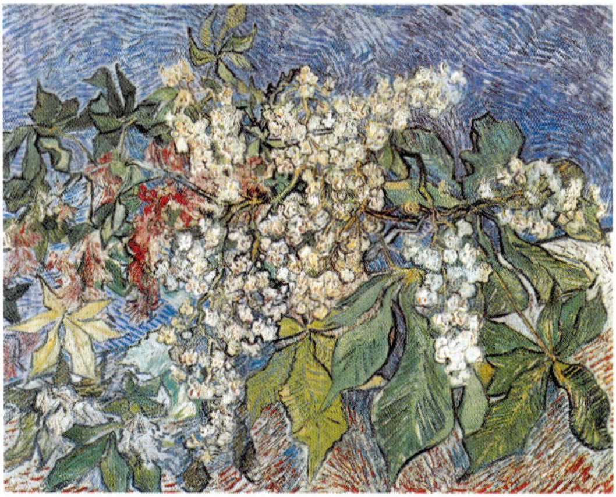

Regarding the painting *Branches de Marronniers en Fleurs* [*Chestnut Branches in Blossom*] (JH2010, F820, left) 72 × 91 cm, Landais roundly declares that when Vincent painted branches they looked like branches but those in this picture do not. The painting is far too systematic and unnatural.

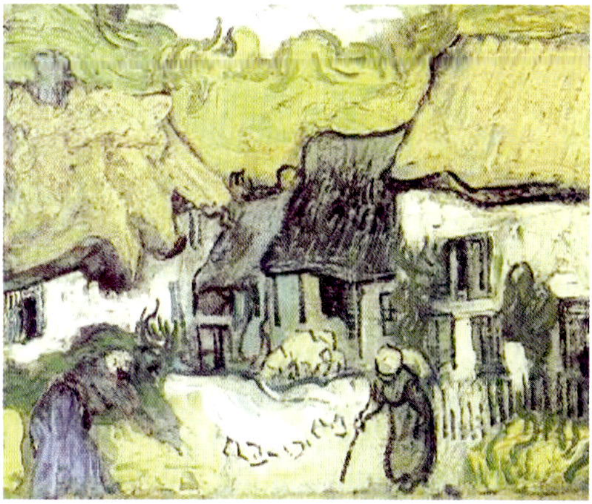

Of *Les Chaumes de Jorgus* [*The Thatched Cottages at Jorgus*] (JH2016, F758, right), Landais comments, "A very ugly painting, undoubtedly the shoddiest canvas from Auvers". (Large areas of roof in this small painting resemble peanut butter spread on a sandwich by a child.)

An article in the Paris *Le Figaro* had declared the painting a fake shortly before it was to be auctioned by Sotheby's in New York on behalf of the Readers Digest Collection on 16th November 1998. Sotheby's must obviously have been alarmed but maintained that they were confident that it was a genuine van Gogh despite the provenance declaring Dr Gachet as first owner. They knew that there was some confusion about the title of the painting, which was originally *Thatched Cottages at Jorgus*—Paul Gachet had crossed out '*de Jorgus*' in the title on the back of a photograph of the painting, as he had obviously recognised that the site and the image on the painting were not compatible. Another anomaly in the provenance listed in the sale catalogue was that the painting was said to have been owned at one time by the Wildenstein Institute in New York. This the Institute denies!

Sotheby's nevertheless decided to go ahead with the auction, and the small painting, renamed *Thatched Cottages at Auvers,* fetched some $4 million. Sotheby's guaranteed its authenticity and will assist the buyer in having the painting examined by the Van Gogh Museum Research Project. If the verdict goes against it, they will rescind the sale and refund the purchase price. We must patiently await the day when this research project, apparently not yet off the ground, begins to function and can provide the buyer with the required expertise.

Landais is equally devastating about other attributions, but each of his criticisms is extensively, clearly, and convincingly explained. Consequently, he has a considerable following and many experts share his beliefs.

The exhibition showed not only paintings attributed to Vincent van Gogh and to other well known artists such as Cézanne, Renoir, Monet, and Pissarro, it also showed a multitude of known copies by the Gachets senior and junior and, especially, by Blanche Derousse. It gave a good impression of the kind of 'copy factory' the Gachet household had been.

The museums do not appear to have been able, or even to have tried, to refute Landais's and other critics' reasons for publicly labelling various paintings as fakes. They seem to have decided just to call the critics 'amateurs' and to expect their own reputations to enable them to ride the storm.

The task of defending—against all odds—existing attributions fell to Anne Distel, curator of impressionist paintings at the Musée d'Orsay, and Danièle Giraudy, a chief curator in the French National Museums Service, whose laboratories had been responsible for the scientific research. Mme Distel admitted to having had the greatest difficulty with the attribution of the Lille *Cows* to van Gogh. She concluded in an interview with Geraldine Norman—surely in an effort to avoid embarrassment all round—that it would be "more logical to accept that painting as an unsuccessful sketch by van Gogh himself".

This is not the place to go into details about all the possible misattributions in this exhibition. Landais believes there were about thirty in all, not only of van Goghs, but he prefers not to stray outside his chosen field.

* * *

A few paintings from the Gachet stable need special mention, however. Perhaps the most important is the copy of the *Portrait of Dr Gachet* in the Musée d'Orsay. There is another version in oil on canvas with this title, the whereabouts of which are unknown at present.

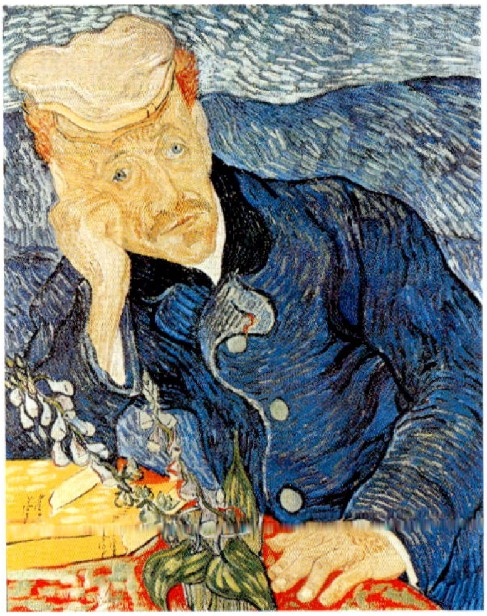

The original *Portrait of Dr Gachet* (JH 2007, F 753), 66 × 57 cm
Present location unknown

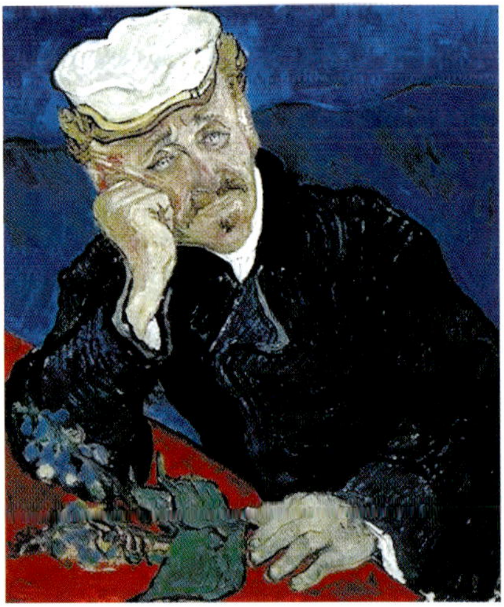

The copy of the *Portrait of Dr Gachet* (JH 2014, F 754), 68 × 57 cm
Musée d'Orsay

The original painted by Vincent van Gogh is famous and amazingly impressive. As Vincent described it to his brother, "The face is weary with the heart-broken expression of our time." This painting fetched a record price at Christie's in New York in 1990 when it was bought by a Japanese businessman, Mr Ryoei Saito, for some £51 million. The new owner kept it in a vault, and never allowed it to be on view.

The Times reported on 31 January 1998 that Sotheby's had bought the painting back for about £6.2 million after Saito had died. I wrote to *The Times* about this, and they replied that they had meant to say that it had been bought back for £6.2 million ($10 million) *less* than the £51 million ($82.5 million) paid for it at auction in 1990. Sotheby's in New York would not confirm to me having reacquired the painting, and it now somehow seems to have disappeared off the face of the earth.

Mme Distel said they had wanted to show this original version of the *Portrait of Dr Gachet* in order to hang it, and compare it, with the version owned by the Musée d'Orsay, but this indisputably genuine version could not be located. It has been suggested that the painting may never have left Japan or may have returned there. The mystery is rather odd for an investment of more than £50 million.

There has also been a report in the press that the painting had been bought in 1938 by the grandfather of a Christine Königs. He apparently knew the Mr Kramarsky whose son sold the painting in 1990 through Christie's in New York to Mr Saito for $82.5 million. The painting reportedly appears in the books of Walter Feilchenfeldt senior, who moved to Amsterdam when the national socialists gained ground in Germany. In these records Kramarsky's bank, Lisser & Rosenkranz, is given as the owner. Both Christine's grandfather and Kramarsky senior lived in Amsterdam at one time. Export of the painting to the USA would seem to have been a sensible move in those days, but it is not clear what they, who knew each other well, arranged between them. The Kramarskys apparently fled to the USA in 1939. There appears to be a record of purchase of the painting by Königs in 1938, but no record of his selling it. He may have placed the painting with Lisser & Rosenkranz as collateral. Be all this as it may, the rumour goes that if the painting surfaces Christine Königs may claim it.

If the two versions of the *Portrait of Dr Gachet* could have been brought together for comparison the impact would have been as dramatic as would be the bringing together of the three versions of the *Fourteen Sunflowers in a Vase*—always provided, of course, that on such an occasion both sides of the argument were given a fair hearing.

The artist who wrote about a portrait he had painted that "the face is weary with the heart-broken expression of our time", is not likely to have painted the version of the Gachet portrait now in the Musée d'Orsay collection which was in the 1999 Paris exhibition. The copy does not have the depth of sentiment of the original. Apart from the expression in the face, however, the background landscape, the foreground still life, the coat, the hands, the colours, all leave no doubt that these two paintings are not by the same artist. Mme Distel probably knows that too, and this may have been reflected in the secondary place the painting occupied in the Paris exhibition at the Grand Palais, even though it was used for the front cover of the exhibition catalogue.

Blanche Derousse painted a third version of the *Portrait of Dr Gachet* in watercolours, in 1901. This is also in the collection of the Musée d'Orsay. It has been suggested that this watercolour is a copy of that museum's oil-on-canvas version, which is supposed to have been painted, like the undisputed version, directly from the sitter.

Looking at the progressive deviations from the original, as Landais persuasively reasons, it is more than likely that this watercolour, dated 1901, was painted *before* the oil-on-canvas painting in the Musée d'Orsay. If this is the case Vincent, who died in 1890, can hardly have painted the latter.

The second painting requiring special mention is the painting *Cows* (JH2095, F822, 55 × 65 cm, below), still attributed to van Gogh. This painting is after a work in oils by Jordaens in Lille, of which Dr Gachet himself, under his pseudonym Paul van Rijssel, made an etching in 1873. This etching is also in the Musée des Beaux-Arts in Lille, donated by Paul Gachet junior in 1950, who claimed that it had been copied by van Gogh in oil on canvas in 1890.

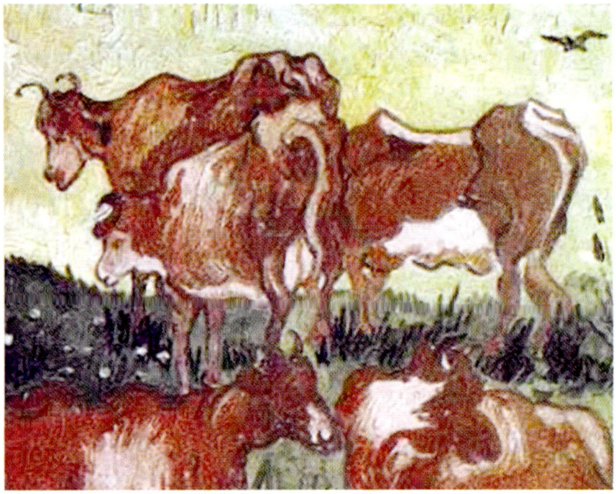

Another copy of the same subject was produced by Blanche Derousse in watercolours, date not given. This is also in the collection of the Musée d'Orsay, acquired as a gift from Paul Gachet junior.

If one carefully studies the original painting by Jordaens, then the etching by Gachet senior, then the oil-on-canvas version attributed to van Gogh, and the watercolour by Derousse of *Cows*, Landais's claim that the watercolour copy was most probably painted before the oil-on-canvas copy is convincing.

De la Faille wrote that he was not convinced that the painting was by Vincent, but Gachet junior had insisted that Vincent had painted it during his stay at Auvers, and on this assurance alone he had been persuaded to attribute it to van Gogh in his 1928 catalogue. The catalogue of the Grand Palais exhibition informed visitors that:

> When Paul Gachet donated this painting in 1950 to the Musée de Lille it immediately gave rise to a debate within the committee of curators appointed to ratify the donation. They deemed the work "not sufficiently representative of the artist's genius to be housed in a

> provincial museum." They recommended that it should be stored in the Louvre's 'documentary rooms'. These were such veritable dungeons that Paul Gachet vehemently refused the proposal in the name of his father's memory.

The catalogue also stated that the decisiveness in the painting hardly suggests the cautious working of a forger. [It is more likely to be a copy in oils of an earlier watercolour by the same artist. It seems to have been the attribution, not the painting, that was a forgery. Someone other than the artist is likely to have arranged the false attribution.] The catalogue continues:

> It seems more logical to accept the work as an original, albeit ill-conceived sketch, created by Van Gogh in the exceptional circumstances that accompanied the end of his career in Auvers . . . This conclusion is supported by the clumsiness of the work, which in no way glorifies the painter but rather draws attention to his limitations.

What a disgraceful slur on Vincent van Gogh in order to avoid having to admit to having accepted a misattribution! Whatever happens in the debate about van Gogh, surely he should no longer be saddled with such an inelegance as *Cows*!

In Landais's opinion, and many agree, the oil painting of *Cows* is by the same hand as the copy in oils of the *Portrait of Dr Gachet.* The finger would seem to point at Blanche Derousse. Vincent's nephew and heir, Vincent Willem van Gogh, was of the same mind. According to Geraldine Norman in an article in the *Daily Telegraph* of 16 November 1998, Vincent Willem van Gogh is reported to have written to the Board of the Van Gogh Foundation in 1966:

> I am now convinced that Blanche Derousse made paintings which passed as paintings by van Gogh. I have no grounds to believe that they were made for this purpose. She died at the beginning of this century and presumably Gachet sold them as van Goghs.

It should be noted that watercolours by Blanche Derousse are marked with the author's initials, but the oils are unsigned. This may have been influenced by the purpose for which the oils were painted—perhaps not her own idea but by request. Could they possibly have been commissioned for the catalogue which Dr Gachet planned but which never materialised?

* * *

As planned, the Exhibition moved to the Metropolitan Museum in New York in May 1999. The very substantial 300-page illustrated catalogue, issued in French for the exhibition in Paris, did not contain an actual list of exhibits but was loaded with relevant and not-so-relevant material and information, including details of the research to attempt to confirm authenticities, and so on.

For the exhibition at the Metropolitan this beautiful catalogue was translated into English and slightly altered and augmented in a few places. One difference was that it contained more and better illustrations than the Paris version had; for instance, *The Garden of the Asylum in Saint-Rémy* donated to Holland by Gachet junior in 1954 was included.

The Metropolitan Museum's catalogue is reasonably frank about doubtful sources of paintings from the collection and among the donations of the Gachet family. It asks how Dr Gachet could have acquired paintings by Cézanne and van Gogh painted before these artists came to Auvers. In the catalogue, Susan Alyson Stein, associate curator of the Metropolitan Museum of Art, suggests that we cannot ignore the possibility of other sources for Dr Gachet's acquisitions.

After the Metropolitan Museum in New York, *The Collection of Dr Gachet* transferred in September 1999 to the Van Gogh Museum in Amsterdam, where it occupied a much reduced space on the second floor of the new 'Yasuda wing', as a relatively small sideshow. This limited space was only adequate because the exhibition had been seriously curtailed and was a far cry from the elaborate show under the same flag in Paris. The exhibits relating to the research done on paintings had been eliminated, as had various others. No catalogue had been prepared. In the bookshop, located in a different part of the Museum, copies of the catalogue from the earlier Metropolitan Museum exhibition were on sale among a variety of other books and catalogues.

The entrance to this particular exhibition had been poorly signposted and was difficult to find. Visitors to the main part of the museum could easily miss the way to the new wing, which starts on a lower level, and as a result many missed this special exhibition altogether. No serious attempt had been made to draw the attention of the visitors to it and most of them seemed happy enough with the mixed exhibition and the fabulous display of van Goghs in the main building. One may wonder if this contrasting low-key treatment stemmed from slight embarrassment at being associated with the exhibition at all.

A notable addition to what had been shown in Paris was the presence of both versions of *The Garden of the Asylum*, the asylum in Saint-Rémy where Vincent stayed before he came to Auvers-sur-Oise (see page 143). One of these two, for which the official provenance records Dr Gachet as first owner, was donated by Paul Gachet junior in 1954 to Vincent van Gogh's nephew, Theo's son. The painting had been kept out of the public eye by the Gachets until 1954. Vincent Willem van Gogh accepted it as a gift but soon doubted its authenticity. He even sent it to an exhibition on fakes in Minneapolis in 1973, after which it returned to the collection of the Van Gogh Foundation in Amsterdam.

In 1987, after apparently misinterpreting several of Vincent's letters, Professor Ronald Pickvance thought that he had 'discovered' that the painting had been mentioned in the letters and he included it in an exhibition *Van Gogh in Saint-Rémy and Auvers* in the Metropolitan, for which he was guest curator. The Van Gogh Museum followed his example and exhibited the painting in the *Retrospective of Van Gogh* of 1990, again advised by Pickvance.

Some years later, Landais, after he had claimed that the painting was a fake, as Willem van Gogh also thought, checked how a fake could possibly have been mentioned in the letters, and Pickvance's misinterpretation was exposed. In 1996 Hulsker, who has studied the painting carefully more than once, and who is the acknowledged world authority on *The Letters*, advanced arguments why he did not believe the painting was authentic and gave it a question mark in his latest catalogue.

Notwithstanding the arguments by Willem van Gogh, Hulsker, Landais, and others, and despite the overwhelming documentary evidence, van Tilborgh has still seen fit to 'reinstate' it as authentic. Amongst his arguments is that 'the yellow light of the sun in the sky is falling beautifully through the crowns of the trees' and, polemically, that Hulsker must have forgotten to look at the painting properly. In reality, in the Amsterdam version, 'the yellow light of the sun' looks as though it has been thrown at the trees from the opposite direction, towards the sun, and has got stuck in the branches and foliage. Landais said in an article, "*Une neige de petits points maladroits* [A snowstorm of clumsy little errors]."

Van Tilborgh also cites a letter from Vincent to Emile Bernard as supporting his view that the letter applies better to the Amsterdam painting than to the undisputed authentic version (now in the Museum Folkwang in Essen). That could support the view that the copyist is believed to have painted the second version from a black and white photograph and the description of colours in this letter. It is very unlikely that the genuine painting in Essen was the model for creating the Amsterdam version. Important remarks in this letter clearly apply to the Essen version.

Johanna van Gogh is the recorded first owner in the official provenance for the genuine painting in Essen, which was never in the Gachet collection, let alone among the Gachet donations, and therefore did not really qualify to be in this exhibition.

There is also a watercolour by Blanche Derousse of the same subject, as well as a black and white rendering of it. The Amsterdam version has two important similarities with the watercolour copy by Blanche Derousse—the absence of a farmhouse in the background and of windows in the asylum building.

It was thus an unexpected but pleasant surprise to find the indisputably authentic version owned by the Essen Museum Folkwang—never in the Gachet collection, never a Gachet donation—hanging next to the version the Van Gogh Museum had received as a Gachet donation, in an exhibition announced to be in homage to Dr Gachet. It certainly facilitated comparison, and their close proximity did not do the Amsterdam version any favours. The differences, especially obvious to those who had been alerted to them, stared one in the eye. They do indeed suggest, if not confirm, that the Amsterdam version is a painting by another hand.

Apart from the differences mentioned above, Vincent's letter to Emile Bernard (B21 c. 20 November 1889) describing the painting mentions "a few rosebushes which have finished flowering". This is cleverly reflected in the Essen painting, whereas the rosebushes in the Amsterdam painting appear to be still in a reasonable state of bloom. This letter also mentions the enormous trunk of a tree, which has been hit by lightning and has been sawn off, and Vincent imagines its feeling of hurt pride against the smile of a last rose in the bush of otherwise nearly finished blooms facing it.

Importantly, the letter points out the dark contour lines and other aspects of the painting which are intended to express the feeling of fear from which some of Vincent's fellow-patients suffer. The dark windows in the wall of the building accentuate the sombre atmosphere within.

The tree trunk in the Amsterdam painting is far less majestic than that in the Essen version; there are many roses and not just a single last rose on the bush opposite; and the windows in the asylum building have been left out. Apart from all these and other details, the Amsterdam painting just cannot match the 'feel' of the Essen original.

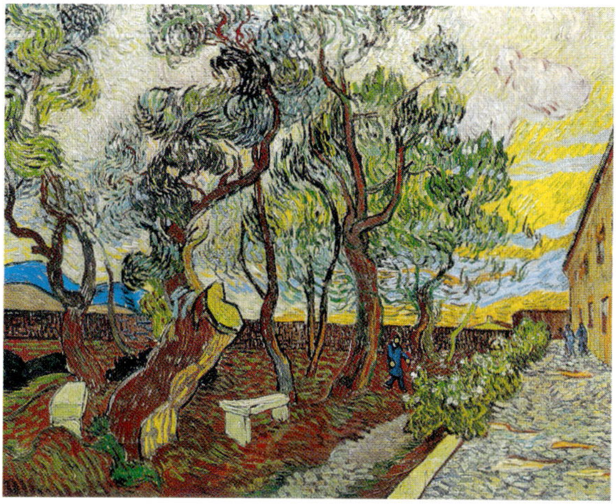

The Garden of the Asylum with a Heavy, Sawn-off Tree
(JH 1849, F 660)
73.5 × 92 cm
Museum Folkwang, Essen

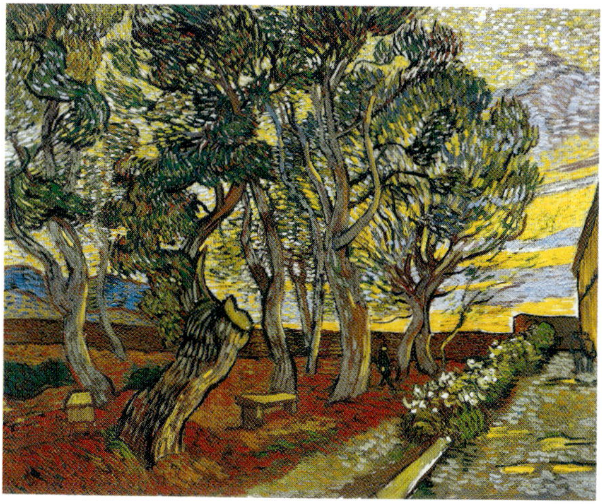

The Garden of the Asylum with a Heavy, Sawn-off Tree
(JH 1850, F 659)
71.5 × 90.5 cm
Vincent van Gogh Foundation, Amsterdam.

A few days before the Gachet donations exhibition opened in Amsterdam the Van Gogh Museum held a press conference on 21 September 1999 about their *The Garden of the Asylum in Saint-Rémy*. The purpose was to defend their current opinion that this painting is an authentic van Gogh. They had done some research on the painting. Van Tilborgh and Ms Ella Hendriks (who replaced Ms Peres) issued a lengthy draft report, dated 21 September and entitled *Van Gogh's* Garden of the Asylum at Saint-Rémy*: Genuine or Fake?*

The report was full of arguments that were unconvincing for anyone knowledgeable, but enough to blind with 'technospeak' many others who tend to accept statements from 'authorities'.

The report suggested that critics had said that the Amsterdam version had been painted by Paul Gachet junior himself, and then compared aspects of the painting with those in a painting known to have been his. And it concluded that there are differences, which, of course, there are. But this is a ridiculous argument, as Gachet junior, if copying a painting, would hardly paint in his own style. Moreover, and perhaps even more importantly, Gachet junior is certainly not the most likely creator of the painting: Blance Derousse is a much better bet, as already suggested by Willem van Gogh in 1966, a view supported by others.

An important point in the debate is the fact that Gachet junior never revealed the existence of this work to the public until 1954, while the report claims that the painting in fact surfaced at a remarkably early stage. It explains that Blanche Derousse was able to make a watercolour copy of it in the period 1900–1903. But even that watercolour was not made public at that time either, and it would be interesting to know when that was donated to the Louvre, or when it surfaced. Neither the report, nor the exhibition catalogue, seem to reveal this. That Derousse was able to make the watercolour of the same subject some ten years or more after the death of Vincent hardly disqualifies her from having been able to paint the oil painting around that time as well. What is meant by 'remarkably early' in that case about the surfacing of either watercolour or oil painting? What nonsense!

The Derousse watercolour of *The Garden of the Asylum* has important similarities with the Amsterdam version in oils; neither has the farmhouse in the background or windows in the asylum wall that are present in the authentic van Gogh in Essen. There were many other statements about the painting in the van Tilborgh–Hendriks report which may have impressed some journalists but which did not get past those a little more knowledgeable about van Gogh.

For instance, the report says of the Amsterdam copy, which it maintains is by Vincent, "He left out the superfluous, nervous detail of the farmhouse in the right background, and showed less of the asylum façade, as a result of which he perhaps found it unnecessary to indicate the windows." One may ask what is this 'superfluous, nervous detail of the farmhouse', which in fact helps to connect the garden with the asylum buildings. Vincent had written to Emile Bernard that in this painting he conveyed the fear and distress of the inhabitants of the asylum. The more extensive asylum façade with windows is clearly part of this intention, so why leave them out in the so-called better copy? Like other statements in the report, this seems to reveal a lack of understanding of the painting.

The van Tilborgh–Hendriks report was the basis for this press conference, to which journalists had been invited and where these two versions of *The Garden of the Asylum at Saint-Rémy* from Essen and Amsterdam were shown. Critics had not been invited and the event was a one-sided indoctrination by the co-authors.

As in the *Sunflowers* symposium, neither the critics nor the press were given a fair chance to listen to both sides in the argument, which would have enabled them to come to an evenly balanced opinion in both these cases.

The critics did get a chance to put over their point of view, however, as the Belgian TV programme *Canvas* showed in a documentary dealing with suspected van Gogh fakes. The following are translations of extracts from Lien Heytink's report, in the *NRC-Handelsbad*, of the filmed debate where both the 'amateur' researchers and the museums were allowed their say:

> In the documentary certain Van Gogh researchers were given an opportunity to demonstrate why, in their opinion, the paintings could not be by Van Gogh. Their arguments showed that they had not come to their conclusions light-heartedly and they sounded very serious. They pointed to changes in provenance made for the purpose of sales catalogues but especially they also analysed aspects of the actual paintings. The more explanations were given the more the spectators were wondering what the reaction of the official institutions, the auction houses and museums would be.
>
> The auction houses decided not to comment.
>
> One French auctioneer remarked that the commotion was futile.
>
> The American museums who were asked to comment declined to do so.
>
> Only the Musée d'Orsay in Paris and the Van Gogh Museum were prepared to offer their reaction.

The representative of Musée d'Orsay spoke a few hesitant words. According to her, at the end of the day, intuition was the decisive factor in determining the authenticity of a work.

Then it was the turn of Sjraar van Heugten and Louis van Tilborgh. Seldom has there been on TV such a demonstration of condescension as was displayed by Sjraar van Heugten on this occasion. He was given the opportunity to disprove the arguments that had been presented by the researchers, and to provide reasons for his views on the dubious Van Gogh paintings. Or at least he had the opportunity to suggest that in his opinion the matter was too complicated to allow him to comment.

But he did not take his chance. All he offered was that, according to him, the van Gogh researchers were amateurs and he wondered what business of theirs it was to interfere.

Also, he suggested, sensational press reports do nobody any good. And he bragged on like this with the haughty appearance of a man in power who is immune from criticism.

It is clear that if ever the two versions of the *Portrait of Dr Gachet* or the three of the *Fourteen Sunflowers in a Vase* are brought together to compare, it will be absolutely essential to invite the independent researchers, the so-called 'amateurs', as well as those who defend the currently suspect attributions, and to give them all equal status in an open debate. This should also have been done when the two versions of *The Garden of the Asylum* were brought together in Amsterdam. Perhaps there will one day be a second showing with the critics allowed to attend, so the press and the general public will be able to judge for themselves.

Ever since the first artquake, the museums have shown how weak they really are. They employ their formidable reputations and prestige to try and silence all opposition but decline to be drawn into a frank debate with independent researchers.

Museums would be wise, in cases where there is serious doubt about authenticity, to do, and be seen to be doing, everything possible to get at the truth. This is not a matter of what experts like or prefer to believe: it is about reality, it is about the truth.

Chapter Sixteen

Third Time Still Unlucky

I had intended one day to forward a copy of Eastaugh's comments on the second van Tilborgh 'expertise' on *The Diggers* [Chapter 12] to Leighton, the director of the Van Gogh Museum. I finally did so on 14 June 1999.

Dear Mr Leighton,

You will remember that last year in May you kindly agreed to a re-evaluation of my painting *Two Diggers* because of an unsatisfactory letter by Mr van Tilborgh which had purported to be an expertise. You handed the matter over to Mr van Heugten, who sent me an invitation by fax on 8th June 1998. He and I agreed on the mutually convenient date of 17th June 1998 for me to bring the painting from Eton to the Museum in Amsterdam.

I brought the painting on the appointed day at 9 a.m. and was asked to collect it again at 5 p.m. I did not see Mr van Heugten or anybody else with whom I could discuss anything regarding the first expertise or the painting. When I came to collect I was asked to wait and after some time was given the painting with only a message that I would receive a letter in due course.

I received a letter, purporting to be the second expertise, dated 22nd June 1998, signed on behalf of Mr van Tilborgh. But I had to conclude that this second expertise again did not contain any convincing arguments against my painting.

In order to verify my own judgement on this I handed this second expertise over to Dr Nicholas Eastaugh, the specialist whom you had recommended to me, and Dr Eastaugh seemed to agree with my views. I enclose a copy of his response.

Until now I have had only ill-founded arguments from the Van Gogh Museum which are in conflict with the results of extensive technical studies and also with the views of several well known and respected experts on the authenticity of my painting.

As I have a signed Agreement with the Van Gogh Museum, promising me reasonable care in its duties for an expertise, I feel that I have some entitlement to ask you whether you have any suggestions which could help me out of this dilemma.

Could the Van Gogh Museum perhaps be asked to apply reasonable care in studying the positive findings of the other experts and denouncing these with sound arguments? Or perhaps find some greater scope for agreement on these?

You will appreciate that I cannot rest until I have been convinced. I trust you can share that sentiment.

With kind regards,

Yours sincerely

Bouwe Jans

I received a reply five weeks later, on 21 July, not from Leighton but from van Heugten. It was in Dutch and translated as follows:

Dear Mr Jans,

In response to your letter of 14 June 1999 I advise you the following:

You have requested us to give you an expertise on a work of art in your possession and we have given you our opinion. We have nothing to add to this. You are of course entitled to a different opinion and you are free to contact other experts.

Hoping to have informed you adequately,

With kind regards,

signed: Sjraar van Heugten,
Head of Collections.

Van Heugten had been promoted to Head of Collections from 1 June 1999.

His letter only confirmed that the Museum is not in the least embarrassed by having issued a didactic verdict on a work of art without good supporting reasons for the opinion therein. I noted particularly that Leighton had again decided not to reply to my letter personally and had totally ignored the opinions of the expert he himself had recommended to me. He had not even made certain that his Head of Collections had sent me a reasonable answer. Hardly the attitude a Dutchman expects from an Englishman!

This curtness, added to the manner of my recent reception when I brought *The Diggers* to Amsterdam, amounted to a brush-off. Could this mean that in the eyes of the Van Gogh Museum I was now just a nuisance maker who could be given even shorter shrift than before and be treated quite offhandedly?—like 'the amateurs' so often derided, whose opinions and questions are beneath the Museum's dignity?

If so, I was being relegated, in many eyes other than the Museum's, to very distinguished and honourable company.

Chapter Seventeen

Reflections

From an early stage in my attempts to find out who painted *The Diggers* I have been taken aback by the attitude of the director, curators, and staff of the Van Gogh Museum and some of their outside associates such as Dorn and Feilchenfeldt. Their attitude has varied from being just unco-operative and unwilling to being frankly unfriendly at times. It became obvious however, that I was not the only one receiving this kind of treatment and that many others had had the same experience. For a long time I have really been wondering what the reason for this attitude could possibly be and eventually had to conclude that perhaps the 'establishment' has something to hide—incompetence in the management of the oeuvre?—an opinion in which I am not alone.

During my interview with van Tilborgh he had told me that the Museum had to deal with many requests for attribution like mine and that some received a short, others a more detailed answer. Leighton has later stated that the Museum gets about five such enquiries per week. Marije Vellekoop, curator of prints and drawings at the Museum since 1999, has also said that the number of works submitted for authentication in 1999 was about 250 (of which only 10% were drawings).

One could therefore believe that the Museum staff are tired of having to find ostensible reasons for rejecting all submissions, especially when they may well be for genuine works, but whatever their reasons, it still did not really justify the attitude I and others had encountered. Nor did it explain why they had made me wait some nine months for a very short answer, which they had originally promised to supply to me within three months.

The strong recommendations by van Tilborgh and by Dorn that I should stop trying to obtain an attribution to either van Gogh or to an alternative artist added to my suspicion that they did have something to hide. Even more so because they were unable or unwilling to provide any sensible reasons to incline me to comply.

Surely sound reasons for a rejection could quickly be given for the majority of the 250 applications for an authentication per year. Photographs and details of all these paintings, watercolours, drawings, etc., such as I had to submit for *The Diggers* are retained by the Museum, for every application, and these would be interesting to study. They are, however, strictly confidential and may not be examined.

Only very sporadically does one hear of a previously unknown van Gogh being authenticated by the Van Gogh Museum so there must be some 250 rejections a year. Of these no more is heard because, as said earlier, a 'no' from the Van Gogh Museum is almost impossible to argue against; the owner normally gives up after such a deathblow.

But then, what about the known missing works, especially those from the early period? Of the 70 studies in oils Vincent painted in The Hague alone, some 45 are indisputably still missing, and these are part of a much larger number also missing, from the 60 or so paintings on stretchers, 150 or thereabouts loose canvases, 90 pen drawings, and 100–200 crayon drawings reportedly handled by Couvreur. A large number of these have been traced. Mouwen sold most of his, either directly, or through the auction house Muller in Amsterdam. Many of these went to the Oldenzeel Art Gallery, which had been founded by a van Gogh family member, Vincent's Uncle Hendrik. Between Mouwen and Oldenzeel alone some eighty works can be accounted for from the Couvreur sales. But many are still not accounted for yet.

There is also the crate that Schrauwen, the carpenter in Breda, gave to the jobbing gardener, Barend den Houter. Den Houter apparently did not find the contents of the crate, reportedly chock-full, very interesting. He may have sold or given away some pieces or he may have left the contents intact.

When in 1938, at the age of 83 he was moving to a home for the elderly, he had to dispose of those of his possessions that he could not take with him. One of the interested purchasers, a Mr Marijnissen, saw the case, which looked as if it had been untouched for a long time, and on opening the lid he found to his surprise that it was filled with well over 200 rolled-up oil paintings, watercolours, and drawings, some of which were signed 'Vincent'. On learning from den Houter that a carpenter in Breda for whom he had done odd jobs from time to time had given him the case, Marijnissen bought it for five guilders and took it home.

Being an artist himself he more or less realised what he had bought, but owing to the Second World War it was not until 1947 that he was able to arouse any interest in Amsterdam, where at first he was not taken very seriously.

Before the official opening of the Rijksmuseum Vincent Van Gogh on 2 June 1973 by Her Majesty Queen Juliana there had been a few major Van Gogh exhibitions in the Stedelijk Museum in Amsterdam, notably one in 1905 and another in 1930, and many of van Gogh's works hung there on long-term loan.

Mr Sandberg, the director, and Dr Jaffé, curator/deputy director of the Stedelijk Museum, visited Marijnissen a few times to look at the works and after some time took ten pieces away for research by the well known van Gogh expert van Dantzig.

Van Dantzig is reported to have written a preliminary letter to Marijnissen on 10 October 1948 in which he said he needed more time but he was getting more and more confident that the end result would be positive. In a further letter, of 20 October 1948, he declared that to his great pleasure he had finished his research and that indeed the results were positive.

A few weeks later Sandberg and Jaffé visited Marijnissen again and proposed that he offer the ten works to the Stedelijk Museum on a twenty-five year loan. Marijnissen thought this to be a strange proposal, and he made the counter-proposal that they should certify at least one of the paintings so that he could sell that. Being 50 years old at that time he was not very keen to have to wait twenty-five years to see any reward.

Sandberg and Jaffé did not agree to this and left, saying that they would soon make contact again. A few weeks later the ten works arrived back with a short covering letter stating: "We have come to the conclusion, with a probability bordering on certainty, that none of them show sufficient characteristics from the hand of Van Gogh." This in spite of the earlier confirmation of authenticity by van Dantzig.

Marijnissen decided not to take further action and sold most of the works to friends and family for next to nothing. One of these buyers was a Dr Georg Klusmann, a German child psychologist, who interested himself in the affair and who also had an interview with Jaffé. During this recorded interview Jaffé seems to have confirmed that he considered there was no question of forgeries. He explicitly said, "I know that there were a large number of genuine van Goghs in the Marijnissen collection", continuing that the crux of the matter really was that they had not had the courage to authenticate the entire collection. He also said that at the time they were very busy and did not have the chance to study the collection adequately. Moreover there were not enough experts sufficiently knowledgeable about the very early works. He had added that with present-day knowledge and technology the chances of authentication would be much better. He suggested that it would certainly be worthwhile researching the Marijnissen collection again and in greater detail.

With Jaffé's co-operation, Klusmann had one of his paintings researched technically in Münich, where it was confirmed that the materials used in the painting and the age of the work were compatible with works by van Gogh, not that this helped his case decisively.

Klusmann was disappointed and no longer wanted even to talk about the Marijnissen van Goghs any longer. He had met with so much lack of understanding, unwillingness, and arrogance that he died a frustrated man, but not before he had written a book about his experiences. He is not alone in having become frustrated for the same or similar reasons.

Perhaps most sensible people would throw in the towel in such circumstances, but a relative of a former neighbour of Marijnissen, whose family has access to some fourteen works from that collection, has recently decided to delve further. I suspect that there may be some interesting revelations from this gestating artquake in due course.

On reflection, there can be little doubt that many very early works by van Gogh from the Couvreur sales and the Marijnissen collection in Breda are still around somewhere. But at one stage it seems to have been decided that it would be counter-productive to authenticate such a large quantity of works and include them in the oeuvre of Van Gogh. No one then and no one since has had the courage to face the upheaval such a move would create. Anyone ever considering it seriously and genuinely could meet with insurmountable resistance. Rejecting all of them may still seem to be the easiest way out.

If that is indeed the case, perhaps it becomes understandable that, whenever one of these Breda orphans turns up on the doorstep of the Van Gogh Museum, it is not very welcome. After all, at one time, they had also been rejected and discarded as worthless by the van Gogh family.

This situation is most unfortunate for *The Diggers* and many other works with a similar background, but at least it may be the explanation of the adversarial attitude of the Van Gogh Museum that I and others have experienced thus far.

I fear that, for the time being at least, all very early works by van Gogh with a Couvreur-Marijnissen-Breda label attached to them will continue to be rejected by the Van Gogh Museum, either because they are unable to recognise them as genuine or from fear of opening the floodgates.

Chapter Eighteen

A Provisional Provenance

Early on, van der Wolk, the curator of the Kröller-Müller museum, had pointed out to me that a good provenance is almost indispensable for art historians and curators of museums to authenticate works of art. But, as we have seen in this book, provenances can be and have been manipulated and can also be misread. According to Landais, a de la Faille provenance is normally correct when the title of the painting is not ambiguous, but when there is a series of paintings with the same or similar subject matter and therefore with the same or similar titles the provenances can become misallocated. Landais adds that Feilchenfeldt has been able to correct some of these errors, but he also believes that Feilchenfeldt has occasionally himself misread documentary evidence, adding to the confusion. What makes the task even more difficult is that, like paintings, provenances can also be faked and forged.

For a work by Vincent van Gogh, the best provenance available is proof that it is mentioned in records from the artist's lifetime or that it is listed in the earliest records of Theo van Gogh's widow, Johanna van Gogh-Bonger.

The first, and sometimes many, years of the existence of quite a number of paintings attributed to van Gogh are a mystery. The first *catalogue raisonné* by de la Faille, not published until thirty-eight years after the painter's death, depended, in many instances unreliably, on a motley of informants and owners. The differing stories told by Paul Gachet junior on various occasions about the same subject matter, for instance, must classify him as untrustworthy and cast doubt on the provenances he persuaded de la Faille to record in his 1928 catalogue.

A de la Faille listing of E. Schuffenecker or A. Schuffenecker as the first owner of a painting, was at one time all that was required for a work to still be believed to be a genuine van Gogh. It was only later that Schuffenecker provenances became suspect and a record of first ownership by Johanna van Gogh or another member or close friend of the van Gogh family became the most secure confirmation of authenticity.

We have seen that for some important paintings, around the time when owners wished to arrange a sale by auction, an original de la Faille provenance quoting a Schuffenecker as first owner was changed to make the first owner a much more acceptable van Gogh family member or members—with, one might conjecture, quite a beneficial effect on a painting's commercial value.

It becomes worrying when the reasons given to justify these changes in a provenance appear to be flawed. It would seem important that, even if the changes and reasons for them have been accepted by auction houses, they should still be fully investigated and either formally confirmed or otherwise.

Many provenances have been recorded on the basis of information from owners, and if nothing better is available these have to be accepted until proved incorrect or suspect. Whether such information is given one-hundred-and-five or thirty-five years after the death of the artist should in principle be immaterial.

The same should therefore apply to a provenance for *The Diggers.* Such a provenance. derived from *The Letters,* with support from the findings of Landais, Hulsker, Eastaugh, Cadorin, and others, could read as follows.

> *Two Diggers in the Afternoon Sun.*
>
> Painted as a study by Vincent van Gogh in The Hague in August/September 1882.
>
> A print of the etching by Millet of two diggers was pinned up in his studio at that time.
>
> The painted study was also pinned to the wall of his studio with drawing pins until September 1883.
>
> Stored in a loft in Schenkweg, The Hague, with some seventy other studies and some chattels in September 1883 when he left for Drenthe (letter 385 [320] 6–7 September 1883).
>
> Fetched by van Gogh from The Hague in December 1883 and transported to Nuenen where he then lived for nearly two years.
>
> Left behind in Nuenen with his other belongings when he left for Antwerp on 24 November 1885.
>
> Packed up into crates with his other belongings by his mother when she also left Nuenen in May 1886, and sent for storage with a carpenter, Mr Schrauwen, in Breda.

By 1902–1903 Schrauwen, having already disposed of at least one crate earlier, had opened some others and as the contents seemed of no value, the whole lot were heaped up in a corner and treated as rubbish, *The Diggers* amongst them.

In 1903 Schrauwen persuaded a rag and bone merchant to take this 'rubbish' away without payment. The scrap merchant, a Mr J.C. Couvreur, and his brother took the lot to their premises in the Stallingstraat, Breda. After weeding out the least interesting and unwanted items they loaded the remainder into their cart and, nailing a few samples to the outside, they offered them for sale to the public at the nearby market for next to nothing. The excessive number of pinholes in the canvas of *The Diggers* (see Landais's report, Appendix E) might indicate that it was one of those nailed to the Couvreurs' cart.

The Diggers, like many other paintings sold off this way in Breda, ended up in private hands at this time and was treated the way many works are when acquired for next to nothing. The buyer may have appreciated the painting; he may even have been the one who had it put on a stretcher, even in a frame perhaps; and he may possibly even have hung it in his home.

The Diggers was probably 'third time lucky' and ended up either in the new owner's loft, or later in that of one of his children in Breda, after the owner had died and the family's waning appreciation for the work failed to keep it hanging on their walls.

From the painting's present condition it is likely that it was kept in darkness for a considerable period.

In or before 1990 or 1991 it was bought at a flea market near Groningen, from a family who had moved many years earlier to Groningen from Breda, where they had acquired it. This new owner sold it at an auction of household effects in Groningen in May 1993, where it was bought by the present owner.

This provenance is perhaps incomplete, lacking owner's names from 1903 up to 1990. Any help in filling this gap will be welcomed and rewarded.

Chapter Nineteen

Not Quite the End

The Diggers is now perhaps one of the more exhaustively researched paintings, art-historically and scientifically, in the entire oeuvre of Vincent van Gogh. In other cases of work rightly or wrongly attributed to van Gogh, enormous prestige and vast amounts of money may be at stake. In the case of *The Diggers* a modicum of prestige may perhaps be involved, but not so very large an amount of money, as the early works are much less valuable than those painted later.

The involvement of these mundane considerations in most of the disputed authentications, however, means that while one day a solution must be found, it is these very aspects that are more than likely the reason for past and present procrastination. The delays are an indication that the establishment has no effective procedure yet for dealing with controversial issues other than, ostrich-like, hoping they will go away. Until an acceptable conclusion emerges disagreement will have to continue.

Some artquakes have shaken the foundations and done their damage, leaving experts and owners to lick their wounds; others are rumbling on beneath the surface. Aftershocks will continue because too much interest has been fired up in too many knowledgeable people.

The matter is not only important for owners, it is also of importance for the reputation of the artist and for the entire art-loving population of the world. Surely museum visitors are entitled to be told the truth about the paintings they have come to see? At the moment, it still looks as if, in major disputes on the attribution of paintings to van Gogh, David is fighting Goliath. In reality, however, the establishment is beginning to resemble a rickety edifice facing an approaching tornado.

The time for specious arguments and for turning a completely deaf ear to the voices of serious researchers and scholars must surely be over. The Van Gogh Museum should no longer publish articles such as the 21-page attempt by Dorn to bolster up the authenticity of 'the Yasuda' in the 1999

Journal of the Van Gogh Museum—the most remarkable conclusion in which was the suggestion that perhaps Vincent left the Yasuda *Sunflowers* unsigned so that it could be distinguished from the other versions.

"What next?" one might ask—and, indeed, the article went on to compare the total of six genuine sunflower paintings from Arles with six apples on the ground under an apple tree and to suggest that every schoolchild would agree that these six apples would not necessarily represent the entire harvest and therefore why could there also not be more sunflower paintings? "What next?" I hear you cry.

The long-suspected close relationship between Dorn and van Tilborgh was confirmed in a recent article in the New York *ARTnews* magazine, Timothy W. Ryback wrote of the duo:

> Roland Dorn is a prolific German scholar living in Zürich who advises the Van Gogh Museum in Amsterdam . . . "Whenever I have a question or doubt about something," says curator van Tilborgh, "I simply call him on the phone."

And it is still the Van Gogh Museum and Dorn who continue to be—for auction houses and other museums—the most acceptable opinions on authenticity. If they do not believe in, or do not want to admit, the authenticity of a painting, even though other experts believe it to be genuine then, illogically, their word almost invariably still carries the day.

Is it not high time that the market, the auction houses, and the museums, woke up to reality and stopped blindly accepting as infallible opinions that today look distinctly shaky?

But good news is on the way. In the same article, Ryback went on:

> Van Tilborgh now considers this intense scrutiny of Van Gogh's oeuvre, by experts and amateurs alike, a 'healthy exercise' . . . "By researching the paintings in such detail," he says, "we are gaining a much deeper understanding of Van Gogh's work as a whole."

This would be a startling but welcome departure from the previously declared stance of 'we at the Museum have our own opinions, and that has to be accepted'. But while it is one thing to become more open to future attributions, it is another to face the embarrassment of admitting previous error. This requires strength of character and, perhaps, the taking to heart of Vincent's own words, "You sometimes find the correct way through your earlier mistakes." Vincent also wrote once to an artist friend, of one of his own paintings:

To make it, I had to accept a month of illness but at least I know that it is a work that you and I and perhaps another odd person [or two] will understand in the way we want it to be understood.

He knew that his work was sometimes beyond the full understanding of many. To have made a mistake in judging his work is therefore not necessarily shameful at all, provided it is admitted once there is evidence to prove it. We all have to live and learn.

There is now further good news. Despite the written declaration in 1997 that the Yasuda company would not participate in any further research on the authenticity of their painting, not to mention the director of the Van Gogh Museum's assertion that it was too fragile to travel, it was officially announced on the Web on 13 September 2000 that:

> The Yasuda Fire and Marine Insurance Company Ltd will lend its famous version of Van Gogh's *Sunflowers* to Chicago and Amsterdam. The picture will be shown in the major exhibition *Van Gogh & Gauguin: The Studio of the South* at The Art Institute of Chicago (22 September 2001–13 January 2002) and the Van Gogh Museum in Amsterdam (9 February–2 June 2002). This marks the first presentation of the painting outside Japan since the company acquired the work in 1987.
>
> The Yasuda *Sunflowers* will be displayed in Amsterdam alongside the versions from the National Gallery, London, and the Van Gogh Museum. This is the first time the three versions of the *Sunflowers* from Arles will be shown together. It represents a unique opportunity for the public to compare these works and to discover what van Gogh was trying to achieve when he decorated the Yellow House in Arles.
>
> Research relating to the *Van Gogh & Gauguin* exhibition will be published by the Van Gogh Museum in 2002.

By the time this book appears, the Yasuda *Sunflowers* and the Amsterdam original will be hanging, with the *Berceuse* in the middle as a triptych, in Chicago, and at least the art world, aware of the problems of its provenance, will have the opportunity to compare these two versions of *Fourteen Sunflowers*. Although the Chicago exhibition did not open to the public until 22 September a press conference was scheduled for 12 September, though after the appalling events in New York on 11 September this never took place. Members of the press had been invited by the Van Gogh Museum on a press tour to Chicago and offered free tickets. There was no sign, however, of any independent scholars and researchers having been invited for this conference, let alone being offered a free ride. There would thus have been ample time for the journalists to publish their reports on what they had been told by museum sources at the press conference well before the exhibition opened to the public, but they would not have had the benefit of simultaneous explanations by independent researchers.

It seemed to have been an attempt to repeat the *Garden of the Asylum* press conference procedure when the press was told that the Museum declared that painting genuine, but independent scholars and researchers believing that the painting was not by Van Gogh were kept at bay and were not invited, and thus only the one side of the argument, the opinion of the Museum, was heard by the press.

Apparently some journalists had decided not to take advantage of the offer of a free trip to Chicago to see the Amsterdam and the Yasuda versions of the *Fourteen Sunflowers in a Vase* together, preferring to wait till February 2002 when all three versions will hang together in Amsterdam.

* * *

Prospects for an honest and open and reasoned debate on the two opposing opinions as to whether the Yasuda version is genuine or not therefore did not look too good. In order to try and get a more satisfactory result during the Amsterdam exhibition I had written an open letter to John Leighton, the director of the Van Gogh Museum, which appeared in the Dutch newspaper, *Het Parool* of Saturday 8 September 2001 and translated as follows:

Open letter to: Mr. John Leighton,
Director of the Van Gogh Museum, Amsterdam.

September 2001

Dear Mr Leighton,
A dark cloud continues to hang over the authenticity of a number of well-known paintings attributed to Vincent van Gogh. Although the Van Gogh Museum and others declare them authentic, their authenticity is still disputed by many independent and reputable researchers and scholars.

One of the most controversial paintings in this debate is the third version of *Fourteen Sunflowers in a Vase*, owned by the Yasuda Fire and Marine Company of Tokyo, who bought this painting at Christie's, in London, in 1987 for £24.75m.

After considerable international publicity suggesting that the Yasuda painting is not by van Gogh, you announced the intelligent plan to hang this Yasuda version, and the two undisputedly genuine paintings of *Fourteen Sunflowers in a Vase,* the one owned by the National Gallery, *the other* by the Van Gogh Museum, together in the National Gallery, in London. However, the announcement of this promising plan was soon followed by a statement that the Yasuda painting was too delicate to travel and, instead of bringing the three canvases together, a Van Gogh Sunflower Symposium was held in May 1998, in the National Gallery. That symposium devoted minimal attention to the authenticity of the Sunflower painting that is in doubt and did not solve the issue.

Apart from the *Sunflowers* there are other doubtful attributions to van Gogh. Articles about these appear in the press, sometimes followed by opposing views in later articles. No positive conclusions can be drawn from all the individual articles in the various newspapers and magazines, sometimes published at considerable intervals. The unsatisfactory situation of doubtful attributions persists. Selling, buying and/or judging a 'van Gogh' continues to be a precarious activity. Too many are tainted. It is welcome news that the 'Yasuda' *Sunflowers* will be exhibited in Chicago at the *'Van Gogh and Gauguin: The Studio of the South'* exhibition in September 2001 and that all three versions of *Fourteen Sunflowers in a Vase* will hang together in Amsterdam in 2002.

On that occasion the Van Gogh Museum is expected to publish the results of their investigations into the question. It would be productive if the critics and the independent scholars interested could preview that publication or, better still, participate in it, or at least receive an invitation to contribute their own views and findings to it, before it is presented. Would it also not be a good idea if both the 'establishment' and their critics could be brought together, with the three paintings, in public? The polemic would then become an open dialogue, demonstrating the good faith of the Van Gogh Museum. This might even herald the start of a new era in which the Museum's experts are prepared to discuss attributions more openly in the future.

May I recommend the above to you for your kind consideration?

Yours sincerely,

Bouwe J. Jans

A copy of this draft letter was shown to the following, who confirmed in writing that they support and effectively join me in this attempt to achieve greater clarity in the current authenticity status for a number of van Gogh paintings.

Dr Jan Hulsker, author of the latest *catalogue raisonné, The New Complete Van Gogh*, and author of: *Van Gogh en zijn Weg; Vincent and Theo Van Gogh: A Dual Biography; Vincent van Gogh, Een leven in brieven; Dagboek van Van Gogh*; and other titles;

Mr Benoit Landais, who has studied van Gogh intensively for over 10 years and is an acknowledged expert on his oeuvre, author of: *Délire à bord; L'Affaire Gachet;* and of many articles in *Connaissance des Art* and in the French and Dutch press and other publications on disputed attributions to Van Gogh;

Mrs Jill Grossvogel, author of: *Claude-Emile Schuffenecker: Catalogue Raisonné;* former curator at the Art Museum of the State University of New York at Binghamton; and Schuffenecker consultant for international galleries, museums, and private collectors;

Mr Frits Bolkestein;
Mr Hanspeter Born, journalist, who has intensively studied the fake van Goghs:
Mr Alain Tarica, art dealer;
Mrs Julia Cave, Producer/Director of the award winning TV documentary *The Fake van Goghs.*

Mr Leighton's reply, entitled *Everyone may look at works of art and participate in the debate,* was published in the same issue. Translated it read:

Dear Mr Jans,

We agree with you that the exhibition 'Van Gogh and Gauguin' (Van Gogh Museum, 9 February–2 June) will offer a unique opportunity to stimulate new research into these painters and their fascinating artistic relationship. There will be more than 120 works from these two artists on show, many for the first time, and we want to make use of this opportunity to gather new insights into what is justifiably called the most important cooperation in 19th century art.

One of the highlights of the exhibition in Amsterdam is the presentation of the three versions of the *Sunflowers*, including the canvas from the collection of the Seiji Togo Memorial Yasuda Kasai Museum of Art in Tokyo. The authenticity of this last work—accepted by a large majority of Van Gogh experts—has received a great deal of attention in the press in the last few years.

Now everybody, both academics and the broader public, can for the very first time form their own opinions by studying the painting at close quarters and by comparing it with the other versions.

During the exhibition in Amsterdam an international symposium will take place from 7–9 March, dedicated entirely to recent research on the life and work of Van Gogh and Gauguin. An international group of speakers will participate and there will be an opportunity for discussion on the *Sunflowers*. Anyone interested is more than welcome to attend the lectures and the discussions.

Although the symposium will throw light on many of the aspects of the art of Van Gogh and Gauguin it will be directed especially to the specialities. We believe that a wide section of the public will wish to learn more about the *Sunflowers*.

Because of this, relevant information about the subject will be available during the exhibition on the dedicated Van Gogh & Gauguin website (www.vangoghmuseum.com, on line from the end of September). Also in the exhibition attention will be given specifically to the *Sunflowers*.

With regard to supporting publications, the catalogue for the exhibition will be available from next week. This contains a considerable quantity of information on the research on Van Gogh and Gauguin, including new material about the still lifes with sunflowers.

The results of the research undertaken by the Van Gogh Museum in co-operation with the Art Institute of Chicago on the *Sunflowers* will be published before the symposium in Amsterdam. As is customary in the scholarly world, many specialists will be consulted and when the work has been completed it will be made available to the outside world. After publication it will be in the public domain and everybody will be free to formulate his or her opinion. We encourage this wholeheartedly.

In conclusion: there will thus be every opportunity for all interested parties to study and admire important works of art, and to participate in live and open discussions. This is by no means a new development, but a continuation of our policy to stimulate and to undertake serious scientific research and to make the results thereof available to a wide public.

John Leighton,
Director, Van Gogh Museum.

The editor of *Het Parool'*, Jhim Lamoree, added an article entitled: *Van Gogh stands behind the 14 Sunflowers:*

The Van Gogh Museum now knows for certain: the *Fourteen Sunflowers in a Vase* in the collection of the Japanese insurance company Yasuda is not a fake but was painted by Vincent van Gogh. Or so claims John Leighton, Director of the Van Gogh Museum, in his response to an open letter from eight disgruntled Van Gogh lovers. They contend that this version of the *Sunflowers* was painted by Claude-Emile Schuffenecker, contemporary of Van Gogh and connoisseur of his paintings.

In a few months time the Museum will publish an investigation into the authenticity of the Japanese Sunflowers in the *Van Gogh Museum Journal*. Next year, it will organise a symposium on 7–9 March in which this matter will be dealt with extensively.

The American Schuffenecker expert Jill Grossvogel asks, however, whether the Van Gogh Museum is the right authority to research the authenticity of the Japanese *Sunflowers*. As we know, the Museum received 37.7 million guilders from Yasuda for the construction of its new wing.

Leighton resolutely denies such an innuendo: "We cannot possibly allow such an accusation to pass. It is not right to say that we are not objective. That is mud-slinging. Moreover, we do this kind of research in co-operation with many other museums."

The eight signatories to the open letter in this newspaper refer to a similar symposium in May 1998 in the London National Gallery which in their opinion was not satisfactorily organised.

Leighton resolutely denies malpractice. He does not want to go into detail at this moment except to say that the research will extensively concern the jute canvas used for the painting, which is supposed to be the reason why the style differs from Vincent's other sunflower paintings from Arles, of which there are five.

Before long everybody will be able to go and see the painting for themselves. The Japanese version of the *Sunflowers* will be included in the exhibition on the co-operation between Van Gogh and Gauguin starting on 9 February in the Van Gogh Museum. In the catalogue an accurate attempt will be made, for the first time, to determine the chronology of the paintings made by Van Gogh and Gauguin in Arles. According to the authors the Yasuda *Sunflowers* was painted in the week of 5–12 December 1888. The painting is even supposed to have acted as something of a lightning rod for Gauguin's mixed feelings towards Van Gogh. A crucial painting therefore, its different style of painting being blamed on the use of coarse jute.

Will the chorus of critics of the research of the Van Gogh Museum be silenced? Jill Grossvogel suggests that research on pigment, paint, and canvas, as carried out by the Van Gogh Museum, rarely produces sufficient proof. "Schuffenecker, a contemporary of Van Gogh, could acquire the same materials; he was a friend of Gauguin; he was familiar with the work of Van Gogh, he had, if you please, one of the *Sunflowers* in front of him for restoration. Moreover he felt he was underestimated and possibly had financial problems—a perfect profile for a faker."

Responds Leighton: "Everyone who knows the work of Schuffenecker can see that he would not have been able to paint the *Sunflowers.*" Grossvogel is convinced of the opposite.

The response from Mr Leighton, Director of the Van Gogh Museum, to the open letter I wrote on behalf of eight independent van Gogh scholars and devotees, as well the statements he made when interviewed by Jhim Lamoree for his article, did not provide a satisfactory answer. Indeed, it confirmed my innermost fears that the Van Gogh Museum was not likely to change its policy of trying to suppress the inconvenient findings of qualified scholars and researchers on the authenticity of the paintings like *Fourteen Sunflowers in a Vase* bought by the Japanese Yasuda Company in 1987.

To recapitulate:
This painting is currently being presented as a Vincent van Gogh masterpiece in the *Van Gogh and Gauguin, The Studio of the South* exhibition at the Chicago Art Institute. At the same exhibition the Amsterdam version of the painting, which many believe to be the original version painted by Vincent in August 1888, is also on show. Both paintings will also be in Amsterdam when the exhibition moves there in February 2002. They will then be joined by the London version painted in January 1889, which many believe to be the only copy of the original *Fourteen Sunflowers* that Vincent van Gogh himself made. The present owners of the Japanese version bought their painting at Christie's in 1987 for a then record sum of some £24.75 million. Four years later the same owners made the generous offer to the Van Gogh Museum of some £15 million for a new wing, which has now been built and is likely to house their painting in 2002.

Ever since the sale serious doubts have arisen about the authenticity of this painting, which is universally accepted to be inferior to the other two; it is the only one of the three not signed; it is the only one never mentioned by Vincent in his letters (according to *The Letters* he only ever painted the original and one copy); it has many features quite untypical of van Gogh's style, some of an unnatural nature which cannot possibly be ascribed to van Gogh; it is a dull painting unlike van Gogh's other work, and so on. According to the original (1987) Christie's sales catalogue it was painted at the end of January 1889; this was later generally agreed to be incorrect, and an article by Dr Dorn in the *Van Gogh Museum Journal 1999* then suggested that it had been painted in February 1889, either in a 3–4 day period early in the month, or in a similar period at the end of it. This was also shown to be impossible as Vincent, in between spells in hospital by order of the police, was working on other projects, like the *Berceuse*.

The catalogue for the Chicago exhibition now suggests that it was painted between 5–12 December 1888. All these varying dates attest to the difficulty of dating a painting of doubtful authenticity. The latest suggestion in the catalogue is so preposterous that I shall not be surprised if a further formal revision is made before very long.

These are just some of the many reasons for doubts about this work, which independent scholars and researchers have declared to be by another hand, possibly that of Claude-Emile Schuffenecker, who had the London version in his hands for some six months to restore it before an exhibition held in Paris in 1901.

Some time after receiving the offer of the generous gift for their new wing, two curators of the Van Gogh Museum were invited to see the painting in Japan. They returned with the verdict that they had found no reason to suggest that the painting was not by van Gogh. The doubts, however, have continued and have increased. The critics have seemingly unassailable reasons for their belief that the painting is not by van Gogh, and the Van Gogh Museum has really done nothing to disprove their arguments: they simply say that they know better, that they can read van Gogh's 'handwriting' in the painting, and that the scholars are amateurs who should not interfere.

But admirers of van Gogh like myself would like, and are entitled to see the dark cloud over his oeuvre removed. This is why, in my open letter to the director of the Van Gogh Museum, I asked for the cogent arguments of independent scholars and researchers to be honestly and publicly debated at the symposium or, alternatively, that at least the critics' arguments be included and analysed in the report the Van Gogh Museum is to publish before the March 2002 symposium.

A symposium on this burning issue a few years ago was totally unproductive and from Leighton's response to my open letter it seems that the March 2002 symposium may again have to cover such a vast amount of material that there may be too little time left for a proper debate on the three versions of *The Sunflowers*. Nor does there seem to be much likelihood that the opinions of independent scholars will be given appropriate space in the Museum's report. Leighton says that their research on *The Sunflowers* will be done in co-operation with the Art Institute of Chicago and that many specialists will be consulted and that only after that research is completed will it be made available to the outside world. There is no indication that these specialists to be consulted by them, for their report, will include any of those who have inconvenient points of view.

I also note that Leighton has already decided, without waiting for the research results, that the painting is definitely by van Gogh and the difference between the Yasuda and the two undoubtedly authentic versions is due to the jute canvas used—though the Chicago catalogue says that the canvas has not yet been examined. Also, as he must well know, most of the arguments of independent researchers have little or nothing to do with the type of canvas used and other paintings by van Gogh on the same type of canvas do not show similar weaknesses.

Despite vague promises, at this moment, the old policy of trying to suppress opposing opinions and unwelcome truths still seems unchanged. One can only hope that the press and public have now been hoodwinked once too often and will all join together in demanding that both sides of the argument will receive equal prominence at the symposium in Amsterdam.

It will be sad if the memory of Vincent van Gogh has to suffer on the altar of the prestige of those who pretend to represent his best interests.

Postscript

The 3-day programme for next March's Symposium has now been published and seems set to fulfill the above predictions. On the afternoon of the second day, in a session on `Authenticity', Roland Dorn will speak for 35 minutes on Van Gogh contributions (second versions) and Louis van Tilborgh for 35 minutes on Van Gogh: problems of authenticity .

As the last item that afternoon, from 16.15-17.00, Louis van Tilborgh and the only 'outside' scholar invited, Benoit Landais, will each have a maximum of 10 minutes to present a statement on the authenticity of the Yasuda. After that just 25 minutes will remain for general discussion of perhaps the most important doubtful attribution to van Gogh today[M]provided, of course, that the programme is not by then running late.

Once again it seems that the playing field will be very uneven; no other external scholar or expert will have any opportunity to put forward at reasonable length the cogent results of years of study; and it looks very much as if the problem, after the briefest discussion, will once again be swept under the carpet.

Appendix A

Vincent van Gogh—biographic summary

1853	30 March. Born in Groot-Zundert, in the south of the Netherlands, eldest son of a priest.
1857	1 May. Birth of his brother Theo.
1861–68	Fragmented school education.
1869	Recommended by his Uncle Vincent, employed by at art-dealers Goupil & Co. in The Hague.
1872	August. Starts a regular correspondence from The Hague with his brother Theo.
!873	January. Theo starts employment by Goupil & Sons in their branch in Brussels.Vincent is transferred to London in June, Theo is transferred to the branch in The Hague in November.
1874	Vincent transferred to Goupil's headquarters in Paris.
1876–79	April. Vincent loses his job at Goupil & Co. After that he teaches in Ramsgate, undertakes religious studies, and works as an evangelist in the Borinage.
1880	Finally chooses an artistic career, and moves to Brussels where he meets the artist Anthon van Rappard. In the meantime Theo has been transferred to Goupil's headquarters in Paris.
1881	Moves in with his parents in Etten and practises drawing. In November spends a few weeks with his cousin, the artist Anton Mauve, in The Hague and does some work in his studio. Returns home but arguments with his parents lead him to move to The Hague around Christmas.
1882	Rents a studio in the Schenkweg in The Hague, has medical problems. Produces first watercolours in June and his first painted studies in oils in August. Owing to financial restraints and lack of materials, his painting in

oils that year only lasted some six weeks. It ended in mid-September. After that he concentrates on drawing.

1883 Still in The Hague, takes up painting studies in oils again in August but again only for a period of some six weeks. On 11 September leaves for the province of Drenthe but after three months decides to go home to his parents, then living in Nuenen, and arrives there on 5 December.

1884 Stays with his parents in Nuenen till May when he rents a studio in the same village. Paints watercolours and studies in oils, mostly of farmers' heads, weavers, and local churches but also still lifes.

1885 Vincent's father dies in Nuenen on 27 March. Vincent completes the final version of the *Potato Eaters* in April. He leaves Nuenen on 24 November for Antwerp, leaving all his work behind, including the studies he painted in The Hague. He never returned to the Netherlands.

1886 Vincent's mother, having been allowed to live in the vicarage for a year after the death of her husband, also leaves Nuenen. While in Antwerp Vincent works hard and takes instruction in drawing and painting at the Academy there, perhaps mainly to take advantage of the free models at the Academy. He leaves Antwerp on 1 March to go and live with his brother Theo in Paris where he meets various artists of that time. Paints amongst other subjects floral still lifes and local scenes.

1887 Organises an exhibition of Japanese prints in Café du Tambourin and meets, amongst others, Toulouse Lautrec, Gauguin, Guillaumin, Pissarro, Seurat, and Emile Bernard.

1888 Tired of the busy atmosphere in Paris, departs for Arles on 19 February, and there paints the famous blossoming orchards and fruit trees, most of his sunflower paintings, portraits and landscapes with wheat fields etc. Rents the Yellow House where Gauguin joins him on 23 October. On 24 December Vincent cuts his left ear and ends up in hospital. Gauguin leaves.

1889 Released from hospital, returns to the Yellow House on 7 January but is readmitted to hospital in February.

On 18 April his brother marries Johanna Bonger in Amsterdam.
On 8 May Vincent obtains voluntary admission to the psychiatric asylum St Paul-de-Mausole in Saint-Rémy-de-Provence, where in July and at the end of December he suffers from renewed mental disturbances.

1890 Birth of Theo's son, Vincent Willem, on 31 January in Paris. Vincent goes back to Arles on 22 February but suffers a further attack which lasts till the end of April. Having recovered, he departs on 16 May, via Paris, where he meets Theo's wife and son, for Auvers-sur-Oise. He arrives there on 20 May. He meets the homoeopathic doctor and hobby painter Dr Paul Gachet, who is to keep an eye on him. Vincent rents a room in the Auberge Ravoux and a period of great productivity follows. Is visited by Theo and Johanna and their baby son in Auvers on 8 June.
On 6 July Vincent travels to Paris to discuss various problems with his brother, returns to Auvers.
On 27 July shoots himself in the chest and dies from his wounds on 29 July, with Theo at his deathbed.

1891 His brother Theo dies, not yet 34 years old, six months after Vincent's death.

Appendix B

The oil paintings of The Hague 1882

The eleven paintings in oil which have surfaced, out of a total believed to be thirty, from the six weeks Vincent painted in oil in 1882 are:

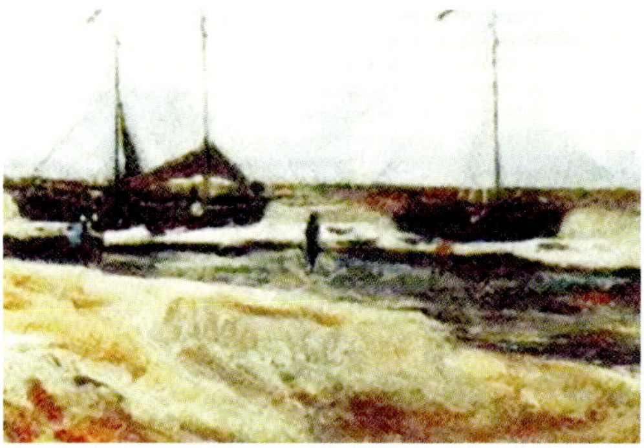

JH173 (F2)
Beach and Sea, paper on panel, 35.5 × 49.5 cm, dated 10-12 August 1882. Present location: private collection.
Provenance: C.Mouwen jr, Breda; then Gallery Oldenzeel in Rotterdam. (Gallery Oldenzeel in Rotterdam was owned previously by Hendrik Vincent van Gogh, one of Vincent van Gogh's uncles.)
The painting appears to show large areas of little impasto, light colours, and only a few very small figures and three fishing boats under a clouded blue sky. It is definitely not a figure study.

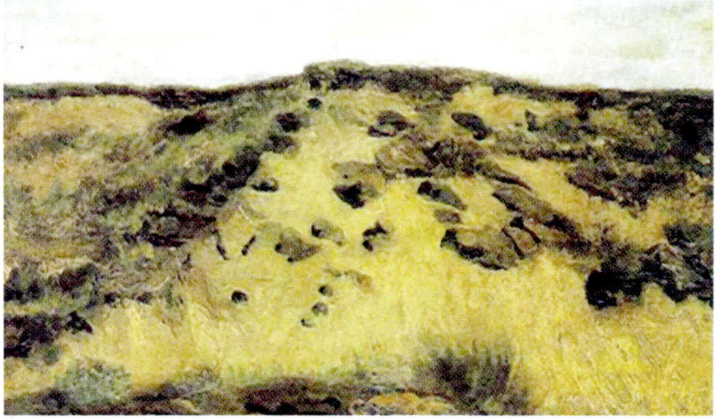

JH176 (F2a)
Dunes,
paper on panel, 36 × 59 cm, dated August 1882.
Present location: private collection in Amsterdam.
Provenance: Oldenzeel Art Gallery, Rotterdam, 1904.
The painting shows a dune under a partially overcast, lightly painted sky, without heavy impasto in the sky, there are no figures and no sun.

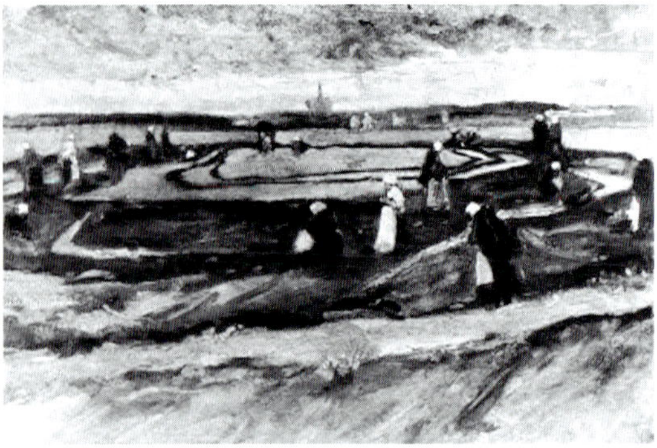

JH178 (F7)
Women mending Nets in the Dunes, paper on panel, 42 × 62.5 cm, dated 20 August 1882.
Present location: not known.
Provenance: C. Mouwen jr, Breda; Oldenzeel Art Gallery, Rotterdam.
The painting shows some twenty small figures mending nets in a wide landscape under a totally overcast sky, with no sun. This cannot be called a figure study and the weather and light conditionsare totally different from those pertaining to *Two Diggers in the Afternoon Sun.*

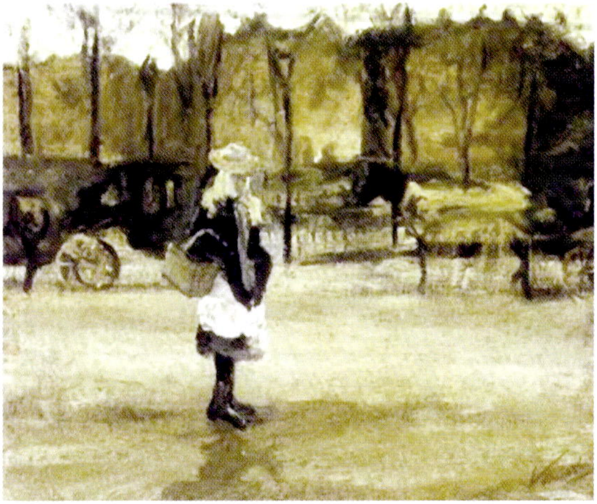

JH179 (F13)
A Girl in the Street, Two Coaches in the Background, canvas on panel, 42 × 53 cm, dated second half of August 1882.
Present location: collection of Mrs L. Jägli-Hahnloser, Winterthur, Switzerland.
Provenance: A. Hahnloser, Winterthur, who is said to have bought this painting before 1914 from an unknown Dutch miller.
The painting shows a girl standing in a street with two horse-drawn carriages and trees in the background.
According to Drs Martha Op de Coul, Head of the Department of 19th Century Art at the Netherlands Institute for Art History in The Hague, this painting is not by Vincent van Gogh. Some other van Gogh experts and scholars are in agreement with her on this. Notwithstanding these opinions Dr. Roland Dorn included it in the 1996 exhibition *Van Gogh und die Haager Schule*, in Vienna and as far as I know he has not been publicly criticised for this.
This painting obviously offers no scope for comparison with *The Diggers*.

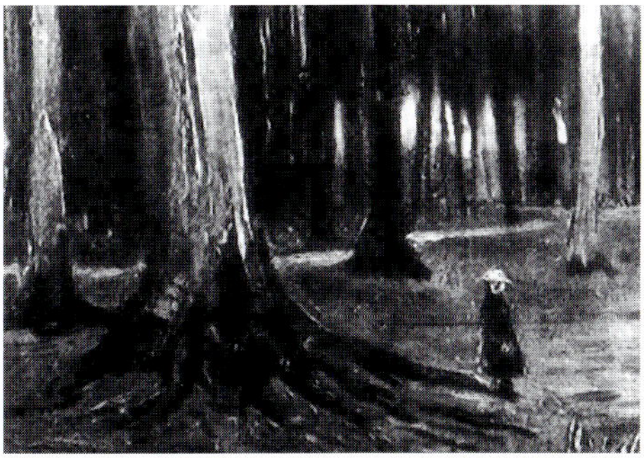

JH180 (F8a)
A Girl in a Wood, paper on panel, 35×47 cm, dated second half August 1882.
Present location: private collection.
Provenance: C. Mouwen jr, Breda; Mouwen put it in a sale in Amsterdam (F. Muller) in 1904 where it was not sold; Oldenzeel Art Gallery, Rotterdam.
The painting shows a little girl standing, a little forlorn, in a wood. Very little sky is visible through the trees. It has not been painted in heavy impasto.

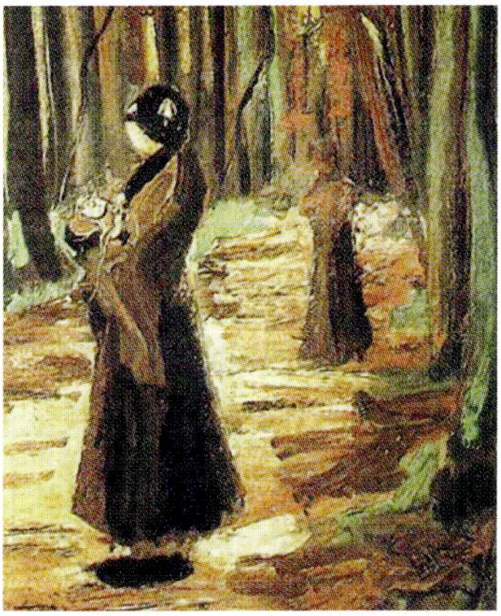

JH181 (F1665)
Two Women in a Wood, paper on panel, 31 × 24.5 cm, dated second half August 1882.
Present location: private collection, Paris.
Provenance: H.P. Bremmer, The Hague.
A small painting. The entire background is filled with trees, all penetrating the top of the painting.

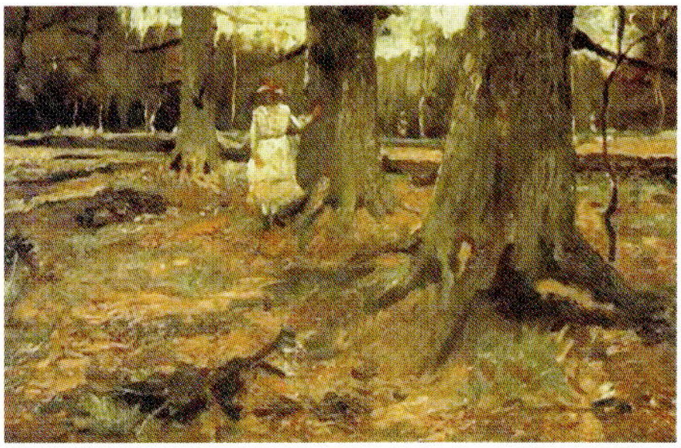

JH182 (F8)
A Girl in a Wood, canvas, 39 × 59 cm, dated second half 1882.
Present location: Collection Rijksmuseum Kröller-Müller, Otterlo.
Provenance: L.C. Enthoven, Voorburg; Enthoven sold it at auction in Amsterdam (F. Muller) in 1920.
The painting shows a girl in white, leaning her left hand on the lower part of the middle one of three tree trunks, which dominate the painting. The entire background is filled with trees some of which do not reach the top of the painting where a small area of a heavily clouded sky can be seen with a little blue. There is also a sketch of the same subject in a letter.

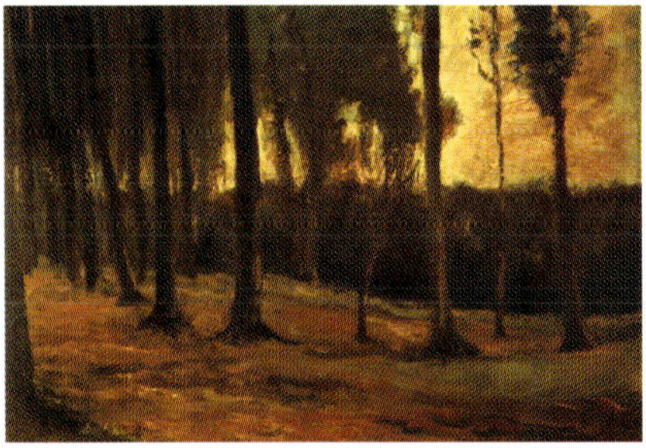

JH184 (F192)
Edge of a Wood, canvas on panel, 34.5 × 45 cm, dated September 1882.
Present locantion: collection Rijksmuseum Kröller-Müller, Otterlo.
Provenance: C. Mouwen jr, Breda; Mouwen put this painting in a sale in Amsterdam (F. Muller) in 1904 where it was not sold; Oldenzeel Art Gallery, Rotterdam; Oldenzeel sold it in a sale (Biesing) in The Hague in 1909; Rijksmuseum Kröller-Müller, Otterlo.
This is not a very significant painting. It shows a large number of trees penetrating the top of the painting, with a further distant wooded area, on a lower plane, for a large part with a dull sky above, spanning the breadth of the painting in the background. It has been painted with little impasto, not unlike *The Diggers*.

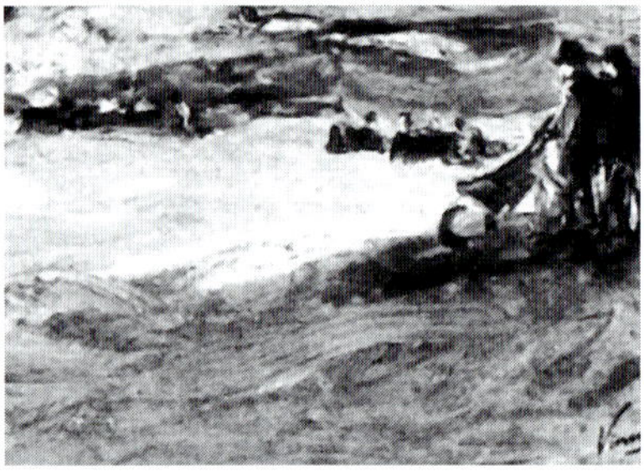

JH186 (F3)
Dunes with Figures, canvas on panel, 24 × 32 cm, dated late August 1882.
Present location: collection H.R. Hahnloser, Bern.
Provenance: A. Hahnloser who is supposed to have bought it from an unknown Dutch miller before 1914.
The figures in this small painting are very small. It cannot be called a figure study. The signature on the bottom right of the painting shows great similarity to the signature in the same position on JH179, which has an identical provenance.

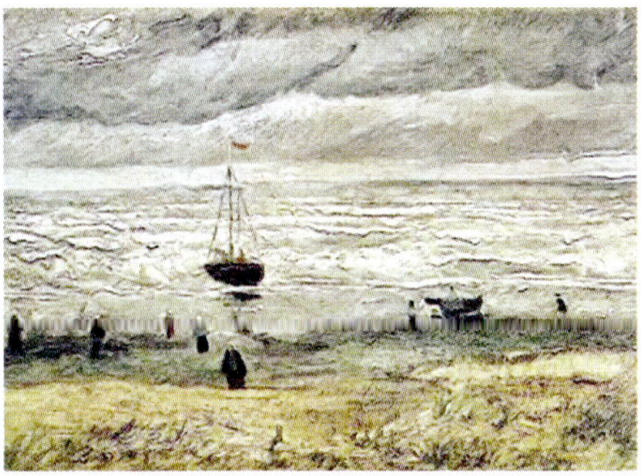

JH187 (F4)
Beach with Figures and Sea with a Ship, paper on canvas, 34.5 × 51 cm, dated late August 1882.
Present location: collection Vincent van Gogh Museum, Amsterdam.
Provenance: Oldenzeel Art Gallery, Rotterdam, 1903.
In certain areas this painting shows a generally heavier impasto than the others from this period. The ten or so figures in it are very small and this painting cannot be called a figure study.

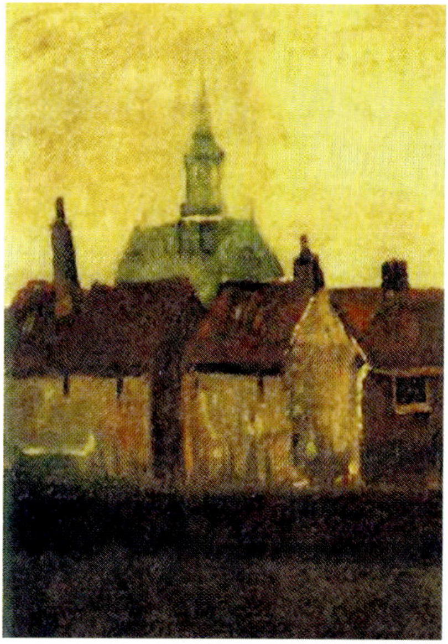

JH190 (F204)
The New Church and Old Houses in The Hague, canvas on cardboard, 35 × 25 cm, dated August 1882.
Present location: unknown.
Provenance: Oldenzeel Art gallery, Rotterdam; acquired by Jan Smit, Kinderdijk, Netherlands in 1905, in a sale in Amsterdam (Mak van Waay) 10.2.1919; L.J. Smit, Kinderdijk; sale New York (Parke-Bernet) 20.11.1968 (present owner unknown).

These eleven paintings comprise all the known paintings attributed to Vincent van Gogh in 1882 in The Hague, in which year he is believed to have painted at least thirty studies in oils.

It is believed that *The Diggers* was painted in the same year, around the end of August/first half of September.

Appendix C

The oil paintings of The Hague 1883

The fourteen paintings attributed to Vincent's 1883 output in The Hague, out of a total, believed to have been, in excess of forty, are:

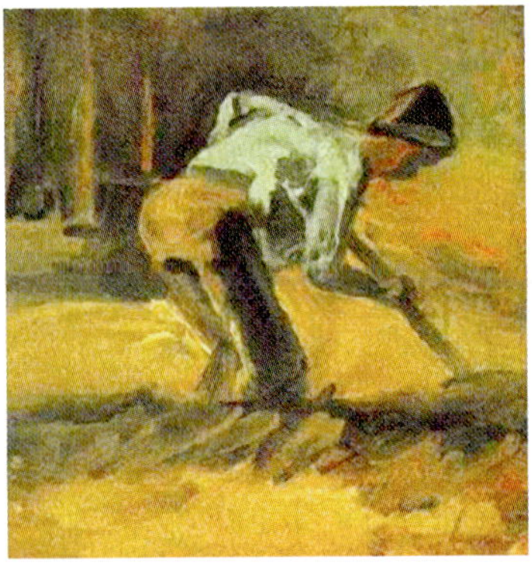

JH185 (F12)
Man stooping with a Stick or Spade, paper on panel, 31 × 29.5 cm, dated originally August 1882, but reassigned to 1883.
Present location: Private collection U.K.
Provenance: Oldenzeel Art gallery, Rotterdam, incomplete reference which could not be checked. This painting is supposed to have changed hands at least twelve times, to have been auctioned by amongst others Sotheby's in 1957 and in Paris in 1960. The painting received a "?" from Dr Hulsker in his: *The Complete van Gogh* of 1996. The painting shows what the title says. It is a study of a man, stooping forward as if digging. It is painted in a very fluid manner with a simple palette.

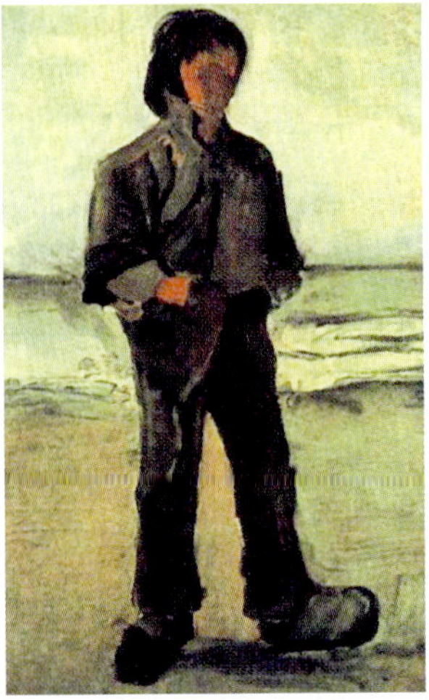

JH188 (F5)
Fisherman on the Beach,
canvas on panel, 51 × 33.5 cm, dated originally 1882 but reassigned to 1883.
Present location: Collection Rijksmuseum Kröller-Müller in Otterlo.
Provenance: Oldenzeel Art gallery, Rotterdam 1903; H.P Bremmer until 1920; then Rijksmuseum Kröller-Müller.

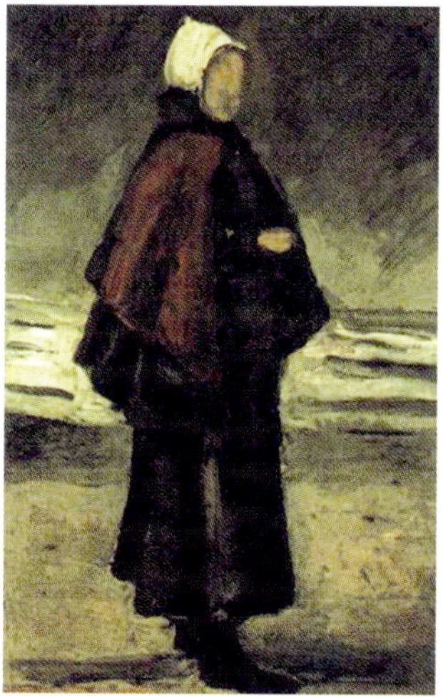

JH189 (F6)
Scheveningen Woman,
canvas on panel, 52 × 34 cm, dated originally 1882 but reassigned to 1883.
Present location: Rijksmuseum Kröller-Müller in Otterlo.
Provenance: Oldenzeel Art gallery, Rotterdam 1903; H.P. Bremmer until 1920; then Rijksmuseum Kröller-Müller.

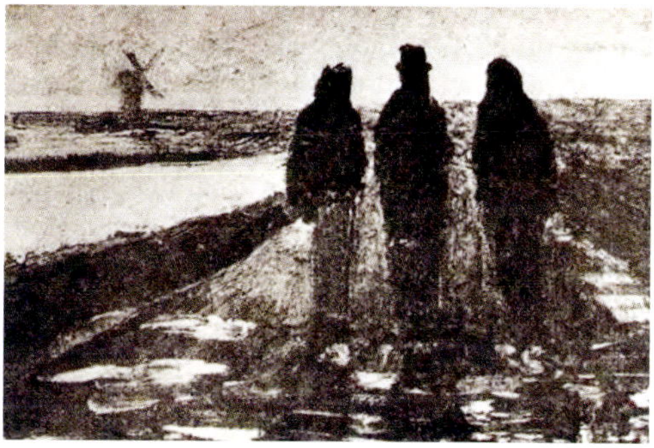

JH383 (F1666)
Three Figures near a Canal with Windmill, medium not known, size not known, dated August 1883.
Present location: not known.
Provenance: not known.

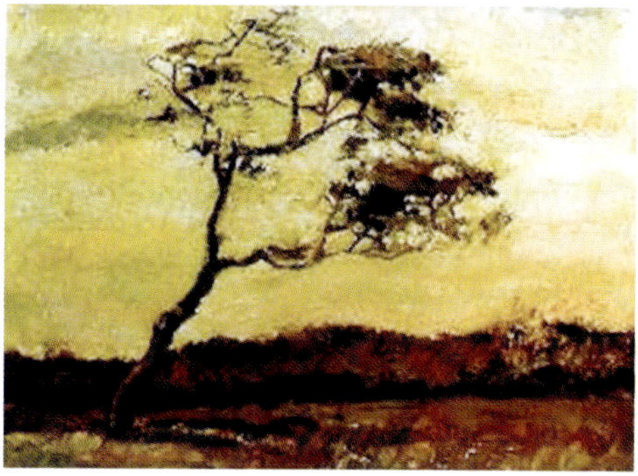

JH 384(F10)
A Windswept Tree, 35 × 47 cm, dated August–September 1883.
Present location: not known.
Provenance: Oldenzeel Art Gallery, Rotterdam, exhibited in Rotterdam in 1903; L.C. Enthoven; sale in Amsterdam (F. Muller) 18 May 1920; Buffa Art Gallery, Amsterdam; J. de Vos jr, Bussum; sale in Amsterdam (F. Muller) 26 January 1944; Neupert Art Gallery, Zürich (before 1964).

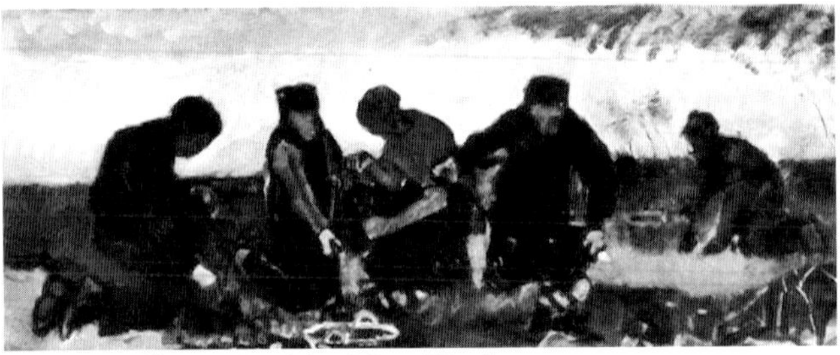

JH385 (F9)
Potato Grubbers, FivePersons, 39.5 × 94.5 cm, dated August 1883, medium not known. Present location: collection of Mr & Mrs. Julian J. Raskin, New York.
Provenance: exhibited Rotterdam 1903; J. Hidde Nijland The Hague; sale at The Hague (Pulchri Studio) October 1937; Nieuwenhuizen Segaar Art Gallery, The Hague; Miss T.B.van Baaren, Utrecht; van Wisselingh Art Gallery, Amsterdam; thence present owners 1964.

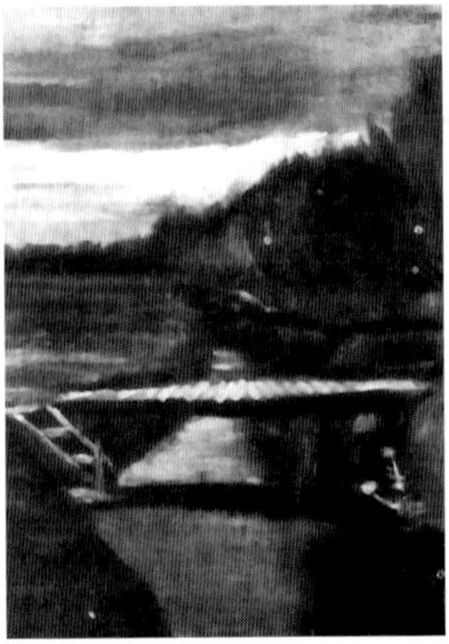

JH386 (F189)
D*itch with Little Bridge*,
canvas on panel, 46 × 34 cm, dated August 1883.
Present location: not known.
Provenance: C. Mouwen jr, Breda; sale in Amsterdam (F.Muller) 3 May 1904; Oldenzeel Art Gallery, Rotterdam; H.J. Nieboer, Rotterdam 1905; thence via Nassau Galleries, Andover, Massachusetts; Sotheby's sale in London 27 March 1957; and later Paris (Stiebel Gallery) to a sale in New York (Parke-Bernet) 15 April 1959; Chagrin Falls, Ohio, Mrs Gordon Stouffer.

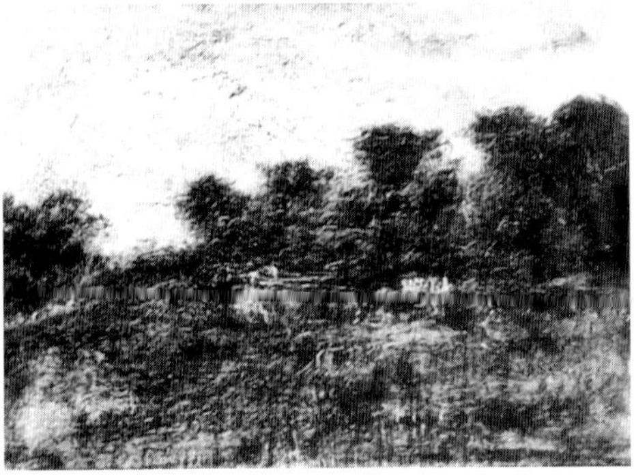

JH387 (F15)
Cows in the Meadow, canvas on panel, 31.5 × 44 cm,
dated August 1883?
Present location: not known.
Provenance: Oldenzeel Art Gallery, Rotterdam 1904;
H. Sijthoff, Wassenaar; sale at Sotheby's, London, 4 December 1968; Brook Street Galleries, London; New York Hirschl & Adler Galleries Inc. 1970.

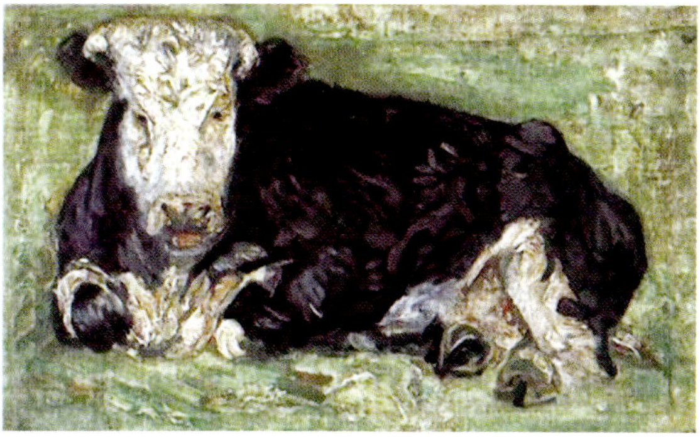

JH388 (F1b)
Cow lying down,
30 × 50 cm, dated August 1883?
Present location: not known.
Provenance: Oldenzeel Art Gallery, Rotterdam; sale Rotterdam 30 April 1912; The Hague, A. Brandsma (1912).

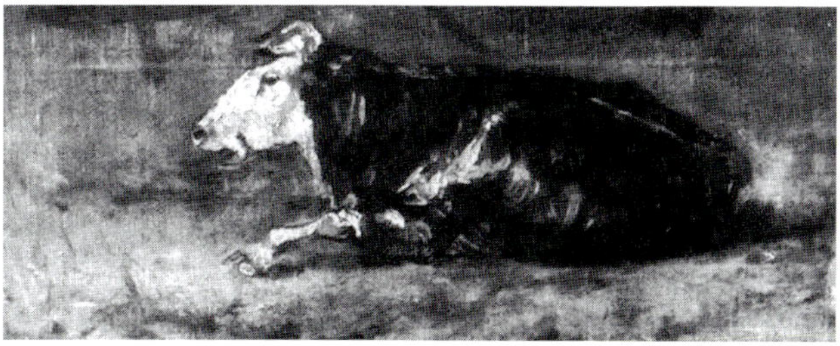

JH389 (F1c)
Cow lying down,
19 × 47.5 cm, dated August 1883?
Present location: not known.
Provenance: Ed van Biema, according to him formerly in collection of C. Mouwen jr, Breda and M. Janssen, Breda; F.P Hirschel, Amsterdam; Private Collection; sale in New York (Parke-Bernet) 11 November 1959; present owner unknown.

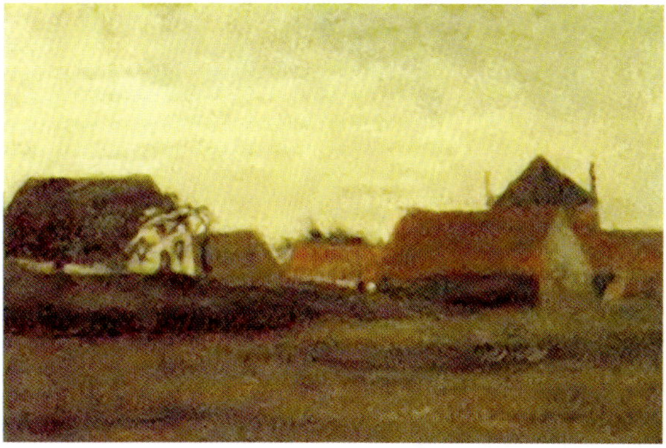

JH391 (F16)
Farm in Loosduinen near The Hague,
33 × 50 cm, canvas on panel, dated c. 4 September 1883.
Present location: collection Centraal Museum, Utrecht, (on loan from Museum van Baaren Foundation).
Provenance: exhibited 1904 in Rotterdam; 1956 in Amsterdam; H.P. Bremmer, The Hague; Nieuwenhuizen Segaar Art Gallery, The Hague 1955; L.H. van Baaren, Utrecht, Museum van Baaren, acquired 1956.

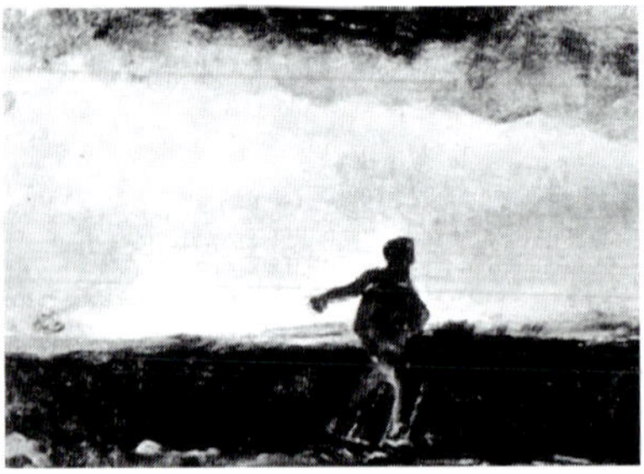

JH392 (F11)
The Sower,
19 × 27.5 cm, panel, dated September 1883?
Present location: not known.
Provenance: L.C. Enthoven, Voorburg; Sale in Amsterdam (F. Muller) 18 May 1920; J.E. Goldschmidt, Amsterdam; sale in Amsterdam (Mak van Waay) 1 May 1923; E. Alexander, Paris.

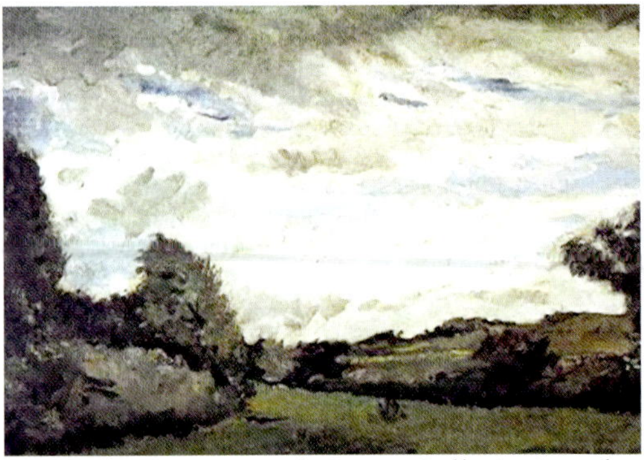

JH393 (F15a)
Landscape with Dunes,
panel, 33.5 × 48.5 cm,
dated September 1883?
Present location: not known.
Provenance: Oldenzeel Art Gallery, Rotterdam 1904; H. Sijthoff Wassenaar; sale The Hague (van Marle en Bignell) 21 May 1963; Private collection in the Netherlands; sale in London (Sotheby's) 4 December 1968; Brook Street Galleries London; New York, Hirschl & Adler Galleries 1970.

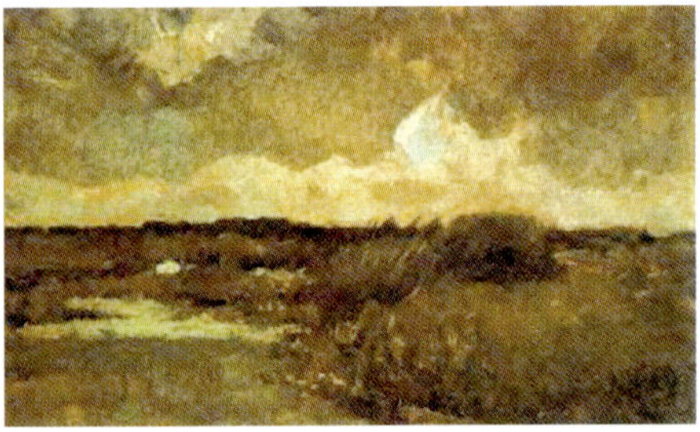

JH394
Marsh,
27 × 45.5 cm, medium not known,
dated September 1883.
Present location: not known.
Provenance: not known.

As can be seen from the above, among the paintings of the 1883 Hague period, little is available for study. None of these paintings really offers conclusive or substantive comparison material for *Two Diggers in the Afternoon Sun*. There is no painting in this period with comparable light or subject matter. One can find areas of comparable brush stroke and impasto. Whatever comparison material is available from this period can possibly be of positive but not of negative significance.

Appendix D

The oil paintings of Drenthe 1883

The seven known paintings from the Drenthe period, September to December 1883, are:

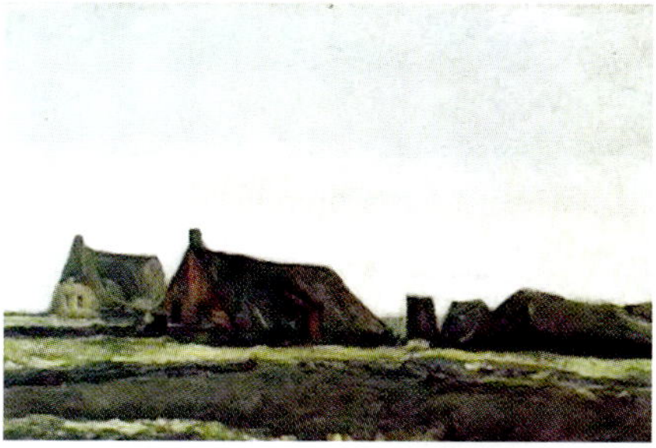

JH395 (F17)
Farms,
36 × 55.5 cm, canvas on cardboard, dated September–October 1883.
Present location: Vincent van Gogh Foundation.
Provenance: Johanna van Gogh Bonger; Vincent Willem van Gogh, Laren.

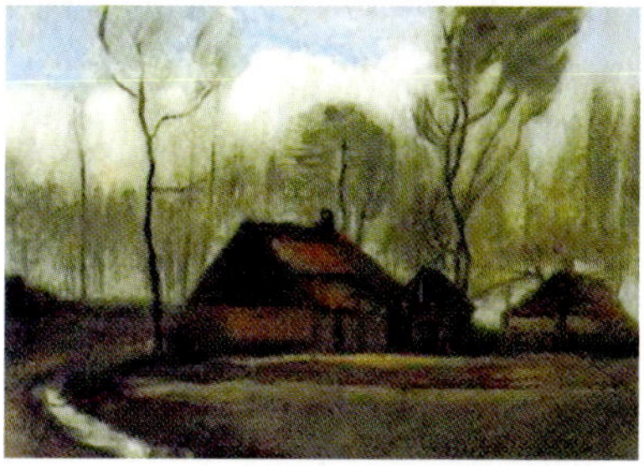

JH397 (F18)
Farms between Trees, 29 × 39 cm, canvas on panel, dated October 1883.
Present location: Museum Jana Pawla II, Warsaw.
Provenance: C. Mouwen jr, Breda; sale Amsterdam (F. Muller) 3 May 1904, not sold; Oldenzeel Art Gallery, Rotterdam.

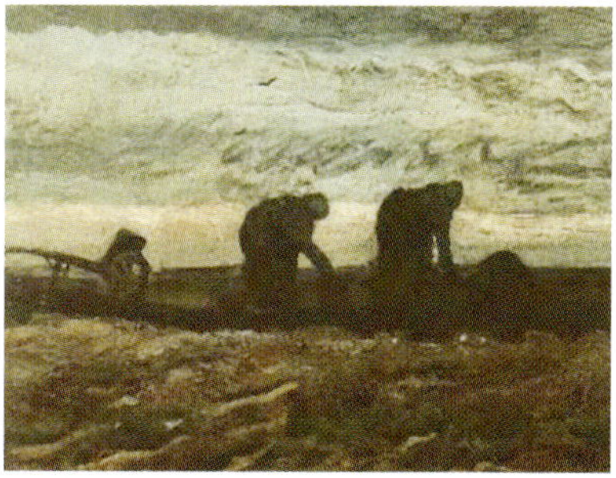

JH409 (F19)
Two Women working in the Peat, canvas, 27 × 35.5 cm, dated 6–7 October 1883.
Present location: Van Gogh Museum, Amsterdam.
Provenance: Mrs. Johanna van Gogh-Bonger, Amsterdam; V.W. van Gogh, Laren; Vincent van Gogh Foundation, Amsterdam.
This painting evokes feelings similar to those evoked by *Two Diggers*, which is thought to be earlier. Two working or bending figures, set mainly above the horizon, face the same direction in relation to the light source.

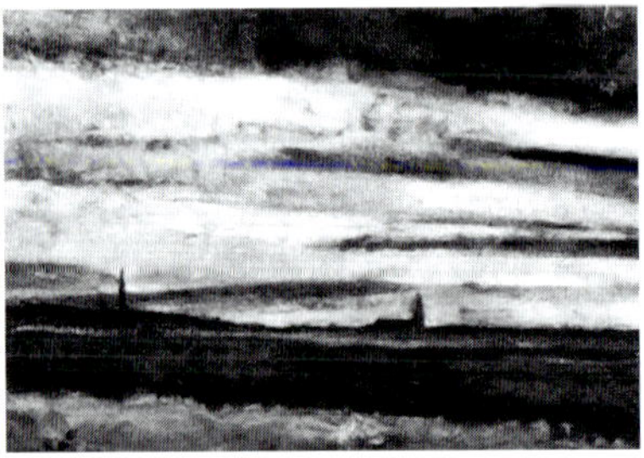

JH413 (F188)
Landscape at Nightfall, cardboard on panel, 35.5 × 52 cm, dated October 1883.
Present location: not known.
Provenance: Oldenzeel Art Gallery, Rotterdam, 1903.

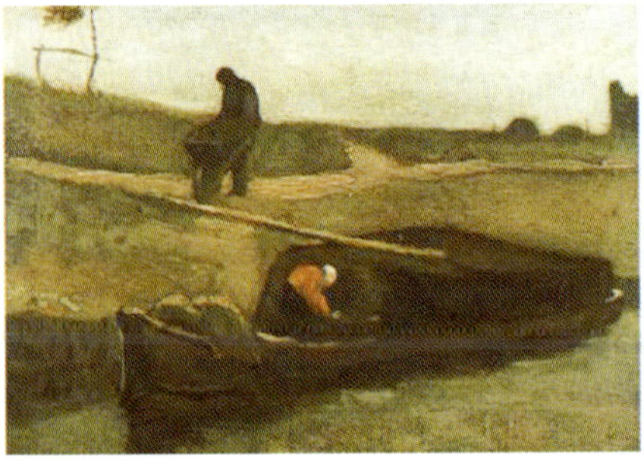

JH415 (F21)
Peat Boat with two Figures, 37 × 55.5 cm, canvas on panel, c. 22 October 1883.
Present location: Assen Museum.
Provenance: Oldenzeel Art Gallery, Rotterdam, 1903; J. van Hoey Smith, Rotterdam; Mrs J. van Hoey Smith-van Stolk, Rockanje (1965); R.W. van Hoey Smith, Rockanje (1968); Assen Museum.

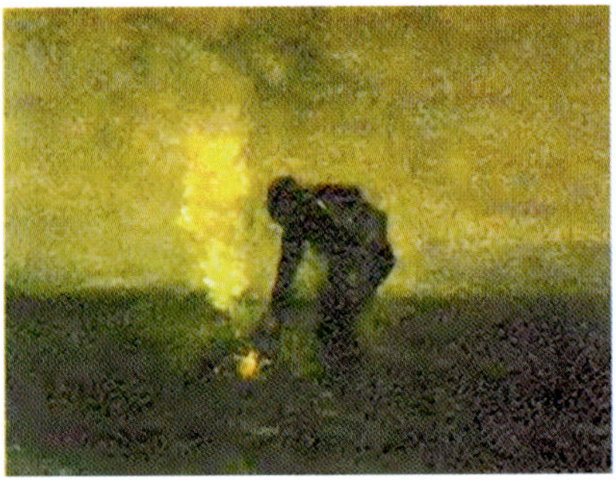

JH417 (F20)
Peasant Burning Weeds,
panel, 30.5 × 39.5 cm, dated c. 22 October 1883.
Present location: not known.
Provenance: C. Mouwen jr, Breda; sale Amsterdam (F. Muller) 3 May 1904; Herman Gorter; Bussum 1905; via various; Tj. Bendien, acquired 1941, Almelo.

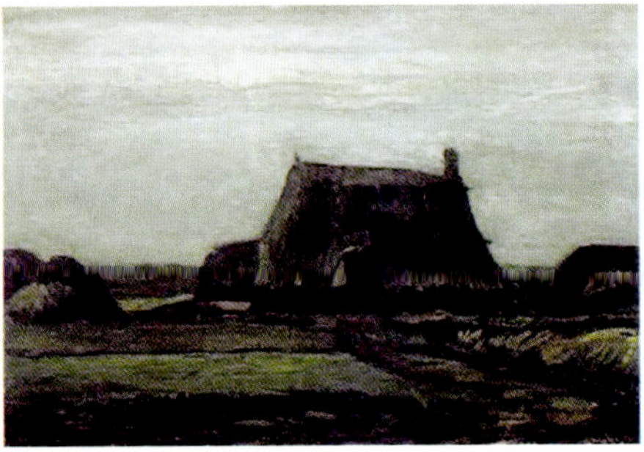

JH421 (F22)
Little Farmhouse with Piles of Peat
canvas on cardboard, 37.5 × 55.5 cm, dated November 1883.
Present location: Van Gogh Museum.
Provenance: Mrs Johanna van Gogh-Bonger, Amsterdam; V.W. van Gogh, Laren; Vincent van Gogh Foundation.

Appendix E

The Benoit Landais report

Introduction

Towards the end of 1997, Mr Bouwe Jans showed me his painting of *Two Diggers*. His question was whether the painting could possibly be by Vincent. At first glance this possibility looked very promising. I immediately saw many of Vincent's characteristics and soon told Bouwe Jans that I was almost certain that the painting was indeed by Vincent, a very early painting.

During the discussions that followed I gave my main arguments: subject matter, depth of field, colours, composition, style of drawing, full-face sun, simplicity, general balance, perspective; everything confirmed my first impression.

However, I had to mention two possible obstacles in the drawing. The first one was the undulating yellow line on the back of the digger on the left, which seemed a bit too loose. The second was the unclear connection between the hand and the handle of the shaft of the spade of the digger in the foreground.

I no longer see these two observations as obstacles. The first one I dismissed because Vincent has occasionally actually contained a surface of colour by using a line following the contour of another surface. Furthermore it appears to have been his method in this case, because one finds the same sort of treatment in the two 'windows' of light (between the diggers and under the arm of the first digger), though without concern about following the contour.

The second of the two observations above I now also reject as an obstacle after seeing an infra-red photograph that shows the preliminary sketch, which clearly reveals that the handle of the spade was not yet drawn before it was painted, and after reading that Vincent said he was sometimes lost when the paint covered up his original sketch.

It is very probable that the choice of colours was influenced by the prevailing circumstances at the time of execution of the painting and it does not seem reasonable to me to maintain any objections, however small, in that respect either.

I have since analysed the information I could find in the *Letters* and in the catalogues of the oeuvre to verify the relevance of my arguments.

What I have found has fully confirmed my initial feeling: all these clues build to a network of precise elements, all leading to the same conclusion, all revealing in an increasingly forceful way the features of Vincent's specialities, the latter distinguishing themselves from more common approaches.

Over and above the documentary evidence, what one can see in the painting only brought more and more grist to the mill; a hundred relevant elements lead to certainty: what could be seen on the canvas was also to be read in the letters—only Vincent could have painted these two diggers.

Throughout my research, I tried to look for identifiable stylistic signs in attributed paintings of the same period. Because these are always difficult to demonstrate, I have only included them in this report in a general manner. On the other hand, I have quoted almost all extracts from Vincent's letters between April 1882 and the end of 1882, which describe his preoccupation with matters corresponding to what I read and see in the painting.

The subject matter

In the middle of a Millet-like bare landscape, two figures are placed in stable balance, seen from behind, digging under a full-face sun.

Everything is there. Vincent's Holy Trinity is there: God—Millet, God—labour, God—sun. Also to be found are his well-known roughness, the vitality inherited from the great draughtsmen, and *the prosaic frugality and intended simplicity* taken from English draughtsmen. (Even though the sources of inspiration are numerous, one of the main sources, if not *the* main one for Vincent as a beginner is Millet, who is mentioned very many times in the *Letters* and celebrated in various ways.)

Vincent's concerns are identical to those of Millet. Vincent accurately summarises the link between: "*. . . the end result of several studies, that is, a general type emerging out of many individuals. That is the Art of Arts, this is the point where Art can transcend nature . . . for instance, there is greater soul in a Sower by Millet than in a common Sower lost in the middle of a field*" (LT 257, to Theo, 3 Jan 1883).

Vincent starts painting in 1882. He wants to represent *the character*, the different *types* of labourers and, above all, *diggers*. He advocates a labour-glorifying ideology (at the same time, in order to spurn contempt for workers and as a follower of the Calvinistic concept of exemplary effort leading to redemption) and rejects easy emotions ("*I do not expect my characters and landscapes to express a kind of sentimental melancholy*").

He rejects the traditional way of representing labour by featuring figures at rest. "*You know that resting figures, like the ones that are very, very often drawn, are very pretty. They are more often drawn than figures at work. And it is tempting to draw resting figures, because it is very difficult to express action, and in the eye of many the effect is 'more pleasant' than something else*" (LT 251, to Theo, c. 3/5 Dec 1882).The suppression of potentially distracting anecdotal elements leads him to conceal faces—which is consistent with the concern of "*touching up to make figures and landscapes more or less unrecognisable*" (LT 226, to Theo, 19 Aug 1882)—and even profiles.

In order to represent *types of characters,* and not to depict specific characters who could be identified, Vincent begins, in The Hague in 1882, to represent figures in profile or from behind. In order to cover different types at the same time, he gives a round form to one head and a more angular one to the other, thus showing his skill. This also explains the clever concealment of the second digger and by doing that he kills two birds with one stone: the attention one would pay to the face of the second digger is diverted to the powerful arm of the first digger which conceals it.

This suggests movement right in the centre of the composition. *Man* is still the main subject; if the spades evoke labour here, they do so without insistence and are placed in the middle ground.

The landscape, a bare land

The landscape has by no means been neglected. Though basic, it conveys a feeling of depth of field, despite the apparent uniformity of the foreground. One understands that the painter's preoccupation is not exclusively with the figure, but equally with the landscape. Rather, it is precisely the reconciliation between these two which preoccupies Vincent in 1882. His preference is for the figure but his concern and effort to combine figure and landscape, to place figures into the landscape or to create a landscape-background for his figures, is a permanent preoccupation (as we shall soon see, for instance in his touching up of his lithographs). So much so, that soon landscapes are regarded as "*backgrounds*", "*on which the tone of the figure and of the entire effect . . . depends.*"

The lack of embellishment which characterises the way the field has been dealt with reminds us of Vincent's interest in barren subjects, especially those which are forbidding and inexpressive; for instance a piece of ploughed land (which we shall come across later on), a field, a river bank, a dune—trying his best to render that which he is able to feel and see.

The authenticity

It is drudgery to try and 'breathe air' into clods of earth or into a *body clinch* with nature; yet this corresponds to Vincent's leanings, to the 'peasant from Brabant' side of his personality, to his austere poetry, to his love for the soil, to which he feels united *by a thousand bonds,* which will be found in metaphors all through his life until he writes in the penultimate letter to Theo, *"mais ma vie à moi aussi est attaquée à la racine même . . ."* ["but my existence itself is threatened at its very root"]. His quest for truth and authenticity via the representation of things he actually experiences, will become one of the hallmarks of his work.

The harshness

The intended harshness and ruggedness are clearly expressed in the painting. The first break in the monotony of the field is hardly sketched out and is purposely relegated to the line of horizon.

A subtly constructed horizon, created by the discontinuity of the dark element, which does not extend to both edges of the painting, and by the little patches of clear sky held under the first line of clouds, characteristic of sea climates. The harsh setting helps to accentuate the importance of the figures and gives them the 'presence' (which the drawings by Mesdag, which Vincent saw, lacked).

In order to prevent the landscape from interfering, Vincent took great care to have all the planes independent of each other, by making sure that there was continuity in the second plane (the colours on the right side of *The Diggers* are also found between them and to their left).

What Vincent rejects is clear enough in the painting. Because he refuses any kind of *slickness/polish* or *agreeable aspect*, he even goes so far as not to represent the gesture of *The Diggers* in any *elegant* way.

This same rejection of *elegance* which he applied in the painting is also observable in his other choices: he prefers a rough carpenter's pencil, and rejects refined language. It also leads him towards a nature which he sees as *severe, rough, austere*, but fair. He is seeking the *darker sentiments* and he wishes to express *prosaic frugality* and *simplicity;* he favours robustness and *virile* solidity in his brush strokes; and all this combines to form the base for his rigorous expressionism.

In view of the concern to represent workers, the usual bareness in the landscape, the quest for genuineness, the harshness, one could probably follow this direction a bit further; one can recognise the stamp of Calvinism in this committed art. *"Art, as we know, is looked down upon with distrust. There are reasons for this recession: not only does art have a bad influence on weak people, but it is also gratuitous, and it has no social usefulness. This is an automatic point of view that can easily prove disastrous for every artist, because it forces them to make a committed or dogmatic work of art!"*, says Janine Garrison in *L'Homme Protestant*.

One could object by saying that Holland was a Calvinist country at the time, and that this point does not really link the *Two Diggers* with Vincent.

True, but firstly the painter comes from Brabant and the painting from Breda—a town of this province where Catholics outnumber any other religion; and secondly, Vincent's Calvinistic upbringing as son, grandson, and nephew of pastors, and then as an evangelist and a student in theology, was particularly strong. And the latter led him towards pictorial 'dogmatism' to start with, towards a value-advertising form of art—the values that are to be found in his writings. In some ways, he has discarded this *horrible religion*, ever since he saw the *dessous des cartes* [ever since he saw through it], and he is now free. But deep inside him, he has kept most of the values of *the religion that formed him,* a religion which 'exalts daily labour, no matter how humble it is'.

Outline first, then filling in

Even though Vincent represents labour, he does not absolutely idealise it. The digger raises his arm, but not too much, and the poses are by no means exaggerated. As a thinker, he knows that people like to find fault. He is also aware that his views do not represent the mainstream and also that he cannot fall back on earlier work for seeking to validate their pertinence.

In the summer of 1882, he is first and foremost a beginner trying to define his own goals, wanting to paint things that have *hardly been painted by anyone so far*. He joins the modern painters: *"Here is what I wanted to say when I stressed the difference between older art and modern art: it may very well be that modern artists are much more thinkers"* (LT 218, to Theo, 21 July 1882).

He longs to paint coherent subjects. He does not seek the finish. He makes studies rather than finished works. "*It seems to me that working for the sake of selling is not the right direction, but a way of making 'fools' of art lovers*" (LT 221, to Theo, c. 1 August 1882).

He comes to painting after having drawn a great deal, in this rich and varied manner which gives him satisfaction.

One of the most forceful arguments demonstrating the authenticity of the painting is given by the photograph under infra-red light (see next page). This shows very clearly that the figures were drawn before they were coloured in.

One is tempted to conclude that the painting is the picture of an artist still working as a beginner: *'the other way round'*. It will dawn on Vincent the following year, when he writes with a bit of hindsight:

Letter to Theo 308, c. 2 August 1883

Recently a great worry has fallen off my shoulders. Last year I repeatedly tried to paint figure studies but I became desperate over the way they turned out. I have started again now and I don't have any problems with the execution now because I draw with much greater ease than last year. At that time I often got confused if I lost the drawn sketch whilst painting.

The first two figures I painted this year I did just like I tried last year—first drawing and then filling in the outline. This is what I would like to call the dry method. The other method is that one actually does the drawing last and starts by first searching out the tones without worrying too much about the drawing, except to get the tones as near as possible in their correct place and slowly making the form and the subdivision of the colours more precise. The result is then a figure as if surrounded by space and somewhat softer. You will see the difference if you see the first two I have now made, if they remain in their present state.

The drawing and the line

But for the time being he is still learning on his own: "*What one learns on one's own may take a little longer, but it is imprinted more deeply*" (LT 232, to Theo, 18 September 1882).

The vigorous execution of the placing of the figures demonstrates Vincent's ability as a draughtsman (the positions are right; in other words, there is no error in the drawing—even if the second figure seems to be depicted in an awkward position).

One should be careful in judging a position to be awkward, for sometimes certain positions are rejected as wrong only because they are different from the usual way of representing them, which is not always what is seen in reality, but it echoes Vincent's writing very faithfully: look for the *line*; equip oneself with the *meaning of the contour* of a preliminary drawing, which is for him the basis of everything, the actual *backbone* of the whole composition.

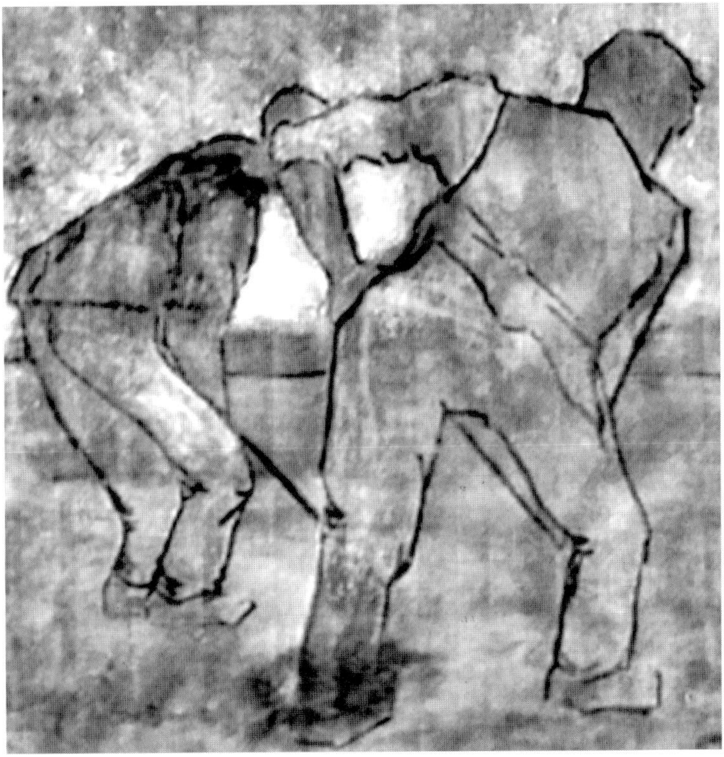

IRR/DIP Image from the Eastaugh report (page 37)

To adapt the drawn lines to the painting will subsequently present him with a problem: these lines are too wide because of the brushes he uses. He will look for more appropriate tools: *"Next time I receive money from you, I'll buy some marten brushes; they are real drawing brushes—for drawing a hand or a profile in colour"* (LT 226 to Theo, 19 August 1882).

Where did he get the idea of marten brushes from? Quite simply, from a lesson on perspective he read in March: 'We recommend red marten brushes as excellent.'

Painting in oils

It became more and more pressing to actually paint in oils. Theo visits him in August 1882 and, after seeing Vincent's investigation of colour in his watercolours, gives him the means to equip himself. He then starts painting, trying to find shades and hues both in oil and watercolours.

The perspective

In March 1882, Vincent reads Cassagne's guide to drawing. He will find a great many pieces of advice enabling him to make rapid progress. The main problem being of course the very question he keeps thinking about, which is the connection and relation between proportions.

In his book, Cassagne explains, with a drawing of skittles, how to situate the horizon, and what is the *'field of perspective—which consists of the space between foreground and the horizon (the line of intersection between the horizontal space and the vertical space, in which the objects in the paintings are placed)'.* Cassagne also explains how to draw and use receding lines and how these meet.

It is interesting to see how the *Two Diggers* is a mechanical application of Cassagne's principles, especially where the receding lines are concerned which are led out of the picture to meet on the horizon.

In fact, one can draw two lines the first one joining the tops of the heads of the diggers, and the second one through the centre of their basis of support and these two meet on the horizon.

One should add to this that Vincent stresses the importance of studying *anatomy and perspective.*

Apart from the effect of perspective borrowed from Cassagne, Vincent adds another very geometrical element to the composition in *The Diggers*: the diamond-shaped area (the lozenge) of light, which includes practically all the yellow coming from the sun and the lighter areas on the ground, the upper vertex, the summit, of this lozenge being the sun.

Two other vertexes of this *lozenge of light* lie on the line of the horizon and the fourth corner is at the bottom of the painting, on the left foot of the digger in the foreground.

This way of representing the sun, full-face, will later become very typical of his art. It is a technique which will bloom fully in Arles, his use of concentric haloes for sources of light, and we can see here that this chosen manner was already established. We see here again the preoccupations of a scrupulous observer of nature and also the mark of a solid artist who solves problems.

The sun is not 'just placed there', but has been closely observed, has been dimly shrouded in a pink-white cloud, preventing it from being perfectly round.

Vincent has not yet achieved the sun of Arles, but it is not the first time he has faced the sun, instead of working with it behind him. The resulting *light from the background* allowed him to give free reign to the contrasts between darkness and light—*violent effects of light*—but above all, to progress in his research on colours.

The invasion of white

The research into colours done by the painter gives us more information about Vincent's specific choices at the time. The report by Dr Eastaugh confirms the presence of lead white in the colours, and not only demonstrates that the author of *The Diggers* did not have a large variety of commercial colours available to him, it also brings us back to Vincent's mixing of colours and his fascination with the *infinite variety of greys*, and his observation that *white and black are present in the composition of all other colours.*

The correlation is even more forceful between the red-brown colour of the soil, and the letter in which Vincent says he has composed (in another painting) a field of *"a red-brown colour, darker here and lighter there"*.

By taking a close look at the terrain in the painting of *The Two Diggers* one notices that the red-brown colour covering the ground is actually not of a uniform shade. It is the result of research into colours which, but for the touches of blue and green, is identical to a passage in his letter LT 228, to Theo, of 3 September 1882: "*To paint it was quite a job. For the ground I needed one large tube and a half of white—yet the ground is very dark—then red, yellow, brown, ochre, black, terra sienna, blackish brown, and the result is a reddish brown, with variations from blackish brown to deep wine-red and to pale, blond russet shades.*"

To underline even more the degree of closeness between the *Letters* and what can be seen in the painting, one can quote: *"And all that falls back on the problems of light, brown and perspective."*

If it is possible to find echoes of Vincent's colour research in the way the ground has been treated in *The Diggers*, then one also must emphasise the apparent waste of energy on that research, for obtaining, what appears to be, at first sight, a lacklustre result.

The question is not to discuss here the learning method Vincent used, but rather the treatment of the ground, telling us that we are dealing here with a beginner who has not yet picked up all the tricks of the trade. Gaining knowledge and experience on how to handle colours will soon enable the artist not to have to go to such great lengths to obtain such a modest result and having to use so many colours.

The sky

The treatment of the sky and the resulting subtleties of the very thorough colour research by the artist present fewer problems. One notices in passing that there is green throughout the ochre plain, the blue in the sky counterbalances the yellow of the sun, and that the pink cloud is right next to the green, which reveals the 'thinker'.

Vincent was already very familiar with handling clear, transparent colours from using these for his watercolours.

The play of colours in the sky of *The Diggers* corresponds with a description by Vincent for a sky for another painting made around the same time:

Letter to Theo 225, 14 August 1882

But it was entirely a matter of colour and tone, the variegation of the gamut of colours in the sky, first a lilac haze, in which the red sun, half covered by a dark purple cloud, and with a sparkling red fine edge; near the sun reflections of vermilion, but there above a strip of yellow, which turned green, and higher up bluish, the so called cerulean blue and then, here and there, lilac and gray clouds catching reflections of the sun. The ground was a kind of tapestry of green, grey, brown, but full of variegation and vibration, the water in the ditch sparkles in that colourful background.

The green

The Eastaugh report is right in pointing out that Vincent does not mention the presence of green in the description he gives of the paints he purchased.

However, the very detailed descriptions of his research into colours and on the multitude of shades to be derived from primary colours, and his concern to show green, largely compensate for the absence of his mentioning green as a readily bought colour available to him.

One could also, perhaps, feel that quotations about green are superfluous for a painter painting nature on the spot in the green Netherlands.

The seascape, the marine

The fact that a seascape was painted on the canvas first, before it was overpainted with *The Diggers*, constitutes another close link with Vincent's interests at the time. In the summer of 1882 he was as much preoccupied with seascapes at Scheveningen, as he was with diggers.

For boats, prows, beach, moorings, masts, etc. see Eastaugh report Dip image fig 5, Xray by Dr Cadorin, and sketches in Vincent's letters: JH159 in LT 220 and JH174 in LT 224.

Scraping off, repainting, brush strokes, and impasto

As a beginner, Vincent reuses his canvases when studies prove unsatisfactory. He frequently scraped off a painted study, partly or completely, and then repainted the canvas.

The superimposition of two of his favourite subject matters in this painting makes the connection with his interests even closer.

The brush strokes, consistent with what we can see in other paintings, show no contradiction with Vincent's ways of handling pigment. In some places one can easily see that the colour was hardly mixed on the palette.

The impasto appears also to conform with Vincent's hesitations between heavy impasto and saving paint.

The canvas

One cannot find any specific reference to the purchasing of canvases in the correspondence of the time. However, Vincent does not only paint on paper or on panel in this early period, he also mentions canvas in his letters and, as well, a few paintings on canvas from the period are known.

The format

One might find it surprising that the painting is as large as it is, especially as one could presume it to be the exercise of a beginner. But self-taught painter Vincent was no ordinary beginner, his impatience pushes him very early towards larger formats.

Satisfactory result and perseverance

One could also judge the painting to be too modern, but here again, the answer lies in Vincent's originality. Even though he loses himself occasionally in colour styles which we today see as too sombre to be appreciated, his ideas are precise from the beginning and he himself also judges his early works to be aesthetically satisfying.

If we accept the belief that his satisfaction is not just an idle boast, then it is hardly surprising not to find the common awkwardness and faults of the work of a beginner in one of his early paintings.

Vincent's perseverance, well known to those familiar with his correspondence, enables us, continually, to measure the time he takes from getting an idea to its implementation, much like a man who works hard every day.

His main preoccupations can be found in *The Diggers*, which summarises the essence of his style and technique at the very beginning of his painting career:

• an intended simplicity, a safe drawing, as if executed with a billhook, like the straight line on the first digger's right arm, the power of the drawing having been partially masked by the later over-painting and filling-in;

• colour contrasts are still a little uncertain and proceed by trial and error;

• labour is celebrated, enriched by the raised positioning of the central arm; lines and execution are spontaneous;

• depth of field well rendered;

• colours are intrinsically powerful, in an almost frightening sort of way, like in his quest for the red-brown which we come across again later in his oeuvre;

• the sun full-face; concentric haloes intensifying its presence;

• the subtlety of the sky, which permits the use of all the resources he can master from his palette; and

• last but not least, Vincent's affection for darkness, to which he will pay homage for the next four years—"*my way of painting and colour will change a lot and I will more likely paint a little darker than lighter*"— dates from October 1884 (LT 383), less than six months before *The Potato Eaters!*

All these above preoccupations are embodied in *the man who intensely feels things*, the gifted man with *a delicate sensibility*, the man that he knew he was.

Therefore it is no surprise to see that the canvas is signed.

The signature

Dr Eastaugh and Dr Cadorin have established that the signature has been scraped. Observations and deductions lead Dr Cadorin to some reservations. His idea is that, if scraped when the paint was fresh, the vertical drop on the edges of the 'cliffs', which one can observe under binocular examination, should be more rounded. Their verticality opens the question of the date of the scraping.

From observation of areas left unscraped, for instance, the line which cuts the 't', I was unable to understand such a 'selective' scraping. I expressed my doubts to Bouwe Jans.

Because of Dr Cadorin's observations and mine, and in order to solve this very specific question and to check if it were possible to get information about the presence of the 'greyish varnish' (see Dr Cadorin's report, Chapter 5) over the scraped areas, which would push back the date of scraping to very early, Bouwe Jans very recently took the *Two Diggers* back to Dr Eastaugh for further microscopic examination and more specific conclusions. I do not yet have Dr Eastaugh's conclusions in writing, but I already know that any doubts about the reality of scraping are absolutely dismissed and that Dr Eastaugh will give new arguments in favour of a very early scraping.

At this point, the question seems to turn on whether scraping would be in conflict with what we know of Vincent's practices. We have to exclude any conflict, the *Letters* speak about his 'scraper'; he did scrape paintings at the time and reworked on drawings by scraping: *"like one does when painting"*. Furthermore, in some cases, when the background in the first plane was dark, as happened now and then in works of that period, Vincent signed by scraping. That is true for at least two other drawings with colour (JH286 and JH301).

We also know of other oil paintings where Vincent placed his signature by incision, rather than adding it in colour. Examples of these are, for instance, JH1178 (F238) *Terrace of a Café*, *'La Guinguette'* and JH1247 (F213) *Fritillarias in a Copper Vase,* both in the Musée d'Orsay. Scraping, in these particular cases appears as a clever and discreet way of writing one's name.

The position, the handwriting, and the graphics in the *Letters*

There is nothing wrong with finding the signature on the right, even though most signatures by Vincent are on the left. Vincent usually preferred the left-hand side, but several of his works of the period have the signature on the right. In fact, throughout his oeuvre one can find some 90 signatures on the right.

Perhaps one should also ask oneself, whilst assuming that an artist signs his work so his name may be seen, whether, if the two figures in the painting look towards the right, it would also not be more compatible if the signature were also placed on the side of greater interest?

The entire signature, ***V i n c e n t***, under close examination appears to be very typical:

• the **V** has the correct opening angle;

• the **i** is detached and a bit more tilted to the right than usual, but this is nothing strange. It is short; it seems also to have its dot; and it does not go as far down as the **V** does. All these elements can also be found in other signatures by Vincent;

• the first **n** is slightly taller than the **i**, as is often the case in Vincent's signatures. It is traced in conformity with Vincent's habit, first a vertical line, then a downward stroke—the latter sometimes coming back a little, as is the case here;

• the **c** is flat and only just closed and that remains the norm throughout his life;

• the **e** is only just readable, as it most often is, and the upper part is a small closed loop;

• the second **n** is smaller than the first one, as it should be. But the downward stroke does not come back as it does in the first one. This peculiarity (similar to the signature in JH306 and in some others) certifies that this is no copied or reproduced handwriting, but a spontaneous action. An imitator would have made the two **n**'s identical, and:

• the **t** should have been slightly smaller if it had been faked.

•the underline—the angle obtained by linking the bases of all the letter (which is also consistent with other signatures by Vincent) and the underlining line are both similar to others to be found in many signatures of the same period.

Lastly, I know of no other painting or drawing from which the signature on *The Diggers* could have been copied in its entirety.

A study for the studio, pinned on the wall?

This study, the painting of *The Two Diggers*, despite the achievement it constitutes, cannot have been intended to be for sale. Such a possibility is contradicted by, on the one hand, the work done on the canvas to realise *The Diggers* and on the other hand that the painter 'forgot' to blot out all the evidence of the underlying marine scene.

This cannot but lead to the hypothesis that the painting is purely a study—which must be judged *from a viewpoint other than that used for paintings*—and therefore it was destined to remain in the studio.

The drawing pins

One other detail to be found on the canvas seems to be in conformity with *a study for the studio.* A close examination shows at least three drawing-pin holes in each corner (and at least thirty-five in all on the face of the canvas), which are evidence that the canvas has been pinned down several times. Some of the pinholes have been made after the paint had dried (causing the paint to flake), some others were made before the paint had dried.

One should then try and figure out what the reason could have been for pinning down the canvas several times before it was finally placed on a stretcher by a professional.

A first pinning down could have been when the original marine scene was painted on it. A second is likely to have been for the purpose of painting *The Diggers.* Another was most probably when Vincent pinned it on the wall of his studio (some pinholes in the front correspond to holes on the side, which could be the sign of folding of the edges before pinning it up).

Vincent's letter say that to paint he pinned onto a stretcher and then, to decorate, he pinned on the walls of his studio.

The Van Gogh Museum's expertise

The short conclusions were short-lived, as Mr van Tilborgh, the head curator at the Museum who signed the 'expertise' on *The Diggers*, had to withdraw two of his six reasons for non-attribution— the 'gay colours' and the lack of impasto he saw on the photograph—when he saw the painting.

He then disqualified his entire expertise by his own statement when he declared, of another painting, that "the opinion of anyone who has not seen the actual painting before declaring it not to be genuine should be disqualified".

His colleague Sjraar van Heugten confirmed this apparently new policy of the museum: "the fact alone that someone has not seen an actual painting deprives him of the right to pass an opinion" ["*Alleen al het feit dat iemand een schilderij nooit in levende lijve heeft gezien ontneemt hem het recht van spreken.*"]

Certainly an expert can work from good photographic documents—

though van Tilborgh issued his expertise on *The Diggers* after only having seen a small amateur photo—but it is at his own risk and he has to substantiate his views by valid arguments. It is difficult to share any of the arguments he presented:

• '*the colours in the sky' being considered different*

This statement is denied by another painting and also by the *Letters*. Vincent said, in September 1882, *"every artist certainly has his own particular colour scheme. But nobody had that from the very first day and it does not show up so very immediately in studies made in the open air . . . So that, from any work I might be able to send you now, you should not give an opinion yet on my use of colour"* (LT 233, to Theo, 19 September 1882).

• *the non-commercial factory prepared canvas*

That could only make some sense if we knew at least that Vincent bought any commercially prepared canvas instead. His unorthodox beginning leaves all the possibilities wide open.

• *the weave of the cloth*

That would only make some sense if at least some research had been carried out on the canvas Vincent used for his paintings at the time or even for later periods, to produce useful knowledge for comparison.

• *the clumsy, not very lively method of drawing*

That would only make some sense without the IRR/DIP image (Eastaugh report Chapter 12), which shows a tremendously sure and quick method of drawing.

• *the painting does not show any of his characteristics*

A further nonsense.

The opinions of Mr Feilchenfeldt and Dr Dorn

According to them, the *treasure hunt* is over. They predicted that no further works by Vincent (among the hundreds missing) can emerge—it does rather look as if they were trying to make their own prediction come true.

They believe themselves to be specialists on provenance, and that is the only aspect they will pay attention to for attributions. In this particular case, the lack of an original written provenance gives them very few arguments, for or against, to offer. It explains, at least partly, Dr Dorn's statement (after seeing only a rather poor photograph), *"I see absolutely no way of attributing the Two Diggers to Vincent"*.

They can see the hand of Vincent in fakes which are supported by erroneous provenance, and equally they have been known to reject genuine works, again on the basis of a lack of documentary evidence.

Apart from themselves providing further evidence of their own confused opinions—the account of Bouwe Jans's contacts with them is rather educational in this respect [appendix D to the full report, not reproduced here]—I can see no further relevance in their remarks on *The Two Diggers*.

The forgery hypothesis

Some suppositions made by sceptics, derived from errors of reasoning, can be rejected.

The limited success of Vincent's works from the Dutch period, and also the lack of the references that would be needed for being able to produce a pastiche containing so many of his various characteristics, make the desire to believe in the eventuality of a forgery, made prior to the publication of Vincent's correspondence in 1914, an excessive attitude.

The publication of his correspondence would not be enough, though, because the link between painting and writing is one-way. It is easy to write an appropriate line about a painting, but it is not so easy to produce, in the very painting style of the writer, an image corresponding to particular correspondence.

The absence, in the correspondence, of an exact description of a painting with two diggers in an afternoon sun removes a starting point for an eventual faker; it is no great loss for authentication either, as it would be too much to hope for, to get an 'automatic' authentication from the *Letters*. The history of the authentication of many fakes shows that an interpretation of a sentence can make a masterpiece of a daub.

Anyway, the letter to Theo 229 of 9 September 1882 perhaps provides a clue:

> *But I equally love the more sturdy, the more rugged side [of autumn], those strong light effects, for instance, on a digger who is sweating in the afternoon sun.*

Miscellaneous observations

The painting is in generally good condition, old but well preserved. It has not been on display, but instead has lived a life outside the commercial circuit.

The absence of visible retouching by the painter indicates that he had no hesitations whilst painting it and that the study would have been painted in one go.

No comparable painting has, as far as is known, ever been submitted before for a formal attribution and/or has been turned down for an authentication.

The signature, which was hardly legible, spells the name 'Vincent', which was not the name under which he was generally known at the time. This may have contributed to the fact that the link between the painting and V*an Gogh* was not established until a collector/art dealer saw a painting that appeared to him as being of special interest.

The provenance

The 'absence of provenance' always frightens specialists and historians who lack the aesthetic wherewithal to understand painting. Let them be assured this time.

A logical sequence of happenings can be advanced, in fact a highly logical one.

Vincent paints the study in The Hague, but he does not send it to his brother (we know that his brother preserved a great many paintings, but the *Two Diggers* are not to be found anywhere in the records of or in the collection of the Van Gogh family). Then he probably pinned it on the wall in his studio in The Hague.

There it is left behind, with his other studies, in the loft of his studio, when he leaves for Drenthe on 11 September 1883. After 3 months in Drenthe he decides to move to his parents' home in Nuenen, Brabant, where he arrives on 5 December 1883. Then he went back to The Hague to pick up all his studies.

No further mention seems to have been made of these 'belongings from The Hague', now incorporated in the Nuenen body of his possessions and works, until a letter to his sister Wilhelmina speaking about the belongings he had left behind when he left Nuenen and which the family had later stored away with a carpenter in Breda.

Letter to Wilhelmina W4, c. 22 June 1888

Tell me, talking about rubbish, maybe it would be worthwhile to rescue whatever is useful out of my rubbish, which, according to Theo, is still in a loft somewhere in Breda.

In 1903, Couvreur, a rag and bone man sold many of them but . . . soon

. . . tried to buy them back, once he became aware of their commercial value, and then sold the lot to an art dealer, C. Mouwen.

At this moment, or perhaps a little later, the new owner of *The Diggers*, who bought it from Couvreur—this seems to be the only possibility—and who liked the picture for what it is, and without worrying about the name of the painter, which would in any case not mean much to him, has it put on a stretcher. The paint, already dry by then, cracks here and there on the edge of the stretcher (see Cadorin report).

According to the latest information from the auctioneer, J. van den Enden, the painting was bought at a flea market near Groningen in or around 1990 from a family who had moved to Groningen many years earlier from Breda, where they had acquired it. The name of Breda as place of origin provides the missing link of some eighty-five or less years.

The buyer at the flea market, believed to be from Beilen in Drenthe, brought the painting to J. van den Enden in 1993.

This auctioneer sold the *The Diggers* through his provincial auction house in Groningen, where it was auctioned along with other items of household inventory.

The present owner, the first wise collector/art dealer to spot it, bought it at this Groningen auction on 17 May 1993.

Dr Cadorin concluded that the painting was at least 80 years old, but probably older.

Dr Eastaugh could not find any components or pigments which were not already available in the early 1880s and agreed to the possible dating to the end of the 19th century.

Mr Nicholas Penny, of the National Gallery in London, estimated that the painting could be as little as 100 years old, but that it would probably be older.

All this evidence combined is in conformity with Vincent's preoccupations in the late summer of 1882 and presents no contradiction to what could be learned from the available documents.

Any possibility that one could be dealing with a forgery in this case is in my opinion strictly excluded.

The date of execution

The sentence: "*But I equally love the more sturdy, the more rugged side [of autumn], those strong light effects, for instance, on a digger who is sweating in the afternoon sun*" (LT 229, 9 September 1882) is very likely to be, though it is not entirely certain, the written connection with the execution of the *Two Diggers in the Afternoon Sun*.

Of course it does not necessarily imply that a painted study of two diggers under an afternoon sun had yet been made. But one is forced to admit that Vincent has in any case already visualised the scene.

And we know how impatient he was, and how he would show that impatience in sentences such as, "... *here is the plan ... which I have started to carry out already*".

Therefore, if the picture was not yet painted on the 9 September, then it was just about to be painted.

On the other hand, the painting could have existed on the 9 September and since Vincent writes in the same letter that he is out of paint —"*In the meantime, my paint is finished*"—so it is more likely that the painting was already completed.

Also considering that Vincent mentions a digger under the 'autumn' sun, one cannot justify placing the date of execution somewhere in August, which is normally still held to be 'in summer'.

For that reason one should place the date as much as possible later towards early autumn, 9 September being the latest.

The date of completing the execution is very likely to have been 'c. 9th of September 1882'.

Copies of the complete report, with all appendices, were sent to Mr John Leighton, Dr Jan Hulsker, Mr van Tilborgh, Mrs A. Tellegen-Hoogendoorn, Dr Martha op de Coul, Mr Feilchenfeldt, Dr Dorn, Professor Pickvance, Mr Johannes van der Wolk, Dr Paolo Cadorin and Dr Eastaugh.